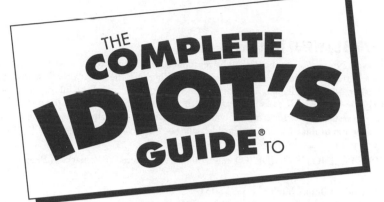

THE COMPLETE IDIOT'S GUIDE® TO

Grant Writing

0 4 - 508

by Waddy Thompson

ALPHA

A member of Penguin Group (USA) Inc.

International Standard Book Number: 1-59257-151-4
Library of Congress Catalog Card Number: 2003112966

05   04   03   8   7   6   5   4   3   2   1

Interpretation of the printing code: The rightmost number of the first series of numbers is the year of the book's printing; the rightmost number of the second series of numbers is the number of the book's printing. For example, a printing code of 03-1 shows that the first printing occurred in 2003.

Printed in the United States of America

Most Alpha books are available at special quantity discounts for bulk purchases for sales promotions, premiums, fundraising, or educational use. Special books, or book excerpts, can also be created to fit specific needs.

For details, write: Special Markets, Alpha Books, 375 Hudson Street, New York, NY 10014.

Publisher: *Marie Butler-Knight*
Product Manager: *Phil Kitchel*
Senior Managing Editor: *Jennifer Chisholm*
Acquisitions Editor: *Mike Sanders*
Development Editor: *Michael Koch*
Senior Production Editor: *Christy Wagner*
Production Editor: *Megan Douglass*
Copy Editor: *Molly Schaller*
Illustrator: *Chris Eliopoulos*
Cover/Book Designer: *Trina Wurst*
Indexer: *Brad Herriman*
Layout/Proofreading: *Mary Hunt, Ayanna Lacey*

Contents at a Glance

Appendixes

Contents

Foreword

The news that my friend and former colleague Waddy Thompson had written *The Complete Idiot's Guide to Grant Writing* struck me as a potential windfall for anyone seeking financial support for a not-for-profit cause. Now that I've read the book, I know that Waddy's thoughtful, methodical approach to everything he does has prevailed in a way that will be enormously and practically helpful to both seasoned and first-time supplicants, from both the professional and volunteer's perspective.

I have personally observed and benefited from Waddy's understanding of the fundamental transaction that is fundraising. He nicely defines it in Chapter 1 with a simple, heartfelt letter from college student Jack to mom and dad, reflecting on his experiences at school and how additional funding indeed will make the difference. Waddy carefully leads the reader through the usual suspects, with good information on government sources, foundations, and corporations, but manages to keep the focus on the importance of individual relationships, which in the end will determine your success in securing a grant. Waddy's guide also recognizes that familiarity with a cause is a prerequisite if anyone is going to even thinking about lending it financial support.

A visit to our neighborhood bookstore informed me that the breezy, totally accessible "Complete Idiot" approach has recently been used to introduce curious readers to everything from making CDs, to the Middle East conflict, and even "surviving anything." Waddy has cleverly adapted the format to his topic, clearly outlining a step-by-step process.

I have worked with a number of individuals who were not by profession fundraisers, including scientists, dancers, producers, and social workers. Whether they liked it or not, their role in this capacity was to instill in other people a well-informed interest and concern in their work. Again, in the end it's all about personal relationships, which, wisely cultivated, in some instances over a period of many years, can bring millions of dollars to the service of a personal or institutional mission.

There's no question, precise attention to detail is critical to good grant writing, and Waddy has covered all the bases. His book identifies potential sources, and discusses in detail research, strategies, how to actually write a proposal, and what to do after it has been submitted. There is as well an outstanding set of appendixes, glossary, a CD-ROM, and an indispensable concluding chapter that together represent a compilation of information I can only wish I had access to over the years I have been thinking about and applying for grants.

So read the book and follow the instructions, but, more importantly, take to heart and understand Waddy's basic message: Grant writing may seem technical and esoteric, but in the end it involves some of the most basic instincts and organizational skills, in particular related to oral and written communication, as Jack knew all along, with or without Psych 101.

Steve Dennin
New York City 2003

Steve Dennin has overseen fundraising programs for some of the country's most prominent not-for-profit institutions, including the Twyla Tharp Dance Foundation, Lincoln Center for the Performing Arts, the New York Shakespeare Festival, Planned Parenthood Federation of America, the Whitney Museum of American Art, and, currently, The Nature Conservancy. He has over 20 years experience writing and successfully securing grants which have helped to create new dances, renovate museums, fund free Shakespeare in the Park, and protect biodiversity at sites all over the world. Steve has also served as a volunteer trustee for a range of organizations. He lives in New York City with his wife Anne and son James.

Introduction

Many people have extensive experience in writing grants and don't even know it. If you've ever asked anyone for anything in writing, you probably followed many of the procedures outlined in this book. That's all a grant proposal is.

How can you harness that power for good? Read this book.

Grant writing can be a satisfying and rewarding experience, no matter if you're a volunteer or building a career. It's a great feeling when the check comes in the mail, but there's a lot to do before you can start counting the money.

What's in This Book

Grant writing entails a lot more than just writing a grant. You are developing financial resources for your charity. Grant writing requires knowledge of the philanthropic field, excellent general writing skills, organizational and project management ability, and a personal touch. That's a broad range of talents and knowledge, but you'll find information on all of them here.

Part 1, "Getting Started," provides you with the basics about what it takes to be a good grant writer and what the process of writing a grant will be like.

Part 2, "Where the Money Is," takes you behind the scenes of all the different institutions that make grants to see what makes them tick. I also provide you with a primer in getting a grant from an individual by learning what basic human emotions come into play.

Part 3, "Research, or Just How Nosy Are You," guides you in satisfying your curiosity about funders and all the people associated with them and to then use that information to win them over.

Part 4, "Strategies for Success," teaches you the little tricks of the trade to warm up your prospects before you ask them for money and to get yourself organized so that everything can proceed according to a plan.

Part 5, "Writing the Proposal," finally gets you to start writing. This chapter shows you how to gather the information you'll need from your colleagues and put it into the form the funder wants to receive, including spelling it out in dollars and cents in the budget.

Part 6, "Post-Application," covers what might be the most difficult part of the whole business—waiting to hear how you did. And for those of you who would like the "in-brief" version of grant writing or a solid summary of what you're supposed to have learned from these pages, I've ended the book with a whirlwind grant-writing course.

The appendixes include an extensive listing of online reference resources and a guide to find much of the same information offline, examples of complete grants, and a glossary that covers all the insider lingo.

The CD-ROM that accompanies this book provides you with a quick-and-easy way to access much of what is contained in the appendixes, along with additional examples. The Internet resources on the CD-ROM will enable you to click through to the various websites using your computer's browser.

The Philanthropy Insider

Throughout the book you'll find tips on different aspects of the grant business:

> **How to Say It**
>
> Every business has its own way of saying things. These writing tips will help you avoid sounding like an amateur.

> **Grant Talk**
>
> The philanthropy world has its own language. In these sidebars, you'll get a plain language explanation about what the arcane terms really mean.

> **Philanthropy Facts**
>
> The more you know about the grant world, the better prepared you'll be to take it on. These facts about philanthropy are meant to both clue you in and give you a perspective beyond the grants you're writing.

> **Words to the Wise**
>
> There are two ways of doing things in this business: the wrong way and the insider's way. These warnings will help you avoid the mistakes of others (including me) and set you straight about what is expected in a variety of situations.

Acknowledgments

During the past two decades, I've been fortunate to work for a number of knowledgeable people who have gently introduced me to the philanthropic and grant-seeking world. I've learned so much from each of them, but I also have learned much from the grant writers who have worked for me. They, too, have given me insights into the process of getting a grant, while putting up with my endless editing of their documents.

Kate Taylor and Rados Piletich, my most recent colleagues in grant writing, allowed me to talk through various issues encountered in this book and gave me some great advice.

Rados is also responsible for two of the grants you'll find in the appendixes. I must also thank Theodore Berger, executive director of the New York Foundation for the Arts, for allowing me to include examples from NYFA grants. All examples in this book not related to NYFA are about fictional charities and no funder referred to in any grant-writing example is intended to represent the policies and intent of any actual funder.

Finally, I must thank Chuck and Reba, who put up with constant neglect while I wrote this book.

Special Thanks to the Technical Reviewer

The Complete Idiot's Guide to Grant Writing was reviewed by an expert who double-checked the accuracy of what you'll learn here, to help us ensure that this book gives you everything you need to know about grant writing. Special thanks are extended to Nancy S. Clarke.

Trademarks

All terms mentioned in this book that are known to be or are suspected of being trademarks or service marks have been appropriately capitalized. Alpha Books and Penguin Group (USA) Inc. cannot attest to the accuracy of this information. Use of a term in this book should not be regarded as affecting the validity of any trademark or service mark.

Part

Getting Started

It's always good to get the lay of the land before beginning any endeavor. In this part, you'll discover just what grant writing is all about, including what knowledge, skills, and disposition you need to bring to the practice of grant writing. This part also considers why you might want to write a grant proposal and briefly covers what that process involves.

Although everyone would like to receive a grant, institutions that make grants operate within a relatively narrow compass. You'll learn who is eligible for grants and what kinds of activities will be rewarded with a grant.

The Practice of Grant Writing

In This Chapter

- ◆ Grant writing defined
- ◆ Why grant writing is right for you
- ◆ How the economy affects grants
- ◆ What it means to be a grant writer
- ◆ Time line for success

Grant writing is one of those topics that seems very technical and esoteric, yet you probably already know more about it than you think you do. But before I go any further, let's be clear about just what grant writing is and isn't.

Grant writing is the skill or practice of asking for money in the form of a grant from a foundation, corporation, or government agency by crafting a well-considered document (the proposal) that outlines how the money will be used, what receiving the money will accomplish, and who will undertake the tasks described in the proposal.

Grant writing *is not* about writing a group of friends to get them each to give $25 for the local library (that's called direct mail or unsolicited third-class mail, but never junk mail if you are in the business of raising money).

Grant writing *is* about creating a proposal, which you can send to local corporations or foundations asking for several thousand dollars for the local library. On occasion, proposals will be written to individuals when a four- to seven-figure gift is being sought, and that is covered in this book, too. But for the most part, you're concerned with getting largish sums of money from some kind of institution or other. Grant writing is an important part of any fundraising program, which would likely include at least direct mail and special events as well.

I'll start off with what I think you already know and finish this chapter with the key things you need to know about the practice of grant writing. Then I'll show you how to pursue the technical aspects in the remaining chapters of the book.

You Already Are a Grant Writer!

If you're anything like me, when you were in college or away at summer camp you found it easiest to remember to write home just when your wallet was getting a little thin. Believe it or not, that was your first grant writing experience. (I hope you were successful!)

Asking for money is never easy, but anyone can acquire the skills to ask like a professional fundraiser. This book tells you how to do that, but like so much in our professional lives, the basics were learned earlier in life. In case your memory is fuzzy on what those letters home were like, I've included a "Dear Mom and Dad" letter to refresh your memory.

> **Philanthropy Facts**
>
> There are more than 700,000 nonprofit organizations in the United States with Federal tax-exempt status, hundreds of thousands more with state tax-exempt status, and untold numbers of other groups that are unincorporated.

Dear Mom and Dad,

Thanks so much for the check you sent a couple of weeks ago. It really came just in the nick of time so I could get all the books for the new semester.

College is great! You probably saw the basketball game on TV last weekend. It was really something to actually be there. The College has a terrific series of concerts in the Coliseum, too, with first-class bands.

So many things to do and see, but I recently have not been able to do and see as many things as my friends because I've been running low on funds. If you could send me an extra $100 to tide me over to the end of the month it would really be great!

It's not that I expect to go out every night. Most of my time is still spent studying, especially for Psych 101, which is really tough but which I think is the subject I like the best. Reading the case studies has really brought home to me what great parents you are.

When do you think you'll come up for a visit? Hope it's soon, and if you could help me out with a check really soon, I'd really appreciate it.

Love,

Jack

Like Writing Mom and Dad

There are many things you can learn from that "Dear Mom and Dad" letter that will serve you well as a grant writer. Let's take a close look at the letter to see some of the points of similarity.

Because Jack's letter home was not the first time he had ever asked for money, he was seeking a renewal grant. So Jack naturally started out telling his parents how he had used the last money they sent. And note that his very first word was "Thanks," the magic word that can open so many doors. It is so important to always acknowledge past support. No one—not a parent or a funder—ever wants to be taken for granted.

Jack follows his opening by telling his parents about what has been happening at school to make them feel involved and current. Every funder will be interested to know what significant things are happening in your organization right now, whether they're related to the specific grant or not.

Eventually Jack had to get to actually asking for money, which to be convincing had to include some ideas on how he'd spend this new money. Jack's pretty vague on this, so he must be looking for *general operating support*. Note that he does at least ask for a specific amount. People like to know what you expect of them, so always be specific—don't make them guess how much the new bus will cost or how much it takes to build a website.

Usually, when seeking general operating support, you would make a point of covering a wide range of issues your charity addresses. Jack can assume his parents have an intimate acquaintance with his general operating needs, so he doesn't have to go into detail here.

Jack knows to end on a high note, staying positive and connecting emotionally with his parents one last time to remind them why they really want to write that check. Jack isn't shy about pushing his parent's emotional buttons. (Who knows better where they are; he probably "installed" some of them!)

Words to the Wise

Don't ask a funder for too much or too little. Your best guide to how much to ask for is how much the funder has given to organizations similar to yours. Check the funder's annual report or IRS return for lists of grants.

Grant Talk

General operating support refers to a grant to pay for the everyday expenses all organizations have, such as rent, utilities, and insurance, as well as for personnel who are not involved in programs (like the grant writer). General operating support can also help pay for programs, which is sometimes necessary when a program is just getting started.

Jack's big advantage over you or me writing a grant proposal is that he wrote based on a relationship built up over nearly two decades. The prospects were knowledgeable about the cause to which they were being asked to contribute. And because of the long relationship, they were predisposed to responding positively to his request.

So how do you create a level of knowledge and (hopefully) a predisposition to a positive response? In the fundraising business it's called cultivation, by which you develop the prospect over a period of time so that the proposal arrives on the desk of someone who is well informed about your organization (if not necessarily about your project). Cultivating before you ask is my favorite saw and one that everyone who works for me is tired of hearing about. You don't have to hear too much more on the subject from me until Chapter 10.

Let's take Jack's letter and use it as a guide to write a simple (very simple) grant proposal:

Ms. Betty Smith
Executive Director
Small Town Foundation
123 Main Street
Anywhere, IL 60000

Dear Ms. Smith:

On behalf of the board and all those we serve, I would like to thank you again for Small Town Foundation's generous $5,000 gift to support our after-school activities last year.

Since we received your gift, 75 additional children have become regular participants in the activities offered at our Center. You might have seen the short write-up that appeared in the local paper about us. Although this recognition was important, the looks in the eyes of our children are the true reward.

We are writing now to ask that you renew your $5,000 gift this year. Your funds will be used to further expand the number of children we can accommodate each day by making it possible to retain an additional teacher's aide.

I would love to arrange a visit so that you can see first hand what your gift can accomplish. Please give me a call at 312-555-1212 or email me at execdir@all4kids.org and I'm sure we can find a time to meet. Your kind consideration of this proposal is greatly appreciated.

Sincerely,

Mary Stuart

Mary Stuart
Executive Director

That's a much simpler proposal than you will ever write, but you get the point. There is no big mystery about grant writing. It doesn't require a Ph.D., but you do need to know how to put the parts together, avoid amateurish pitfalls, and convince others of the importance of what you're writing about.

If you were good at writing please-send-money letters home from college, you're going to be a great grant writer. And if you lived at home and never wrote one of these letters, well, congratulations! You have experience in face-to-face solicitation, which is also a good skill in fundraising.

You say you never needed money from your parents? Well, maybe you'll soon be the one making grants. But whatever your experience, this book will take you from simple show-me-the-money letters to fully developed grant proposals.

How to Say It _____

The "ask" usually comes at the beginning of a proposal and is repeated at the end. Always ask for a specific amount, and with renewals, always ask for more unless you know the funder doesn't make larger grants.

Why Grant Writing Is the Answer

No one grows up wanting to be a grant writer (or any kind of fundraiser, for that matter). Most of us fall into it out of necessity, either as part of our jobs or because we want to raise some significant money for a cause we believe in.

You might want to write a grant proposal, for example, if …

◆ You can't face one more bake sale for the soccer team.

◆ You see that your local seniors' center needs a big infusion of cash to keep going.

◆ The local library's new book budget has been slashed by the city and a group of neighbors want to help out.

◆ You're on the board of a new nonprofit group that can't yet afford professional development staff.

◆ You're raising funds for your own arts project.

Whatever your motivation for wanting to be a grant writer, you will want to produce a professional proposal that will withstand the scrutiny of foundation staff *and get funded!*

Despite the proliferation of new foundations in the 1990s, there are still far more organizations and individuals seeking grants than there are organizations and individuals making grants. In fact, nonprofits outnumber foundations by about 10 to 1. There are many, many well-known organizations that have large, well-paid development staffs vying for this money, but that doesn't mean you won't be successful. Fortunately, there are foundations and other grantmakers for every size organization and every conceivable cause.

In this book, I'll cover everything you need to know to write a successful grant proposal. You'll learn how to research prospects, cultivate relationships within and outside your charity, develop a complete

Philanthropy Facts

There are some 70,000 private foundations in the United States that give away as much as $27 billion annually.

proposal in several common formats, create budgets that also tell a story, and end up with a proposal that will stand out from the foundation slush pile.

The Stock Market and Grants

Everyone whom you might approach for a grant lives in the same economic world as you and I. This means that when times are good and the stock market is riding high, foundations have more money to give away, corporations have greater profits from which to support charities, and governments are flush with taxes. Obviously, the opposite is true when times are hard.

If your charity receives a large percentage of its income from foundations and corporations, economic downturns will dramatically affect your funding. Individuals tend to give more to the causes they most believe in during tough times, but might drop charities in which they have less interest. Government funders generally are affected a bit later, when tax income falls. All this, of course, is the best argument for not relying too heavily on one source of funding.

Foundations are required by law to spend only 5 percent of their assets each year on grants and related expenses. Few rarely give more than that, even when their investments are earning three times that amount. When the national tragedy of September 11, 2001, occurred, many foundations did dip into their principle to make large emergency grants—that is, they gave away in 2001 more than they earned on their investments that year, but this was an exceptional time in every regard.

A grant writer should always be aware of how the economy might be affecting those he or she is soliciting. In lean times, foundations tend to take on fewer new grantees, preferring to maintain their commitments to their current charities. When times are tough, one of the first things to go at corporations is corporate giving. And because corporate foundations are usually funded year by year, there is not even an endowment to fall back on. Government funding can be particularly capricious, being affected by the political agendas of those in power as well as the economy. In early 2003, several states cut all funding to their state arts councils, leaving the arts institutions in those states to fend for themselves.

In a slow economy, the grant writer's job becomes much more difficult. The grant writer must spend much more time getting current funders to renew grants rather than sending out lots of new proposals. Just remember, though, that foundations still have to give money to someone, so it might as well be you.

The Complete Grant Writer

A grant writer is someone who is able to craft elegant, clear, concise sentences that can convey passion equally with detailed information. Often you will be called upon to describe technical facts (for example, in a grant for a new computer network) or concepts and procedures about which you know nothing (as in a scientific proposal) or abstract concepts that lie well outside your daily life (as in a research proposal).

A good grant writer learns enough about the subject to write intelligently so as to make the subject comprehensible to others who have no background in the subject. The grant writer also takes on passion and enthusiasm from the people who will run the project or program so as to be able to get whoever reads the proposal equally excited about the project.

A grant writer must also be a diplomat who helps the people running programs get their ideas into shape. Many people who run programs are so close to them that they cannot see clearly how to explain them to someone unfamiliar with the project or organization, and many simply are just not good writers. The grant writer takes the words from the program staff and makes them English, but without making the program staff feel belittled. The grant writer often also must be an advocate with senior staff and board members.

A grant writer is a financially savvy person who can make numbers speak as clearly as words. Numbers can tell any story you want them to tell. Your budget should reflect the project's narrative description and include enough detail to be convincing, but not so much as to restrict the execution of the program. Crunching the numbers and presenting the numbers are very different talents. The grant writer needs to do both, but more of the latter.

Words to the Wise

Don't be shy about asking program staff about their program. They will probably be thrilled to know someone is interested in what they do. And remember—they need you more than you need them.

Philanthropy Facts

In response to the September 11 tragedy, Americans contributed an unprecedented $2.6 billion to relief efforts. $309 million of this came from foundations and $682 million from corporations. Source: *Giving in the Aftermath of 9/11: An Update on the Foundation and Corporate Response* (November 2002). The Foundation Center.

A grant writer is also full of curiosity, willing to go to any length to ferret out information on funders to find the right match for his or her organization. A grant writer is interested in people—those for whom he is trying to raise money as well as those from whom he hopes to get the money.

But mostly, a grant writer needs passion for the cause at the heart of the proposal. After all, if you don't really care about your project, why should the funder?

Although "grant writer" might sound like a solitary activity, you will actually interact with a wide range of people in the course of preparing a grant proposal, including program and executive staff at your charity, members of your board of directors, and staff at foundations and corporations. On the other hard, it is also something that can be done on a part-time basis working from home.

Grant writing can be quite lucrative as a profession. The positions at different charities go by a variety of names, including Grants Officer, Institutional Giving Manager, Foundation/Corporation/Government Affairs Manager, Director of Development for Institutional Giving, and many others.

Salaries for grant writers vary widely, according to the type of charity you work for and the size of the charity's budget. Generally, fundraisers of all kinds at health charities and in higher education make the highest salaries, social services charities tend to pay the least, with the arts somewhere in between. Expect to make from $30,000 with a small organization away from major metropolitan areas to $100,000 for someone at a major institution who writes grants and supervises others.

If you are considering doing grant writing as a consultant, be aware that in many states all fundraising consultants must register with the state Attorney General. In some extreme cases, you must also register with the state in which any funder you approach is located. If you're considering hiring a consultant to help with grant writing, check with your state's Attorney General's office to see if registration is required, and make sure your consultant has the necessary registration (if any). One final note on consultants: Professional fundraising consultants work for a flat fee, never a percentage of what they raise.

A Week-by-Week Guide

It's important to allow yourself enough time to prepare your grant proposal, especially your first one. The great unknown in preparing a grant is how long the internal review will take. If your executive director is a real stickler who lives to edit some else's prose, allow additional time for review.

The following time line assumes, of course, that you spent at least several months cultivating a range of prospects so that when the right project came along, they were primed and ready to receive your proposal.

Week 1: Most proposals you write will be for specific projects, so you will have to get to know the ins and outs of the project before you can do anything. Allow at least a week to get information from others and digest it. You'll have time during the inevitable rewrites to continue learning and digesting.

Weeks 2 and 3: Conduct research to find the best funder matches for the project and write or call for guidelines (if not available on the Internet). This is the most crucial stage in the proposal process. If you haven't done *all* your homework, you won't stand a chance at success.

Week 4: Complete research, checking to see if anyone connected with your organization knows anyone connected with the funder, and reviewing information received from funders.

Weeks 5 and 6: Write the proposal and share it with program staff and others. Make revisions and more revisions.

Week 7: Make final edits, contact funder when appropriate, and mail the proposal well in advance of the funder's deadline.

Week 8: Relax and wait.

Week 9: Make a follow-up call to see if the application was received.

Weeks 10 through 25 or longer: Patiently wait for news from the funder.

Weeks 12 through 52: Check arrives! General rejoicing!

> **Words to the Wise**
>
> If you need money in less than three months, you are better off approaching an individual using a board or volunteer contact. Institutions move slowly.

As you can see, grant writing involves a lot more than just writing, but that's what makes it interesting and challenging for those of us who do it. I love learning about the new projects I raise money for, and it is so gratifying when a grant is successful and you know that it was *you* who helped buy the books for the library, or provided day care for more kids, or helped people learn to read. But what makes you eligible for a grant and what's a reasonable grant request? You'll find out in Chapter 2.

The Least You Need to Know

- Asking Mom and Dad for money and approaching a foundation aren't all that different.

- Grant writing can produce substantial sums for your community center, soccer team, church, or beginning nonprofit.

- Grant monies for charities decline in a down economy—just like everything else—and rise when times are good.

- The grant writer's best friends are knowledge and passion.

- It's just as important to be persuasive with numbers as with words.

- From concept to grant check can take six months to a year—or longer.

Chapter 2

ABCs of Grants

In This Chapter

- ◆ What a grant is
- ◆ Legal status necessary to receive a grant
- ◆ Project, operating, capital, and challenge grants
- ◆ How to keep your grant from being rejected out of hand

In this and the next four chapters, I'll give you a lot of information on what is meant by a "grant" and the people and institutions that make grants. This is not just background. This is context or, if you will, the *gestalt* of grant writing and grantmaking. An understanding of what lies behind the grant process is key to successful grant writing, or maybe I should say, successful *grant getting*. So on to grant basics.

If I send a $25 check to the local animal shelter, that could be considered a "grant" from me, but we generally think of grants as coming from institutions, whether foundations, corporations, or government agencies. Webster's defines the act of making a grant as "giving to a petitioner, often a subordinate or inferior, something sought that could be withheld." Webster's contrasts this with "award," which it says refers to "the granting of something merited or earned."

The word "grant" historically has been used in a wide variety of contexts, but in every instance an exchange takes place. Not only does someone give away something of value, but the giver expects that the recipient of the grant will do something in return. For example, when England's King Charles made land grants to the American colonists, they were expected to settle and develop the land, in turn producing tax income for the Crown. And when Jack in Chapter 1 received an extra $100 spending money, his parents certainly expected him to stay in school and study.

The roots of modern philanthropy build on the idea of an exchange. When your charity receives a grant, it promises to perform the actions described in the proposal. Many foundations will send you a contract along with the award letter that makes clear the obligations you incur by accepting the grant—usually stated simply by doing everything in your proposal. This is a very good reason to make sure that your organization can actually do everything you say it will do in your proposal. Exaggerated claims or inflated (or deflated) budgets will not help you in the end.

> **" " Words to the Wise**
>
> Being a nudge is also part of a grant writer's job. Reminding those on the program side, politely, of a grant's requirements and its termination date helps everyone concerned. Pose this as "How is that new child care manual coming along?" rather than "Have you written the child care manual yet?"

Today, governments recognize that the practice of philanthropy is good for everyone and therefore give a privileged status to organizations formed for charitable purposes. In many countries, governments exempt money given for charitable purposes from taxation.

Who Can Receive a Grant?

In common practice, "nonprofit," "tax-exempt," "charity," or the more technical "501(c)(3)" are used interchangeably in the United States. They all mean that an organization has been organized for purposes other than profit and that some government agency has recognized that. Other than the few exceptions described in the following sections, only organizations recognized by some level of government as formed exclusively for charitable, nonprofit purposes can receive grants.

> **Grant Talk**
>
> 501(c)(3) status refers to the paragraph in the tax code that defines which types of organizations are recognized to be free from federal income taxes, defined as "organized and operated exclusively for religious, charitable, scientific, testing for public safety, literary, or educational purposes ...."

Recognition by the Feds

The most commonly recognized form of tax-exempt status in the United States is the *501(c)(3)* status conferred by the Internal Revenue Service to organizations formed for educational or charitable purposes and not to make a profit, hence a nonprofit organization. In certain cases, fraternal organizations (501[c][8] or 501[c][10]), cemetery companies (501[c][13]), and some veterans organizations (501[c][4] or 501[c][19]) can also receive grants. Other nonprofit organizations might not be eligible to receive tax-deductible donations (such as grants).

The IRS publishes a list of nonprofit organizations. Look for publication No. 78 or find it online at www.irs.gov/charities and select "Search for Charities". In Canada, the equivalent tax status comes from Canadian Customs and Revenue Agency certifying Canadian Charitable Registration.

Recognition by the State

It is also common for organizations to be recognized as tax-exempt by the state or states in which they run programs or have offices. Your organization probably has (or is seeking) state tax-exempt status as well as federal tax-exempt status because this usually carries exemption from both state income taxes and state and local sales taxes. The state agency responsible for granting tax-exempt status varies from state to state, but the office of the Secretary of State or the Attorney General usually handles this task.

It is not necessary to have Federal tax-exempt status to have state tax-exempt status and vice versa.

Many funders will accept either federal or state nonprofit status. With every grant proposal you submit, you will usually be asked to include proof of nonprofit status. If you have federal 501(c)(3) status, there is no need to also submit evidence of state charity status.

Government Agencies, Schools, and Religious Groups

When receiving a grant for a public school or other government agency (such as a public library), the funder will assume nonprofit status applies (even though these are not 501[c][3] organizations), and will probably not ask for proof of nonprofit status. If, however, a funder receives a proposal from a private school, proof of nonprofit status will be needed. Religious institutions might include proof of nonprofit status rather than have it questioned.

Grants to Individuals

Less than 10 percent of foundations (and an even smaller percentage of corporations) will make grants to individuals. The ones that do make grants to individuals usually do so as scholarships or for research, independent study, or artistic pursuit. Government agencies also offer scholarship funds and research grants. You might also find it necessary to write grant proposals for residencies that provide room, board, and a studio, laboratory, or other facility but no cash.

Philanthropy Facts
The Foundation Center's *Foundation Grants to Individuals* lists 4,300 funders that offer support to individuals (more than 5,000 in their online version at www.fdncenter.org). Compare this to the 80,000 foundations that exist in the United States, and you can see the challenge facing the individual grant seeker.

The grants to individuals you as a grant writer are concerned with are all based on merit, even though some scholarships have a financial need consideration. Many government agencies and nonprofits give financial assistance based on need, but this aid requires only an application form, not a grant proposal.

Although some of the guidelines for these grants call them "grants to individuals," you will find that when it comes to writing the check, it will be paid to the school or research center rather than directly to you.

Whenever money flows from one nonprofit organization to another, there is little room for the transaction to be questioned by the IRS. This is not so when money goes from a nonprofit to an individual. Additional record keeping and rules come into play, and most funders keep life simple by not making grants to individuals.

One of the rules that would affect grants to individuals involves "private inurnment." This means something that would benefit a person who is a close relative of or who has a relationship with a funder. For example, if your parents establish a foundation to provide scholarships to students in the health sciences, and you are attending medical school, their foundation cannot provide you with a scholarship, although it could give your roommate one.

Borrowing Tax-Exempt Status

But what, you might ask, am I to do if the group I'm working for is new and does not yet have nonprofit status or if I'm seeking funds for my own private research, to make a film, or create a work of public art? Fortunately, the law allows for organizations that already have tax-exempt status to accept grant money on behalf of a group (or individual) that does not have nonprofit status.

Grant Talk

Fiscal sponsorship is a formal relationship between a nonprofit organization and an organization that is unincorporated or in the process of seeking nonprofit status or an individual. The relationship is formed so that the organization or person without nonprofit status has access to contributions from foundations, corporations, individuals, and government agencies.

This is called *fiscal sponsorship*. It is a very common means for groups just starting out to receive tax-deductible contributions from the public (including foundation, corporate, and even government funders) while developing their programs and seeking nonprofit status. The fiscal sponsor will usually deduct a service fee from contributions it receives on your behalf, usually 5 to 10 percent, depending on how much service they provide.

Legally, the fiscal sponsor is responsible for the contributions made to it on your behalf, which requires a level of scrutiny and control that makes fees necessary. The services a fiscal sponsor provides can range from simply accepting funds and issuing a check to full bookkeeping services and management assistance.

Individuals, especially those in the arts, also use fiscal sponsorship to raise funds to carry out a project or to provide seed money for a project, which in some cases might then be further funded as a commercial project. Fiscal sponsorship makes possible many, many documentary films. (Note all those credits to funders at the end of every documentary film you see on public television.)

Some agencies providing fiscal sponsorship include …

- ◆ Dade Community Foundation
  200 South Biscayne Boulevard Suite 505
  Miami, FL 33131-2343
  www.dadecommunityfoundation.org/Site/creating/types3.jsp

  This foundation is involved with sponsorship of projects of all kinds in the Miami, Dade County, area. Many community foundations provide this service to area groups.

- ◆ Dance Theatre Workshop
  219 West 19th Street
  New York, NY 10011
  www.dtw.org

  This service group is involved with sponsorship for dancers, musicians, performers, visual artists, and art educators.

- ◆ Film Arts Foundation
  145 9th St, #101
  San Francisco, CA 94103
  www.filmarts.org/sponsoredpr/whatis.html

  This foundation is involved with sponsorship for film projects.

- ◆ New York Foundation for the Arts
  155 Avenue of the Americas, 14th floor
  New York, NY 10014
  www.nyfa.org/fs

Philanthropy Facts
Common fiscal sponsors include nonprofit service organizations, community foundations, and other public foundations (that is, foundations that receive support from a wide section of the public rather than a single individual).

This grantmaking public charity is involved with sponsorship for emerging arts organizations and for artist projects in all artistic disciplines. An extensive list of other arts fiscal sponsors is available at www.nyfa.org/files_uploaded/OtherFSPrograms.pdf.

- ◆ The Rose Foundation
  6008 College Ave., Suite 10
  Oakland, CA 94618
  www.rosefdn.org/grants/fiscal.html

  This foundation is involved with sponsorship of environmental protection and community regeneration projects.

◆ Third Sector New England
18 Tremont St. Suite 700
Boston, MA 02108
www.tsne.org/section/36.html

This service organization is involved with sponsorship for community coalitions and regional or national projects that share their mission of creating healthy, sustainable communities, and active democracy.

Hundreds of organizations offer fiscal sponsorship, and there's probably more than one in your community. When considering an organization to sponsor you, be sure to check them out. You'll want to talk to someone else who has been sponsored by them and take a look at their audited financial statements for the last three years to see if they are financially stable.

Ask an accountant to review the financial statements with you, because these are difficult to understand if you're not used to reading them. It doesn't happen often, but nonprofits have been known to go out of business having spent not only all of their funds but also those of the groups they were sponsoring.

For more information, you might want to read *Fiscal Sponsorship: 6 Ways to Do It Right* by Gregory L. Colvin (ISBN 0-936434-65-1).

What Can You Raise Money For?

No matter what you want to raise money for, there probably is a funder out there who would be interested in making a grant for it. When you begin your research into who your funder might be, you'll need to keep in mind the broad categories that funders use to describe the kind of support they will give.

Words to the Wise

Never put all your eggs in one basket. Apply to several funders at the same time for your project. What, you ask, will happen if they all come through? You should be so lucky to have such a problem, but you can always expand the scope of the project or ask one of the funders to allow you to use their grant to extend the project for a longer period of time.

Project Support

By far the most common type of grant is made to support a particular project, as opposed to operating, capital, and challenge grants, which are described in the following sections. Fortunately, a clever grant writer can make almost any need into a "project."

Funders like projects because projects have a defined beginning and end. This makes it easy to judge if a project has been successful. Funders are wary of a charity coming back again and again expecting support for the same thing. Although renewal grants are fairly common, the funder will almost always make it clear in your grant letter that their grant does not imply any promise of future funding.

Here are some samples of the wide range of project grants (also called "program grants") that I have been successful with over the years:

♦ $10,000 received from a community foundation to provide after-school arts programming to at-risk youth. The grant paid for a writer and a musician to work with the kids, transportation from the homeless shelter in which they lived to the after-school facility, and materials for use in the program.

♦ $25,000 received from a corporate foundation toward the purchase of new computer equipment. The remaining $40,000 for this project was raised mostly from members of the organization's board of directors. The grant paid for hardware, software, and consultants to do the installation. Note that there are some foundations that will pay for software but not hardware and vice versa. We fortunately found one that did not make a distinction.

Words to the Wise

Sometimes the difference between a project and a capital grant lies in how you say it. A small capital project can easily be pitched as a project. Avoid using the word "capital" in the proposal if the funder doesn't fund capital projects and emphasize the short-term rather than the long-term benefits of the project.

♦ $50,000 received from a corporate foundation to expand an internship program over a two-year period. With unemployment at record levels, the corporation was interested in helping people change careers by gaining experience in areas in which their skills were transferable but in which they lacked experience. The grant paid for modest stipends for the interns and for mini-seminars to further develop skills needed in a nonprofit arts organization.

♦ $75,000 received to design a new website and to announce it to the public. The grant covered the fees of the web designers and programmers, advertisements to announce the new site, and also paid for some of the time of regular staff who worked on it.

How to Say It

One of the greatest challenges for a grant writer today is writing a grant proposal for a highly technical subject such as website design or computer networks. Try to integrate definitions into a sentence in a way that does not seem like you are talking down to the reader. Note the subtle difference between "25,000 different people, or unique users, visited our website in January" and "25,000 unique users (i.e., different people) visited our website in January." Placing the tech term second, indicates that you, like the reader, are more comfortable with the plain language description.

♦ $100,000 received for a museum to carry out a pilot program to remain open an additional evening each week and to carry out a publicity campaign to let the public know about the new hours. Funders *love* pilot programs, that is, programs that can be continued or used as an example for similar programs elsewhere. The grant paid for placement of newspaper ads and partly subsidized the cost of remaining open. This grant was one of several for this program. In this case it really paid off: Seven years later, the museum is still open free to the public on Friday evenings.

♦ $170,000 received to provide information services. This grant covered staff salaries to do research to maintain a database of opportunities for artists and to provide personal assistance by phone and e-mail. Office expenses incurred by these staff members were also covered by this grant.

♦ $250,000 received to increase the circulation of a magazine for writers that provides career advice and listings of opportunities. The grant paid for a large direct-mail campaign that would allow testing different approaches and using different designs to see which would be the most successful in attracting new subscribers. This was attractive to funders because it served a dual purpose: It increased the number of writers who were served by the publication, and it increased the *earned income* for the organization, thus making it less dependent on grants in the future.

> **Grant Talk**
>
> Grants that increase **earned income,** that is income not dependent on grants, are popular with funders, because more earned income means less dependence on grants. Earned income can come from service fees, products sold, or even interest income.

Each of these grants was restricted to the purpose outlined in the proposals or the grant contracts. We couldn't change our minds and spend them on something else without the funder's permission.

But what about all those day-to-day expenses that are not part of a particular project? That brings us to general operating support.

Operating Support

The most valuable grant you can receive is for general operating support (known popularly in the business as GOS). This support can be used for basically anything and everything your organization needs to function, including programs, staff salaries (including administrators and fundraisers who are not covered by project grants), rent, utilities, and office supplies.

You would think that because every funder has these same kinds of expenses running their own offices that they would see the need to make grants to cover them, but this is not the case. Consequently, when you find a GOS funder, treasure them, cultivate them, and appreciate them every day.

Funders that provide GOS understand what you do and appreciate its intrinsic value to those you serve. In the best of all possible worlds, these funders will support you over a period of years. But never take your GOS funders for granted. All of them will eventually move on to help other groups.

Many GOS grants will be quite small (as little as $1,000), requiring you to find many of them to pay the basic expenses. This is not necessarily a bad thing—it's easier to replace two $1,000 funders than to replace one $10,000 funder. Spend some time every month looking for new GOS supporters.

Capital Support

Grants to help pay for a new building are the typical capital grant, which is why capital grants are also referred to as bricks and mortar grants. Capital grants, like capital expenses, cover a wider range of needs. Fewer funders make capital grants than make project grants. There are, however, a few major funders that *only* make capital grants.

Capital expenses are usually defined as those that pay for something that will serve the charity over a period of time, from the 50- to 100-year life of a building to three years for computer equipment. Renovations of an existing space and major purchases such as buses or automobiles are also typical capital grant opportunities.

In the previous list of successful grant proposals, you'll remember a project grant for computer equipment. This could have been considered a capital grant, but the scale of the project (less than $100,000 at an organization with a $12 million budget) made it more of a project. "Scale" will depend on your organization's budget and the relative size of the project.

Capital projects are also funded by program-related investments (PRIs). These are usually loans at below market rates (sometimes at zero percent interest). In other cases, PRIs will be made to a nonprofit to develop a program that will create earned income through sale of a service or product. Rather than simply repaying the loans, the nonprofit might pay a percentage of the profits to the foundation, just as a for-profit corporation pays dividends to stockholders. Only a small percent of foundations make PRIs.

Words to the Wise

Never underestimate the value of naming something, anything, for a donor. You don't have to put up a building to cash in on naming opportunities. The coffee machine can be named, or how about the new television for the recreation room? Although a number of donors shy away from naming, others need the extra motivation.

There is a natural attraction to helping bring about something as tangible as a building. The funder and the entire community actually see what has been done. You can reward capital funders by naming anything from a theatre seat to the entire building for them.

Challenge Grants

Funders in general do not like to be the only ones supporting anything, whether it is a project or capital expenditure. A challenge grant allows a funder to make sure that you pursue a broad base of support. The funder provides only partial support for your project and challenges you to find the other funds by withholding the payment of their grant until you prove to them that other money has been raised.

Some funders particularly like to be part of challenges, either as the one making the challenge or by helping to match or fulfill the challenge. A challenge grant can also be a means of encouraging your regular individual contributors (especially board members) to make additional gifts.

> **Philanthropy Facts**
>
> The Kresge Foundation in Flint, Michigan, makes virtually all of its grants in the form of challenge grants for bricks-and-mortar or endowment projects. It funds nationally and generously, so always consider it for a major building project. Kresge has many rules governing the timing of its grants, so get Kresge's information early in the fundraising process.

> **Words to the Wise**
>
> What happens if you are unable to raise the matching funds required by a challenge grant? If you can find a way to still complete the project (even if it's a scaled down version), go back to the original challenger with a revised plan. Chances are they'll still give you the grant. Government agencies, however, are usually not allowed to be so accommodating.

Typically, a challenge grant requires you to raise a proportionate amount of money, either matching the challenge grant equally (a one-to-one match) or greater (a two-to-one or even three-to-one match). For example, with a three-to-one match, the challenger promises to give you $25,000 if you raise an additional $75,000.

For example, the $25,000 grant for computer equipment mentioned earlier was an interesting match—the grant was conditional on our raising the "additional funds to complete the project." This created a wide-open matching situation because we could "make the match" by finding cheaper equipment as well as by raising additional funds, which is exactly how it worked out.

Large capital projects commonly include challenge grants to stimulate both additional giving from current contributors as well as your resolve to find a number of new contributors.

When accepting a challenge grant, be sure you understand all the implications of the challenge, including how many dollars must be raised for the match, the time period you have to raise it, and from whom you must raise the money. The last condition might seem strange. After all, money is money. But if a funder thinks that you have too few donors to support, for example, your new building, they might require that funds come from new donors. Challenge grants help you raise more money, even though all the conditions can sometimes make them seem more trouble than they are worth.

What Funders Look For

It's unfortunate, but I have heard on more than one occasion that funders first look for a reason why they should *not fund a proposal*. Wow! But yes, that's how tough this business can be.

With the huge number of proposals funders receive and the limited staff they have to review proposals, they need to do whatever they can to narrow the field of applicants as quickly as possible. Which brings me to the number one rule of grant writing—*Follow instructions*.

- ◆ If they ask for three copies paper-clipped singly and then clipped together on yellow recycled paper in 13-point type, do it.

- ◆ If they are 20 years behind the times and have an application that must be typed on a typewriter, do it.

- ◆ If they restrict the number of pages or even words, do it.

They next look for a match between their funding interests and your proposal. Too often, grant writers send proposals out to a large number of funders, thinking that at least one will be successful. Wrong. Grant writing is not about luck and multiple submissions. It's about research and focused writing.

Not only will sending a proposal to a funder who does not fund your type of project result in a rejection, but when you later have a project that does meet their interests, they will remember you as the one who didn't do the research the last time.

So the second rule of grant writing is: *Do your research*.

How to Say It

It might sound like grade school, but failure to follow instructions and lack of study (research) doom many proposals before they even reach a foundation board.

When you have passed these two hurdles (which aren't that hard to cross), the funder will likely give your proposal serious consideration. The funder will, of course, also check to make sure you are a nonprofit (or have a fiscal sponsor) and fall within any other restrictions they have (a geographic area is the most common).

I'll discuss the other things a funder will look for when I cover the parts of a proposal, beginning in Chapter 12.

The Least You Need to Know

- Grants can come from foundations, corporations, or government agencies.

- Nonprofit status or a fiscal sponsor is required to receive most grants.

- Individuals can receive grants, too.

- Most grants are awarded for projects, general operating expenses, or for a capital project such as a new building or major piece of equipment.

- Follow each funder's instructions no matter how trivial they might seem or how much they restrict your creativity.

- Approach only funders whose interests could reasonably include your project.

Part 2

Where the Money Is

Billions of dollars are donated every year by philanthropic institutions and individuals. This part looks at each source of grant money—foundations, corporations, government agencies, and individuals—and helps you understand what they are all about.

You have to know what makes each type of funder tick to unlock their vast treasuries. This part also looks at what each will expect from you after you have their money.

Chapter 3

Foundation Primer

In This Chapter

- ◆ What makes a foundation a foundation
- ◆ How the type of foundation influences your approach
- ◆ When a foundation is not a foundation
- ◆ Venture philanthropy: friend or foe?

Foundations have been around since the early seventeenth century, at which time they were largely associated with religious institutions. When we think of a foundation today, the picture that most likely comes to mind includes those set up by the great industrialists of the late nineteenth and early twentieth centuries, such as Andrew Carnegie, Henry Ford, and John D. Rockefeller. Each in his way saw philanthropy as a way to right society's wrongs.

Carnegie in particular was the very picture of the American philanthropist. In his book, *The Gospel of Wealth* (1889), Andrew Carnegie advocated that the rich have a moral obligation to give away their fortunes. Carnegie's philanthropy during his lifetime was wide-ranging, resulting in New York City's Carnegie Hall, The Carnegie (a group of museums, concert hall, and library in Pittsburgh), Carnegie Mellon University, more than 2,000 public libraries throughout the English-speaking world, and several foundations that still bear his name (one confusingly called the Carnegie Corporation of New York).

Philanthropy Facts

At the time of his death, Andrew Carnegie had already given away $350 million of his fortune. He eventually created seven philanthropic and educational organizations in the United States and others in Europe. Today, the Carnegie Corporation of New York (the only one of his philanthropies that is a grantmaking organization) has assets of $1.7 billion and makes around $56 million in grants annually. His other six U.S. foundations are concerned with ethics and international affairs, recognizing heroic individuals and educational policies.

Toward the end of the twentieth century, history seemed to be repeating itself when the titans of the computer world set up foundations bearing their names that quickly took their places among the world's largest. Think Gates, Allen, Hewlett, and Packard.

The creation of foundations was given a boost by the 1913 law that established the income tax, and at the same time exempted organizations that were formed solely for charitable purposes.

The super-rich industrialists weren't the only ones starting foundations in the early twentieth century. Around the same time, the first community foundation was founded in Cleveland, Ohio. The community foundation drew on the wealth of a number of donors who pooled their funds for the support and betterment of their community.

Words to the Wise

If you know that a foundation that supports you plans to "fund out," try to set up a meeting to discuss how a final grant to your charity might be used. Be sure to go with several options, including stabilization of programs they have supported as well as capital projects.

Foundations are usually set up to exist forever. A surprising number of donors, however, establish their foundations with a "sunset clause" that requires their foundations to go out of business at a pre-determined time, usually a set number of years after the founder dies. Donors include sunset clauses, at least in part, out of a desire to have their money given away only by people who knew them (or people who knew people who knew them). In this way, they believe that their money will more likely be used for purposes of which they would have approved.

In the philanthropy business, this is called "funding out" because the foundation gives away all its money; interest and principle. This frequently results in a number of very large grants, which can be a boon to charities. If your organization is not already one of their grantees, however, don't expect to be part of the going-out-of-business bonanza. When they are getting ready to shut the doors, foundations usually will not accept new causes or charities.

Types of Foundations

Foundations today range from small foundations with total assets of $500,000 or even less to the Bill and Melinda Gates Foundation, which, with assets in 2000 of $21 billion, made it the nation's largest. Most foundations fall well in the middle of this dramatic spread. Foundations can be divided into several categories, an understanding of which will help you in researching prospects and focusing your grant proposal.

Typical Foundations

It's hard statistically to justify any model as a typical foundation, but I can describe for you the type of foundation you most often will encounter in your work as a grant writer. One of these foundations will have been founded a number of years ago by a single wealthy individual, making it legally a private foundation. The individual's name or that of a close relative is probably also the name of the foundation. This person might or might not still be living, but even if he or she is, some people not related to the founder will partly compose the board of trustees. Usually, the longer the founder is deceased, the greater the number of nonrelatives on the board.

The foundation probably employs a professional staff of 5 to 200 program officers, assistants, and executive staff. The board of trustees meets several times a year to consider grant proposals. A program officer presents the proposals to the board after carefully screening them according to the foundation's guidelines and interests.

> **Philanthropy Facts**
>
> According to the Foundation Center's helpful FC Stats, in 2000, education captured the greatest share of foundation grants (25 percent), with health coming in second (21 percent), followed by human services (14 percent), the arts (12 percent), and the environment and animals (7 percent).
>
> Source: *Foundation Giving Trends* (2002). The Foundation Center.

Smaller foundations may be administered by the philanthropy or trusts department at a bank or by the donor's lawyer, in which case the bank's or lawyer's employees serve as the foundation staff.

Foundations fitting this very general description will be the easiest for you to learn about and approach.

- They publish guidelines.
- They will at least look at any application that comes through the door.
- They have professional staff that can guide you.

Here are a few examples of my so-called typical foundations:

- The Dana Foundation
  745 5th Avenue, Suite 900
  New York, NY 10151
  www.dana.org

  This foundation's principal interests are in improved teaching of the performing arts in public schools and in health, particularly neuroscience and immunology. They employ nearly 30 people. Grants: $18 million in 2001.

- The James Irvine Foundation
  1 Market Street, Steuart Tower, Suite 2500
  San Francisco, CA 94105
  www.irvine.org

  This foundation gives in California, primarily for higher education, workforce development, civic culture, sustainable communities, and children, youth, and families. It has over 40 employees. Grants: $51 million estimated in 2003.

- The Joyce Foundation
  3 First National Plaza, 70 W. Madison Street, Suite 2750
  Chicago, IL 60602
  www.joycefdn.org

  This foundation makes grants for urban issues in Chicago; improvement of schools in Chicago, Cleveland, Detroit, and Milwaukee; poverty in the Midwest; the natural environment of the Great Lakes; election finance reform; and gun control. They also make grants to individuals whose work falls within these areas. They have 21 staff members. Grants: $43 million in 2000.

- W. K. Kellogg Foundation
  1 Michigan Avenue E.
  Battle Creek, MI 49017-4058
  www.wkkf.org

  This foundation's primary interests lie in health, food systems and rural development, youth and education, and philanthropy and voluntarism. They also make special grants in their local community. They have nearly 200 employees. Grants: $223 million in 2002.

- The Rockefeller Foundation
  420 Fifth Avenue
  New York, NY 10018-2702
  www.rockfound.org

Their wide-ranging interests include the arts; civil society; feeding and employing the poor; medical research, training, and distribution of services; revitalization of the African continent; and more. They also run a conference center in Italy for scholars, scientists, artists, writers, policymakers, and others to conduct creative and scholarly work. Around 175 people manage these programs. Grants: $162 million in 2001.

◆ Robert W. Woodruff Foundation, Inc.
50 Hurt Plaza, Suite 1200
Atlanta, GA 30303
www.woodruff.org

Interests of this foundation include kindergarten through college education; health care and education; human services, particularly for children; economic development; art and cultural activities; and the environment. They prefer one-time capital projects of established charities. Their staff consists of 12 people. Grants: $123 million in 2002.

Words to the Wise

Foundations tend to fund locally, but don't overlook funders outside your area. For example, the Jerome Foundation in Minneapolis makes grants in Minnesota and in New York City. The better foundation directories will have an index of geographic interest to cross check against office locations.

Although these are all very large foundations, their range of interests is not atypical nor is the way they limit their grantmaking to organizations in specific geographic areas. As with all funders, you must do your homework to make sure that your grant proposal meets all of their restrictions.

Family Foundations

A family foundation is one in which the majority of trustees (frequently all) are related to the foundation's founder. Most foundations begin as family foundations, but here we're talking about those that are still governed by the family that founded them. The Council on Foundations estimates that two-fifths of all private and community foundations are run by families. These foundations account for one-third of all foundation giving.

Many family foundations have few or no paid staff and depend on family members volunteering their time. They can easily be overwhelmed with the volume of applications. Be sure to approach them only when you are certain that your organization fits their requirements and you are ready to submit a proposal.

As with any family undertaking, family dynamics frequently come into play at these foundations. At some, the "I'll vote to make a grant to your library if you'll vote to support my hospital" interaction can make for seemingly erratic grantmaking. This makes your research that much harder. On the positive side, if you or someone on your board knows one of the family foundation's trustees, that trustee will likely have enough sway to get your grant approved.

Philanthropy Facts

Family foundations are among the largest foundations in the United States, including the Bill and Melinda Gates Foundation (the nation's largest of any kind). The top ten foundations with "family" in their name contribute upwards of $300 million annually and include families such as the Waltons (as in Wal-Mart) and Hall (as in Hallmark cards). The large family foundations might be staffed more like older foundations, but the personalities of their founders still guide the giving.

The changing of the generations at a family foundation can result in a sharp change in funding priorities. It's only natural that the younger generation will want to differentiate itself from its parent's grantmaking.

When researching foundations, note the surnames of the trustees, if the founder is living, and if he or she is also a trustee. You might have to do a little detective work, because surnames might have changed with marriages.

If it appears that you are dealing with a family foundation, be prepared to …

◆ Forget about applying to one if they do not accept unsolicited proposals, unless you can …

◆ Find a personal connection with a trustee.

◆ Look carefully at the *most recent* grant awards to see how they match (or don't) any published guidelines.

Words to the Wise

If you notice very specific and seemingly erratic geographic restrictions, you'll probably find that family members live in each of those locations. Your research may be able to pinpoint who lives where, allowing you to then discover that family member's local giving preferences, which in turn will help you focus your proposal.

Here are a few examples of the larger family foundations:

◆ The Arthur M. Blank Family Foundation
The Forum, 3290 Northside Parkway, N.W., Suite 600
Atlanta, GA 30327
www.blankfoundation.org

The founder of Home Depot gives to arts and culture, athletics and fitness, education enhancement, environment (including outdoor activities), fostering understanding, and organizational effectiveness in Georgia; Maricopa County, Arizona; Coastal South

Carolina; Park and Gallatin Counties, Montana; and New York City. Thirteen employees run this foundation. Grants: $35 million in 2001.

◆ The Brown Foundation, Inc.
2217 Welch Avenue
Houston, TX 77019
www.brownfoundation.org

The Brown Foundation, Inc. supports public primary and secondary education in Texas; services for children, especially in the Houston area; and the visual and performing arts. They have seven full-time staff. Grants: $62.3 million in 2001.

◆ The Milken Family Foundation
1250 4th Street, 6th Floor
Santa Monica, CA 90401
www.mff.org

Although a number of family members are among the trustees, several nonfamily members are also on the board. Grants are made mostly in education and medical research (especially cancer research) and mostly in California. They make a large part of their grants through awards and fellowships. They list 18 staff members on their website. Grants: $24 million in 2001.

Community Foundations

The United States has nearly 600 community foundations, and Canada has 127, serving virtually every geographical area. These foundations collectively make grants of as much as $2 billion annually, making them an important source to consider for your proposal. Community foundations are considered public foundations because they actively solicit support from a wide range of the public. This is in contrast to the private foundations discussed in the previous two sections, which receive support from one or two individuals.

Community Foundations bring philanthropy within the grasp of those who are comfortably well off, but not able to put millions into a private foundation. This is not to say that immensely wealthy people do not contribute to community foundations; many do, establishing funds at a community foundation in addition to their private foundations. Community foundations also have a general fund made up of contributions from a large number of donors.

A chief characteristic of a community foundation is the many funds that have been entrusted to it, each established by a different donor to benefit some

Philanthropy Facts

Community Foundation Silicon Valley (www.cfsv.org) is one of the fastest growing community foundations in the United States with assets of $583 million in 600 funds. The founders of eBay are among their donors. It serves Santa Clara and southern San Mateo Counties in California, and made $52 million in grants in 2001.

aspect of life in that particular community. The New York Community Trust, for example, has some 1,600 different funds, ranging in assets from $5,000 to $70 million.

So how do you go about deciding which of 1,600 funds to apply to? You don't. You cannot apply directly to most of those funds. Although administered by the community foundation, the donors have retained the right to advise the foundation on what grants should be made. Legally, the final decision rests with the community foundation, but donor recommendations are usually followed when they fall within the guidelines of the community foundation. Theoretically, you could solicit these donors as individuals, but finding their names will be difficult.

Other funds at community foundations might issue a *request for proposal* (RFP) or have formal guidelines. The website of The Greater Kansas City Community Foundation (www.gkccf.org) is a model of clarity in laying out the foundation's different funds and how to apply.

Grant Talk

A **request for proposal** is a means funders employ to encourage proposals for a program established by the funder. In many cases, an RFP is no different from the guidelines a funder issues for grants. With the RFP, the funder is being proactive in soliciting proposals, perhaps for a new initiative or for a program that has not been receiving good proposals. The Foundation Center maintains a free, current national list of RFPs on its website at www.fndcenter.org, which they'll also e-mail you weekly for free.

The funds without donor advisors can be applied to with one application—you simply apply to the community foundation itself, noting its areas of interest, of course. If it finds your proposal both worthy of funding and meeting the restrictions established by a particular fund's donor, your grant letter will tell you that your have received a grant "from the Betty F. and Henry S. Smith Fund of the New York Community Trust." (And yes, if you get a grant from them, you have to use the whole long name in all acknowledgements and donor listings.) Not every grant from a community foundation will be from a specific fund. They also maintain a general endowment from which they make grants.

If a community foundation is on your prospect list …

◆ Research to see if any of your potential individual donors or one of their family members has established a donor-advised fund.

◆ Check to see if the community foundation solicits proposals through RFPs.

◆ Only apply to a specific fund at a community foundation if their guidelines say to do so.

◆ Only apply to a community foundation in your area. They aren't interested in work you might do elsewhere, and community foundations in other areas might be unable to fund you, even for a program that takes place in their community.

Operating Foundations

An operating foundation may make grants, but grantmaking is a small part of what it does. An operating foundation can be private or public. It usually runs one or more research or service programs that are its primary reason for existing. For the most part, these will not be good prospects because they do limited grantmaking and have a narrow range of interests. But if their interests match yours, go for it.

> **Philanthropy Facts**
>
> Depending on which way the stock market tilts on a particular day, the distinction of being the world's largest foundation goes to either the Bill and Melinda Gates Foundation of Seattle, Washington, or the Wellcome Trust in Great Britain. Both have assets in the $21 billion range. An American, Henry Wellcome, one of the founders of Burroughs Wellcome pharmaceuticals, founded the Wellcome Trust in 1936.

Here are a few examples of what you can expect operating foundations to look like.

◆ Russell Sage Foundation
112 East 64th Street
New York, NY 10021
www.russellsage.org

This foundation is devoted to research in the social sciences, supporting scholars who study at its facility or at other institutions. It also publishes books and holds seminars. Grants: $4 million in 2000.

◆ Carnegie Endowment for International Peace
1779 Massachusetts Avenue, NW
Washington, DC 20036
www.ceip.org

International affairs and U.S. foreign policy are pursued through research, discussion, education, and publications by this beneficiary of Andrew Carnegie. Grants: $0.

◆ KnowledgeWorks Foundation
700 Walnut Street, #600
Cincinnati, OH 45202
www.kwfdn.org

Educational initiatives in Ohio are the sole concerns of this foundation, which does make grants. Grants: $1.35 million.

Commercial Foundations

How can there be a "Commercial Foundation?" Well, technically there can't be, but I'm using this term to identify and distinguish one of the most dramatic trends in funding in the last decade.

The very wealthy have always had access to manage their philanthropy through the trust department at their banks. This assistance, however, usually came only to those with seven-figure (or much higher) deposits at the bank. In 1992, Fidelity Investments Corporation realized that many of their clients (both middle class and beyond) would be interested in a way to manage their philanthropy just like they managed their other investments. The result was the Fidelity Charitable Gift Fund.

The *Chronicle of Philanthropy*'s 2001 ranking of the largest charities by total donations received showed that the Fidelity Charitable Gift Fund was the second largest charity in the United States, receiving $1.087 billion in contributions, $353 million behind the Salvation Army, which has long been the largest U.S. charity—but maybe not for much longer. The Fidelity Charitable Gift Fund made $735 million in grants in 2001.

Needless to say, every other investment bank took notice, and today dozens if not hundreds of institutions operate in the same way. Legally, these are 501(c)(3) nonprofits, not foundations at all, even though without any programs and vast reserves of money they certainly look like foundations. (Merrill Lynch, interestingly, decided not to get on this bandwagon. Instead of offering their own donor-advised funds, they decided to work with community foundations to increase giving in local communities.)

> **Words to the Wise**
>
> Don't confuse the Fidelity Charitable Gift Fund with the Fidelity Foundation. The Fidelity Foundation (www.fidelityfoundation.org) is the company foundation that makes grants in areas where they have a major presence to a wide range of nonprofits.

> **Philanthropy Facts**
>
> All foundations do not have "foundation" in their name. Some might use the designation "Fund" or "Trust" or "Charitable Trust," but others call themselves "corporations," like the Carnegie Corporation of New York, mentioned at the beginning of this chapter.

Don't get excited by all that money in the gift funds operated by commercial financial institutions. You can't apply to them for a grant. If one of their investors (I mean, donors) decides to make a grant to your charity, you'll receive a check, possibly accompanied by a letter identifying the donor, possibly not, because the gift funds allow donors to give anonymously. The commercial gift fund administrators do not need to receive your newsletters or anything else beyond the acknowledgement letter required by IRS regulations, because they do not direct the grantmaking.

Foundations in Name Only

There is no legal definition of a foundation. Even the IRS defines a foundation by what it is not. For example, a private foundation is defined as one that does not receive its funds from a wide segment of the public. Some organizations with the word "foundation" in their name aren't foundations, as we understand them. They and other nonprofits that make grants using funds they have raised are called Grantmaking Public Charities by the Foundation Center to distinguish them from private, corporate, or public foundations. The Foundation Center and other funder directory resources include many of them in their publications and databases. Community foundations and local service organizations might be able to point you to others.

Venture Philanthropy

The hot topic at the end of the twentieth century was venture philanthropy. It was used in relation to both foundation and corporate giving. This was a vogue term coined possibly as long ago as 1984 to denote the source of much of this new philanthropic money (venture capitalists who were making a killing in the stock market) and the way they approached their philanthropy (supposedly just like they did their businesses).

The following characteristics are typically attributed to venture philanthropy:

♦ Venture philanthropists seek involvement with the nonprofits they fund, not necessarily as board members or trustees, but as a source of management and technical assistance.

♦ They provide support over a period of years. Just as a business needs time to grow, so do nonprofits—something we can all agree on.

♦ They expect accountability beyond the making of annual progress reports, making fulfillment of specific goals and frequent reporting essential.

♦ Venture philanthropists expect you to plan from the beginning of their support how you will continue the program after their support ends.

♦ They are very pro-technology when it comes to learning to whom to give their money and as a means to solving societal problems.

CAUTION

How to Say It

Strunk & White's admonition in *The Elements of Style* "Do not be tempted by a twenty-dollar word when there is a ten-center handy, ready, and able" could have been written with venture philanthropists in mind. Shed all your jargon and never say anything that could be viewed as talking down to them.

If you apply to a foundation that practices venture philanthropy (and frequently they'll say so if they do), be prepared for the higher level of involvement and for thinking of your grant proposal as a business plan. Also expect to provide some kind of ROI (return on investment), whether that is a social return (through improved services), a financial return (when your charity performs more efficiently), or even an emotional return (warm-and-fuzzy feelings), the venture philanthropist expects something back—for the charity as much as for himself or herself.

Words to the Wise

Financial transparency is key to engaging the venture philanthropists. Have your 990 tax return at the ready to give them, and make sure the information on top staff salaries is included. High staff salaries won't bother them: They expect highly skilled people to be paid well. They will expect full financial disclosure. Don't be afraid to post your audited financial statement and 990 form on your website.

Venture philanthropists have been successful in business and believe they can be successful in other areas (like philanthropy). Provide them with an opportunity for success.

Venture philanthropy seems to have become a less common buzzword with the fall in the stock market that began in late 2000. Some venture philanthropy foundations, however, continue to function and function well, such as the Robin Hood Foundation in New York City (www.robinhood.org).

The Least You Need to Know

- ◆ The way a foundation is set up and managed should influence your approach.

- ◆ Large, long-established foundations are generally more open to your approaching them than those still controlled by the founder or the founder's family.

- ◆ Charitable gift funds run by financial institutions are not foundations and not places to which you can submit a proposal.

- ◆ Operating foundations have limited grantmaking programs, preferring to run their own programs.

- ◆ Many nonprofit organizations, some calling themselves foundations, also make grants to other nonprofits and to individuals.

- ◆ A grant from a venture philanthropist might bring with it technical support, involvement by the funder, a long-time commitment, and greater reporting requirements.

Chapter 4

Corporation Primer

In This Chapter

- ◆ Why corporations give away their money
- ◆ Raising money from companies with problems
- ◆ How sponsorship differs from a grant
- ◆ Outline of a sponsorship proposal
- ◆ Corporate donations other than cash
- ◆ Which corporate door to knock on first

On the face of it, it might seem strange that a corporation would give away some of its profits. After all, a public corporation operates to make money for its stockholders. Corporate philanthropy still remains controversial at some companies for this reason. Corporations, even those with supportive boards and stockholders, must justify their philanthropic expenses as good for the bottom line. This is why, when all is said and done, corporate philanthropy is about public relations and marketing the company's name and products.

Corporations give money to charities ...

- ◆ To improve employee morale by supporting charities the employees care about.
- ◆ To improve their image as good corporate citizens with the public by supporting charities that serve the public.

♦ To improve their image with stockholders by burnishing their image with the public.

♦ To make the communities where they operate better places to live and work.

Formal corporate giving has only been active in a substantive way since 1935 when the tax laws were structured to permit (and encourage) greater corporate giving. Since then, corporate giving has become an important part of funding for charities of all kinds. According to the AAFRC Trust for Philanthropy's *Giving USA 2002* report, analysis of 1998 tax returns reveals that overall, U.S. companies contribute one percent of net income to charity, but the percent varies widely by industry from a high of eight percent in mining (which includes petroleum) to a low of four tenths of one percent in the finance and insurance industries.

Philanthropy Facts

The nonprofit community lobbies corporations to commit to donating 2 percent of net income, although few contribute at this level. Minneapolis, however, started a five percent club in 1976 made up of companies pledged to giving at that level. Today it's called Minneapolis Keystone, and it includes a 2 percent and a 5 percent club. The latter boasts 152 members, including major U.S. companies such as Target, General Mills, and Andersen.

Corporations give their money away through a variety of mechanisms based on how the company is structured and what it wants to accomplish through charitable giving. In this chapter, I'll look at corporate foundations, giving programs, matching gifts, sponsorships, and in-kind gifts.

Corporate Foundations

Corporate foundations usually do not have huge endowments. Instead, the relatively small income for grants produced by the endowment is supplemented (sometimes to the tune of seven figures!) by an annual donation to the foundation by the company. This gives the company the flexibility to make fewer grants in lean years and more grants when business is booming.

Ostensibly, the foundation is independent of the corporation. A corporate foundation is subject to the same laws prohibiting self-dealing and minimum grants made from their assets as is a private foundation. This is not to say that the mission of a corporate foundation is ever far from that of its company. The board of the foundation is usually composed of high-ranking executives from the company, and its policies reflect the public image the company seeks to project.

Corporate foundations cannot receive tangible benefits in exchange for a grant, just like private foundations. But even a simple acknowledgement such as "This program has been brought to you by Local Widget Company, supplying the community with widgets for 30 years" has a great public relations value. Thus, even an independent company foundation can further the goals of better PR for the company.

To concentrate their influence where it will do them the most good, all but the largest corporate foundations fund only in geographic areas where they operate. Corporations that fund nationally operate nationally, such as AT&T, Sears, and Ben & Jerry's.

Many of the larger corporate foundations have developed programs to carry their brand name forward in a targeted manner that they could not achieve with individual grants. For example AT&T:OnStage has supported production of 84 new plays at 56 theatres in the United States, Canada, and the United Kingdom. AT&T also assists with the marketing of these plays to spread recognition of the corporate brand.

Cashing In on Trouble

One of the more cynical (yet effective) means of targeting corporate philanthropy is to look for companies that have a public relations problem. After the Exxon Valdez dumped millions of gallons of oil along the Alaskan shoreline, any environmental group that had asked for a contribution probably would have received it, but few would have wanted to associate themselves with Exxon at that time.

Many corporations take a proactive position and focus their grantmaking on areas of potential controversy or ongoing PR problems. Several oil companies (even those without major ecological disasters to their credit) focus their grantmaking on environmental causes. Tobacco companies are among the most generous corporate sponsors, and they love to support dance and sports—activities requiring great stamina and lung capacity.

Words to the Wise

If you consider applying to a corporation in trouble, be sure your executive director and your board know about it before you get started. You don't want to create your own public relations nightmare by accepting money that would work against your charity's image.

Don't Be Led Astray

Grant writers make one of their most common errors in targeting corporate philanthropy by assuming a corporation makes grants in an area parallel to its own business. It can happen, but just as often doesn't. For example …

- ◆ Lucent Technologies Foundation doesn't fund technology projects. Their grants go for education reform.

- ◆ Gulfstream Aerospace Corporation Contributions Program doesn't fund science or engineering. They prefer to support historic preservation (a popular topic in their home city of Savannah, Georgia), arts, and education.

- ◆ BP Foundation (as in British Petroleum) doesn't fund chemical engineering or even environmental causes (like other mining companies). They support education and humanitarian aid in response to disasters.

So always check carefully what a corporation will fund in a directory of funders or on the company's website. Don't waste their time and yours trying to stretch the limits of their guidelines.

Sample Entry

Entry number

1633
LINCOLN NATIONAL CORPORATION
(also known as Lincoln Financial Group)
Philadelphia, PA

Company name and location

Business activities

Company URL: http://www.lfg.com
Business activities: Operates holding company; sells life insurance; provides investment advisory services.

Corporate financial information including *Fortune* and *Forbes* ratings

Financial profile for 2001: Number of employees, 6,780; assets, $98,001,304,000; sales volume, $6,380,638,000; pre-tax income, $764,139,000
Fortune 500 ranking: 2001—286th in revenues, 137th in profits, and 39th in assets
Forbes 500 ranking: 2001—275th in sales, 133rd in profits, and 33rd in assets

Corporate officers

Corporate officer(s): Jon Boscia, Pres. and C.E.O.; Richard C. Vaughan, Exec. V.P. and C.F.O.; George E. Davis, Sr. V.P., Human Resources
Subsidiaries: The Lincoln National Life Insurance Co., Fort Wayne, IN

Giving statement

Giving statement: Giving through a corporate giving program and a foundation.

Corporate giving program name and address

Lincoln Financial Group Corporate Giving Program
c/o Corp. Public Involvement
1300 S. Clinton St., P.O. Box 7863
Fort Wayne, IN 46802
FAX: (260) 455-4004; URL: http://www.lfg.com/lfg/ipc/abt/cgv/index.html

Corporate giving program financial information

Contact: Patti Grimm, Corp. Public Involvement Prog. Admin.
Financial data (yr. ended 12/31/01): Total giving, $260,764, including $253,474 for 26 grants (high: $35,000; low: $600; average: $600-$35,000) and $7,290 for 16 in-kind gifts.
Purpose and activities: As a complement to its foundation, Lincoln Financial also makes charitable contributions to nonprofit organizations directly. Support is given primarily in Hartford, Connecticut, Schaumburg, Illinois, Fort Wayne, Indiana, Portland, Maine, Syracuse, New York, and Philadelphia, Pennsylvania.
Fields of interest: Arts/cultural programs; higher education; education; youth development; human services.

Types of support offered

Types of support: General/operating support; sponsorships; donated equipment.
Geographic limitations: Giving primarily in Hartford, CT, Schaumburg, IL, Fort Wayne, IN, Portland, ME, Syracuse, NY, and Philadelphia, PA.
Support limitations: No support for public or private K-12 schools, hospitals, hospital programs or foundations, nursing homes, veterans' posts or organizations, service organizations, or fraternal organizations. No grants to individuals, or for religious causes, political causes, or sporting events or tournaments.
Publications: Corporate giving report, application guidelines.

Application information

Application information: The Corporate Public Involvement Department handles giving. The company has a staff that only handles contributions. A contributions committee reviews all requests. Application form required.
Initial approach: Contact nearest company facility for application form
Copies of proposal: 1
Deadline(s): Contact nearest company facility for deadlines
Final notification: Following review

Staff

Number of staff: 1 full-time professional; 2 part-time professional; 1 full-time support.

Foundation name and address

The Lincoln Financial Group Foundation
(formerly The Lincoln National Foundation, Inc.)
1300 S. Clinton St.
P.O. Box 7863
Fort Wayne, IN 46801-7863 (260) 455-3879
E-mail: ao'neill@LNC.com; URL: http://www.lfg.com/lfg/ipc/abt/cgv/index.html

Establishment information: Established in 1962 in IN.
Donor(s): Lincoln National Corp.
Contact: Angela O'Neill
Financial data (yr. ended 12/31/00): Assets, $17,742,697 (M); gifts received, $8,874,899; expenditures, $8,936,967; qualifying distributions, $8,585,889, including $6,836,906 for 565 grants (high: $450,000; low: $250; average: $5,000-$50,000) and $271,373 for employee matching gifts.
Purpose and activities: Giving primarily for arts and culture, education, and human services in communities where employees live and work. Operates the Lincoln Museum in Fort Wayne, IN.
Fields of interest: Arts/cultural programs; education; human services; children & youth, services; community development, neighborhood development.
International interests: United Kingdom.
Program(s):
Lincoln Financial Advisors Matching Gift Program: The program offers matching funds for charitable contributions by Regional Planning Offices (RPO) and Lincoln Financial Group agents. The program is designed to assist charitable efforts that will enhance the quality of life in communities where Lincoln Financial Group has a business presence. Through the program, the foundation matches contributions to qualifying nonprofit organizations across the United States.
Matching College Gift Program: The foundation has a strong commitment to education; nearly a third of the foundation's charitable dollars are devoted to educational programs and higher learning institutions. To further its commitment to education, Lincoln Financial Group matches contributions made by its employees, agents and retirees to accredited colleges and universities across the United States. This program encourages individuals associated with the corporation and its affiliates to support colleges and universities.
Types of support: Annual campaigns; capital campaigns; building/renovation; equipment; land acquisition; emergency funds; program development; conferences/seminars; seed money; scholarship funds; technical assistance; consulting services; program evaluation; employee matching gifts; matching/challenge support.
Geographic limitations: Giving limited to communities where Lincoln National employees live and work, with emphasis on Hartford, CT, Chicago, IL, Fort Wayne, IN, Portland, ME, Syracuse, NY, Philadelphia, PA, and the United Kingdom.
Support limitations: No support for religious or political causes, elementary or secondary schools, hospitals and nursing homes, veterans' service or fraternal organizations, sporting events, or tournaments. No grants to individuals, or for endowments, multi-year funding, operating support, deficit reduction, continuing support, or marketing programs. Support for tickets, corporate tables, and testimonial events is limited.
Publications: Annual report, application guidelines.
Application information: Application form required. Applicants should submit the following:
1) copy of IRS Determination Letter
Initial approach: Letter requesting application and guidelines
Copies of proposal: 1
Board meeting date(s): Quarterly
Deadline(s): Varies
Final notification: Within a week following board meeting
Directors: Jon A. Boscia, Gloster Current, George E. Davis, John H. Gotta, Charles E. Haldeman, Jr., Barbara S. Kowalczyk, Angela O'Neill, D'Arcy Rudnay, M. Joyce Schlatter, Susan Segal, Lorry Stensrud, Westley V. Thompson, Richard C. Vaughan, C. Suzanne Womack.
Number of staff: None.
EIN: 356042099
Selected grants: The following grants were reported in 1999.
$500,000 to Regional Performing Arts Center, Philadelphia, PA. For construction of center.
$500,000 to YMCA of Metropolitan Fort Wayne, Fort Wayne, IN. For facility renovations and new equipment for Old Fort and Southeast Family branches.
$411,000 to Philadelphia Futures for Youth, Philadelphia, PA. For Sponsor-A Scholar Program and Delaware/Lincoln Scholarship.

Establishment data

Foundation financial information

Areas of foundation giving

Specific limitations to giving

Foundation officers, trustees, or members of other governing bodies

IRS identification number

Selected grants

Symbols

‡ Indicates individual is deceased. (L) Ledger value of assets. (M) Market value of assets. * Officer is also a trustee or director

A sample listing from National Directory of Corporate Giving, 8th Edition, David Clark, ed. New York, NY: The Foundation Center (79 Fifth Avenue, New York, NY 10003, www.fdncenter.org), August 2002.

Corporate Foundations Versus Contributions Office

In a number of cases, the company foundation administers limited program areas, leaving other giving to the corporate contributions office. Every company that has two means of giving divides responsibilities for different reasons, but there are two generalizations that might help you in researching them.

- Companies that make significant in-kind donations of services or products usually do so through the contributions office. If you aren't sure if a company donates products, there's nothing wrong with phoning the foundation to ask about it, but they will in all likelihood refer you to another office.

- Although grants made through the foundation must be listed in the foundation's IRS return, which is open to public inspection, contributions made through the contributions office do not have the same reporting requirements. This makes it easier for a corporation to support a cause that is controversial or does not fit within its foundation's guidelines.

Words to the Wise

It's rare for a corporation to make charitable grants where they do not have a corporate presence. To do so would violate the entire community relations angle of corporate giving. Take a look at the business pages in your local paper to see what companies are active in your area—and which are doing well financially—to start your corporate prospect list.

Local Versus National Giving

Some companies make grants through their foundations or contributions office for national programs, but make grants for local organizations through their branch offices or stores. Sears, for example, has a national giving program but also makes grants and in-kind gifts through its local stores. This can definitely work to your advantage, because the manager of a store in your community will likely have a better understanding of the needs in your town and might even be familiar with your charity.

Corporate Matching Gifts

As I mentioned at the beginning of this chapter, one reason corporations give is to improve employee morale. One way of doing this it to allow employees to have some say in which charities receive grants. Rather than influence the major grantmaking activities of the corporation, many companies will match the contributions made to charities by an employee (and in some cases those made by the spouse of an employee or a member of the corporate board of directors).

Mostly, they match dollar for dollar, but some go as high as three to one. You apply for these grants by completing a simple form (supplied by the donor) and enclosing proof of nonprofit status after you have received a contribution from someone associated with the corporation. You don't even have to do a cover letter, much less a proposal.

Corporate Grants Versus Sponsorship

Corporate sponsorship drops the aura of doing good and gets down to an exchange of benefits between the corporation and a charity—cash (or goods) for positive PR and some marketing opportunities. There is big money in sponsorship: The IEG (International Events Group) reported $1.44 billion in 2001 sponsorships of the arts and various causes.

A corporate sponsorship proposal bears little resemblance to a grant proposal. The sponsorship proposal's focus will be on the demographics of your constituents (age, income, occupation, where they live, and even buying habits if you know them) rather than on the details of your programs. Rather than smoothly flowing prose, the sponsorship proposal uses bullet points to highlight the PR and marketing opportunities you offer.

If you cannot describe the people your organization serves in demographic terms, you probably will be unsuccessful seeking sponsorships. You can survey your constituents to gather this information, or you can get general information from the U.S. Census Bureau (www.census.gov). Its website can give you a lot of what you'll need based on city, county, or even city block, and the information is free.

To give you a more concrete idea of what a sponsorship proposal would look like, here's a list of its parts:

1. One-page cover letter summarizing first the benefits to the corporation, secondly your project, and finally a price range for sponsorship—never an exact price.

2. One-page summary of benefits to the corporation and audience/constituent demographics (see the sample following this list).

3. One-page summary of the sponsorship opportunity, such as dates, location, attendance, expected media coverage—everything you would include on an invitation and on a press fact sheet.

4. Samples of press and reports from your own publications of similar past projects.

5. Sample brochures from past events showing prominent sponsor credit.

Do not include books, annual report, or videotapes. The idea is to sell the corporation on your charity with the fewest possible words and pictures. You'll find a template for a complete corporate sponsorship proposal on the accompanying CD-ROM, but here's an example of a fact sheet listing the benefits to the corporate sponsor and the demographics of the charity's audience.

Benefits to Anytown Daily News as Exclusive Media Sponsor of AIDS Ride 2003

- ◆ Exposure to the 2,000 people either participating in or attending the start and finish of the AIDS Ride 2003.

- ◆ Exposure to the 4,000 supporters of Community AIDS Services through the monthly newsletter.

- ◆ Prominent acknowledgement in all press releases, advertisements, and mailings associated with the AIDS Ride 2003.

- ◆ Celebrity participation is likely to draw significant press attention.

- ◆ Status as sole media sponsor excludes any competitors from participating.

- ◆ Opportunity to be associated in the minds of all who hear of the event with the local agency that has done more than any other in Anytown to provide services to people living with HIV/AIDS.

Audience Demographics

- ◆ Riders: average age 31, 60 percent male, household income between $40,000 and $55,000, college degree or higher

- ◆ Start and finish line audience: average age 29, 70 percent female, household income between $40,000 and $55,000, some college

- ◆ Supporters of Community AIDS Services: average age 42, 65 percent female, household income $55,000 to $75,000, some college

---

You would think that sponsorships would not be tax-deductible, but that's not the case. As a grant writer who will be crafting sponsorship proposals, it helps for you to understand what benefits are and aren't tax-deductible. Even though the corporation's decision to sponsor you will be based on market factors, being able to remind them that all or part will be tax-deductible sweetens the deal. A few theoretical examples will make it clear what I mean:

Words to the Wise

Tax deductibility of contributions is a complex subject. The examples given here are not meant to be applicable to any other situations. Always check with your accountant or lawyer to help you determine whether gifts are tax deductible or not.

Example #1: A camera manufacturer gives a sporting event $1 million to be the exclusive photography sponsor. The contract states that the sporting event will not accept money from any other film or camera company, that signs acknowledging the sponsorship will appear prominently at all events, and that the camera manufacturer will have the right to claim "official sponsor" status on all its products for a specified length of time.

Grant or sponsorship? Clearly a sponsorship and not tax deductible because of the considerable benefits the camera manufacturer receives in return: Not only did it receive rights to promote its product at the event and anywhere else connected with the event it chose, but it also kept its competition from participating.

Example #2: An airline gives free travel to the employees of a nonprofit, which in exchange acknowledges it as the "official airline" and provides a link on the nonprofit's website.

Grant or sponsorship? Probably sponsorship, but the IRS has ruled that simple acknowledgment and a logo link on a website do not make the corporation's payment nondeductible. Chances are this money would come through the sponsorship or marketing office, even though the entire donation would be tax deductible.

Example #3: A corporation gives a public radio station $25,000 to sponsor its most popular program. In exchange, the radio station agrees to announce the sponsorship (or underwriting in public radio lingo) three times during each airing of the program for a month.

Grant or sponsorship? This time, the corporation can definitely consider it a grant, taking a full tax deduction because public radio rules prohibit a long list of words (like free, best, biggest, on sale) that would make it an advertisement.

Example #4: A bank makes a $10,000 contribution to be a corporate member of a museum. In exchange, they want all their employees to receive free admission.

Grant or sponsorship? Somewhere in between. The corporation might pay for this one in two checks: one paying for the free admissions drawn on the company account and one covering the balance (what the museum has determined to be the tax-deductible value of the membership) from the company foundation's account.

Philanthropy Facts

The IEG (International Events Group) provides the most complete information on corporate sponsorship. It publishes a newsletter, has a helpful website (www.sponsorship.com), and holds seminars across the United States. The seminars are expensive to attend, but they're worth it for the resource notebook you receive. The notebook contains sample sponsorship proposals as well as a method for figuring out just what your sponsorship opportunity is worth to a corporation.

Tax deductibility aside, as the grant writer you need to determine which office at the corporation will be most interested in your proposal.

◆ Contact the sponsorship/marketing office if you can offer significant public relations opportunities to the corporation in exchange for the money. Regardless of how much ends up being tax deductible, this will be considered a sponsorship.

◆ Contact the foundation or contributions office if you can offer nothing more than a polite acknowledgement of the money.

Free Stuff and Free Consulting

Corporations also make available to nonprofits at no charge the products they manufacture. Giving you $2,000 worth of soup (retail) costs the corporation less than giving you a $2,000 grant. When you receive goods or services instead of a grant, it is known as an *in-kind gift*. You sometimes have to write a proposal for an in-kind gift just as you would for a cash grant.

Grant Talk

In-kind gifts (free goods or services) can be a significant resource for your charity. To benefit your ongoing relationship with the corporation, be sure to send a thank you letter immediately and a follow-up letter a few months later to tell them exactly how the product was used. In-kind contributors should be acknowledged in all your donor lists, in a ranking of equivalent value, or in a separate list of in-kind donors.

Many corporations make their products available to nonprofits through a third-party distributor. The best known of these groups is Gifts In Kind International, with branches across the country. You pay a membership fee to them to receive their catalog. Virtually anything you can think of is in that catalog. Companies donating through them include Home Depot, IBM, Williams Sonoma, and Staples, Inc. Check the Gifts in Kind's website (www. giftsinkind.org) to find the affiliate in your area. Other than the simple membership application form, no proposal is needed when ordering products directly through them.

Philanthropy Facts

Microsoft and several other technology companies make their products available at a deep discount through a San Francisco-based organization called DiscounTech (www.techsoup. org/DiscounTech).

You can also apply to some corporations for a free consultant to work with you, typically on finance or technology issues, because businesses and nonprofits have these issues in common. Their companies might pay these volunteers their regular salary while they work for you.

This is really great community relations for the corporation because they have literally put a human face on their philanthropy. The nonprofit receives help from a highly qualified consultant at no cost. Talk about a win-win situation! Companies handle this in different ways. On Qualcomm's website (www.qualcomm.com/community), you can complete a simple form to find a volunteer. The Gap allows employees up to five hours each month to do volunteer work on company time.

As an extra bonus, some companies will only make grants to charities if they have an employee who volunteers with the charity (this could be one of your board members, someone providing technical assistance, or a volunteer in your soup kitchen). The Gap will make a donation for every 15 hours one of their employees puts in as a volunteer. AT&T's corporate contributions office will make a small grant to every organization that has an employee as a volunteer.

And the Letter Gets Sent Where?

So with all these company divisions competing to give their money to you, how do you decide where to send your proposal? Read everything you can about what each office supports. More and more, company websites offer information that will help you direct your proposal to the right office. Also try calling someone at the division that looks most promising to discuss your project. If they are the wrong one to speak to, they might be able (and willing) to direct you to the person or division most likely to be able to help you.

If you think you can offer substantial benefits, I'd start with the sponsorship office. If they invite a proposal, you'll probably hear back from them within a few weeks if they are interested. In contrast, foundations tend to move more slowly because committees or boards make the decisions, possibly taking months for a response.

Words to the Wise

Getting someone to advise you isn't always easy, but don't let your frustration tempt you to send a proposal to more than one office at the same company. Even if you don't tell them that you are approaching different offices, they might find out, and each will resent your wasting their time. And remember that a grant proposal is not appropriate for a sponsorship office anyway.

Here are examples of some large corporations and how they part with their cash.

◆ AT&T Foundation
32 Avenue of the Americas, 6th Floor
New York, NY 10013
www.att.com/foundation

Grant proposals are accepted by invitation only. They make grants for uses of technology in education, public policy, and the arts and culture. They make no in-kind contributions of products or services. Grants: $39 million in 2000.

◆ AT&T Corporate Contributions Program
295 N. Maple Avenue,
Basking Ridge, NJ 07920

AT&T gives nationally but focuses on the New York City metropolitan area within broad interests. They accept proposals up to three pages. Applications go through the nearest local office, which can be located by writing the preceding address. Grants: $1.5 million in 2000.

◆ Delta Air Lines Foundation
c/o Delta Air Lines, Inc., Department 983
Hartsfield Atlanta Intl. Airport
Atlanta, GA 30320-0852
www.delta.com/inside/community/foundation_guide/index.jsp

They handle employee-matching gifts as well as making direct grants for child welfare, civil rights, community development, and international affairs. There is no staff dedicated solely to the foundation. Their grants are limited by the income produced by the foundation's endowment. Grants: $3.3 million in 2001.

◆ Delta Air Lines Inc. Corporate Giving Program
PO Box 20706, Department 979
Atlanta, GA 30320-6001
www.delta.com/inside/community/foundation_guide/index.jsp

This office covers much of the same territory as the company's foundation, but it also makes grants in the arts. In-kind gifts for free air travel are made through this office. Donations come from allocations of current company revenues. Grants: $2.6 million plus $9 million in in-kind gifts (a good part of it was 9/11 related) in 2001.

◆ The Gap Foundation
2 Folsom Street
San Francisco, CA 94105
www.gapinc.com

Most of the foundation's grantmaking is aimed at programs that assist young people, although it also makes some grants in health, human services, the arts, and the environment. Grants are made "worldwide," according to its website. Grants: $5.8 million in 2000.

◆ Sears-Roebuck Foundation
3333 Beverly Road, Room BC097A-A
Hoffman Estates, IL 60179

They give nationally and will accept unsolicited proposals. Grants are made for programs that encourage community service or volunteerism and affect multiple communities where Sears has stores. They employ one staff member. Grants: $4.4 million in 2000.

Sears, Roebuck and Co. Contributions Program
3333 Beverly Road, D-703
Hoffman Estates, IL 60179
www.sears.com/sr/misc/sears/about/communities/community_main.jsp

This office also funds nationally and employs only four staff members. "Cause-related marketing" and sponsorships come from this office, as well as huge donations in products. Local organizations can apply directly to local stores for contributions. Grants: $7.4 million in cash gifts plus $27 million in in-kind gifts in 1999.

> **Words to the Wise**
>
> If you are working for a grassroots community organization, it is unlikely that you will be able to get a large grant from a major corporation on your first try. It is possible that you could get an in-kind donation (for example, of T-shirts from a local outlet for The Gap) and build on that contact to lead to a cash contribution or volunteer assistance the next year.

Corporate philanthropy has become an important element in the support of all kinds of charities. It still remains controversial to stockholders focused on the bottom line and to nervous charity board members who fear corporate associations will taint the charity's image. But corporate giving is not the only source of funding that can raise eyebrows. Even through we expect our government agencies to support health and education, other causes (such as the arts) can create an animated discussion at any dinner party. I look at public funding in the next chapter.

The Least You Need to Know

◆ Corporate giving is done to enhance the company's reputation with employees, stockholders, and the community.

◆ In all corporate proposals, include how you will recognize the grant or sponsorship. Be creative.

◆ Some corporations make grants nationally but also give money away through their local operations.

◆ The degree of recognition and benefits you can provide to the company help determine if you should seek a grant or a sponsorship.

◆ Never approach different offices at the same corporation at the same time.

◆ Do approach rival corporations at the same time.

◆ Corporations might give you free merchandise and even loan you an employee to help you with the work.

Chapter 5

Government Primer

In This Chapter

- Finding grants at state and local levels
- Types of federal grants
- How government agencies differ from other funders
- How to include operating costs in a government proposal
- How to turn political capital into cash

Governments at the local, state, and federal levels make grants to non-profit organizations to carry out programs that benefit the welfare of the community. They also support research in virtually every area and artistic endeavor. In some ways, getting a grant from a government agency is easier for the grant writer than from any other source:

- Applications for government grants always involve completing forms, which is a lot easier than constructing a proposal.

- The applications limit space for the description of your program. This not only forces you to get to the essence of a program (which will benefit all your foundation and corporate proposals), but it also prevents everyone at your charity who reviews your edits from adding on and on and on to it. I love telling people editing my government proposals that for every word they want to add, they must suggest a word to cut. This takes great discipline for all concerned.

> **Words to the Wise** _____
>
> It can be very useful to establish contacts with your elected representatives' staffs. They might hear of a grant opportunity that has just come out or that you might have overlooked. The better educated you keep them about your charity and its programs, the better they can represent you by supporting legislation that will help your cause, too. Put your elected representatives on your mailing list, and for state and national officials, that means home offices as well as legislative offices.

Governments support nonprofits (and occasionally individuals) through grants, Requests for Proposals, and the distribution of pork, politely known in legislative circles as "special allocations." In this chapter, I'll take a look at each.

Grants

There are so many and varied government grants that both government agencies and private companies publish newsletters to help you keep track of it all. It's important to keep up-to-date on government support at all levels, because new programs become available all the time.

State and Local Grants

Finding local and state grant opportunities might be as easy as going to one of their websites and searching for "grants." A handy website for locating state and local government agencies is www.statelocalgov.net. The resources that you will find on different official state websites will vary greatly. At minimum, you should find access to the websites of state agencies and in many cases county and city government sites as well.

> **Philanthropy Facts**
>
> *Federal Grants and Contracts Weekly* from Aspen Publishers (www.aspenpublishers.com) offers you just what the title says. Although fairly expensive, it is a lot more digestible than the Federal Register. If you see federal grants as an important source of income for your charity, you might want to try a subscription. (They'll send you a sample copy for free.)

♦ On the Illinois site (www.illinois.gov), a search for "grants" returned 35,413 hits! Although you'll never get through all 35,413 links, this might still be easier to deal with than the different ways each state agency organizes its information. The links included a number of actual grant programs as well as a grant proposal that a local fire department used to get a grant for new equipment and had posted for other fire departments to copy. There were also links to listings of nongovernment grant resources various agencies (for example, the libraries) had put together.

◆ The Oregon state website (www.oregon.gov) came back with more than 200 links when I searched for "grants." Noticing a number of listings for "watershed" grants, I went to the agency listings and under the Watershed department also found the details on grant programs for watershed restoration.

◆ On the Texas site (www.texas.gov), a search for "grants" only returned 158 links, many of which were not grant programs at all. (One was an announcement that a library now had a book on getting grants.)

Even if your web searches prove successful, you'll also want to be in contact with the agencies that most closely reflect your charity's purpose, whether that is child welfare, education, senior services, the arts, or prison reform. Ask the agency to put you on their mailing list for any grants or RPFs that come up. It can also pay to look outside your sector, because services for at-risk youth, for example, could be provided by an educational organization, a health service, or even an arts group.

> **Words to the Wise**
>
> Always jump down to the eligibility requirements, especially when looking for government grants. Many of these grants are made only to other government agencies, so save yourself some reading time by checking one of the shortest sections first.

Although the following section on federal grants dwarfs the preceding section on state and local grants, this does not mean that the federal government will be the primary source of public money for your charity. Local and state programs are so varied that it would be impossible to give specifics on any programs or agencies here. A lot of the information on applying for and the ins and outs of federal grants can, however, be applied to local and state grants, so please read on.

Federal Grants

Federal grants come in two flavors: "formula" and "project."

◆ **Formula grants** essentially reimburse your charity for service you have already performed. Local or state agencies might offer their own form of formula grants. Formula grants are awarded based on a mathematical formula that, for example, might multiply the number of your clients by the average cost of providing a service in your city by some percentage the government has decided upon. Note that the majority of formula grants are restricted to other government agencies.

◆ **Project grants**, on the other hand, are competitive. Everyone is not guaranteed a grant, and your application will be judged against every other application from across the country. Examples include grants to help preserve America's jazz heritage, to operate or plan public service programs, and community projects to provide high-quality food to low-income families. There were 901 project grant opportunities listed in March 2003.

There is a lot of competition for project grants. If you are grant writing for an organization that has been around for less than three years or has a very small staff and budget, you probably should not waste you time seeking a federal project grant. If you believe your charity might be able to compete nationally, by all means apply.

Many federal grants require that their grant be no more than half the project's cost, meaning you have to raise the remainder elsewhere—and not from another federal agency, which is not allowed. Also remember that you might not get as much as you asked for, so be prepared to present a scaled-down program if necessary.

Federal grants of both types can be researched in the Catalog of Federal and Domestic Assistance (www.cfda.gov). This site even offers a guide to writing government grants written in classic bureaucratese. You can look up grants by category (for example, agriculture, health, or environmental quality) or by whom your project will serve (for example, youth, senior citizens, or the mentally ill). The Federal Commons section (www.cfda.gov/public/granttopics.asp) provides a user-friendly interface for search by topic.

> **Philanthropy Facts**
>
> In early 2003, the Catalog of Federal Domestic Assistance listed 681 grant opportunities in health, 318 in community development, 261 in housing, and 31 in the arts.

If you are really convinced that there is gold for you in the federal grant coffers, you can also check the daily Federal Register, online at www.gpoaccess.gov/fr/index.html, order a print version, or use the one at your local library. Information on new grant programs appears here first, but you'll have to sort through dozens or hundreds of meeting notices and legislative details to find them. This will be a fruitless labor for most small charities.

Another useful federal site is FirstGov, the U.S. government's official web portal, which includes a special section for nonprofits. At firstgov.gov/Business/Nonprofit.shtml (no "www" with this address), you'll find links to grants, nonprofit registration and tax information, and a number of other topics.

Here are a very few of the federal agencies that make grants and their Internet and mailing addresses.

◆ Federal Emergency Management Association
500 C Street S.W.
Washington, DC 20472
www.fema.gov

FEMA assists in the recovery from natural disasters such as floods and hurricanes, and these days, unnatural disasters like terrorist attacks. FEMA has an office in every state, the addresses of which you can find on the website.

◆ National Endowment for the Arts
1100 Pennsylvania Avenue N.W.
Washington, DC 20506
www.arts.gov

The NEA mostly makes grants to arts organizations, although writers and folk artists can get grants, too.

◆ National Endowment for the Humanities
1100 Pennsylvania Avenue N.W.
Washington, DC 20506
www.neh.gov

The NEH gives grants for scholarly research in literature or history, including documentary films.

◆ National Science Foundation
4201 Wilson Boulevard
Arlington, VA 22230
www.nsf.gov

The NSF is a portal for locating government grants in science and engineering. It provides 20 percent of federal research support to academic institutions.

◆ Small Business Administration
6302 Fairview Road, #300
Charlotte, NC 28210
www.sbaonline.sba.gov

The SBA makes loans to for-profit businesses, but offers limited grant programs to nonprofits and other levels of government to provide technical assistance to small businesses.

◆ U.S. Department of Education
400 Maryland Avenue, SW
Washington, DC 20202
www.ed.gov/index.jsp

The U.S. Department of Education gives a wide variety of grants, mostly to schools, sometimes to nonprofits in partnership with a school, and sometimes to nonprofits all by themselves.

◆ U.S. Department of Health and Human Services
700 Independence Avenue S.W.
Washington, DC 20201
www.dhhs.gov

This is the government's biggest grant maker.

- U.S. Department of Housing and Urban Development
  451 78th Street, S.W.
  Washington, DC 20410
  www.hud.gov

  Grants are available on creating or retaining affordable housing, improving neighborhoods, and the like.

- U.S. Environmental Protection Agency
  1200 Pennsylvania Avenue N.W.
  Washington, DC 20460
  www.epa.gov

  Their grants assist communities with environmental issues and environment-friendly development.

Words to the Wise

When you receive the verdict on your government grant, call the program officer to get the comments of the people who evaluated your proposal. The comments are just as helpful when you are successful as when you aren't. They are required by the Freedom of Information Act to give you this information, and it is critical for preparing your next grant application. Some agencies will require that you request the comments in writing; others will share them with you over the phone.

After you've found a grant program that seems to be a match for your charity, give the guidelines and application materials a thorough read. Afterward (only afterward), don't be shy about calling for answers to any questions you might have. These civil servants have always been more than civil anytime I've needed help. A two-minute call can save you hours of work. Don't be surprised if you get an answering machine. Budget cutbacks mean fewer staff, but they will call you back.

Most government grant applications start off asking for basic information about your charity, including when it was founded, tax status, employer I.D. (like a Social Security number, but for a corporation), budget size, mission, and short statement about your project. The example of a government grant in Appendix F includes a cover page similar to those found with many federal grant applications.

Fortunately, most agencies at all levels of government now provide forms that can be downloaded and completed on your computer, allowing your typewriter to continue to gather dust. There is a definite trend among government agencies at all levels to require grants to be submitted online. I'll cover this kind of application in Chapter 19.

Covering the Bottom Line

Normally, federal grants and contracts allow little or no overhead, called indirect costs. If you plan to work with government agencies on a number of projects, it will be worth it to establish your indirect rate. An indirect rate is the percentage of your general operations that can be considered part of the project budget without itemizing it.

It's a lot of work to complete the process to obtain an indirect rate, but after it's established, you can use it with any other federal agency. You should find instructions in every RFP or grant application for how to establish an indirect rate. The process takes some time and will involve some back-and-forth with the agency, so begin the application procedure several months before the application deadline. When it is completed, you'll receive a "negotiated rate agreement" form. A copy of this is all you'll need when applying to other agencies.

Words to the Wise

In contrast to the stringent guidelines for indirect expenses imposed by government funders, note that most foundations (private and corporate) will allow an indirect expense in your project budget of 5 to 15 percent without question or documentation. But don't put an indirect expense line in lightly. You should be able to back it up if the program officer asks about it.

Spend Now, Get Paid Later

Most federal programs will only reimburse you for actual expenses after they have been paid (or for only a very short time in advance). If cash flow is a chronic problem at your charity, talk with your finance person to make sure this won't create a hardship for your group. This is 180 degrees from the foundation or corporation practice of giving you all the money up front.

RFPs and Contracts

The forms for applying for government grants and RFPs can look a lot alike, so what's the difference?

◆ Grants offer greater opportunity to get your charity's project funded.

◆ RFPs offer your charity an opportunity to carry out a government program.

If you're lucky, you'll have a program that parallels one the government is anxious to have carried out. But mostly, you'll find yourself applying for RFPs that lie somewhere in between: projects that will help your charity serve its constituents, even if the program is not exactly one your program staff would have designed.

> **Words to the Wise**
>
> RFPs are issued not just for your charity to perform a service. They are also issued to provide a service for the government, such as creating a manual or other product that the government can use or offer to other charities. There is some prestige in performing these services, but don't expect to make a lot of money performing them. Despite what you might think about government spending, some agencies are very good at keeping out overhead beyond your official indirect rate.

A successful response to an RFP results in a contract to perform the services described in your response to the RFP. It will include a restatement (and possible revision) of the budget, a time line that must be followed, and the name of the person at the government agency to whom your program leader will report.

It's Never Free Money

Government grants come with a number of requirements and certifications you should be aware of from the beginning.

♦ Government grants create an obligation to keep your financial records in great detail. Make sure your financial people are aware of the requirements. Government audits do occur—by agencies and the IRS—so keep these budgets very real.

♦ You will probably have to sign drug-free workplace and employment nondiscrimination statements.

♦ You might have to certify that your office and/or the facility where the project will take place meet the minimum requirements of the Americans with Disabilities Act (ADA compliance).

♦ You'll probably be asked for ethnic and other demographic information on your board, staff, and constituents, which you probably won't have because federal law prohibits you to collect some of it, but they still ask for it. (You can usually get away with checking "general population.")

Who You Really Know: Line Items

The most controversial means of government's distribution of wealth is through member items, also known as special appropriations, or plain old "pork." Typically, a member of a legislature (from the U.S. Congress to your local city council, and mayors and other executives, too) adds an appropriation for your charity to a bill that is under consideration. Depending on his or her influence and the other machinations that go on in any legislature, this might get approved along with the bill.

These special allocations are common enough that your legislator will probably have forms prepared for you to complete and a staff member who deals with them. In addi-

tion to a short questionnaire, you'll probably be asked for a summary of the project, and maybe a budget.

Although large capital projects get funded this way, many community groups depend on these appropriations from city and state officials to survive.

Naturally, someone at your charity will have to know a legislator really well to get attention for this kind of action. Be aware that when you seek a member item appropriation, you might be doing an end run around the government agency to which you normally would be applying. That agency might not be too thrilled that your appropriation could even lead to a reduction in their agency's funding.

> **Philanthropy Facts**
>
> If you plan to seek a special allocation at any level of government, contact the official's staff as soon as you can for guidance on restrictions (such as regrants are usually not allowed with federal grants), how much you should ask for, and when your request must be in. Legislative calendars have their own logic and if you're a day late, you'll be more than a dollar short.

The Least You Need to Know

- There are grant opportunities at every level of government, but you might have to do some digging to find them all.

- Federal formula grants are given based on a statistical model, not the excellence of your charity or project.

- Federal project grants are highly competitive and are awarded on the quality of your charity and the specifics of your project.

- RFPs are requests to fulfill a government program, whereas a grant allows you to propose a program within general parameters.

- Government grants come with reporting and other requirements you might not expect.

- Federal grants in particular are usually made as reimbursements rather than outright payments.

Chapter 6

Individual Donor Primer

In This Chapter

- ◆ Why people give to charity
- ◆ Why to send a grant proposal to an individual donor
- ◆ How to pitch a proposal to a corporate executive
- ◆ Tax deductibility and individual giving
- ◆ Sample proposals to individuals

A chapter on getting money from individuals might seem out of place in a book on grants. After all, in the second chapter I pretty much defined grants as coming from institutions. Although the checks might come from an institution's bank account, it's still an individual who reads your proposal and decides to make the grant or not. So it's good to understand the motivations behind an individual's decision to give away his or her own money, even if you intend only to send proposals to institutions.

Individuals make more charitable donations than any other sector! It might surprise you to know that according to the AAFRC Trust for Philanthropy's *Giving USA 2002*, 75.8 percent of all donations in 2001 came from individuals—and that's not even counting the $16.33 billion that individuals left as bequests that year. To ignore individuals in your fundraising would be a major mistake.

So where does the grant writer fit into this? In this chapter, I'll first look at why people give and then examine a few situations where a formal grant proposal to an individual makes sense.

Why People Give Away Their Money

Some very basic human needs and desires guide an individual's impulse to give to charity. Chief among these is pride of association. People like to be part of something positive that is larger than themselves. People join clubs and honorary societies for this very reason.

By making a contribution to your charity, the donor will be able to take pride in your charity's accomplishments. If you do your job right, every contributor, large or small, will feel this about your charity. For this reason, I'll remind you throughout this book of the importance of keeping donors (individual donors and all your contacts at the institutional funders) informed about your charity's accomplishments.

Fear of being alone, although perhaps a less noble feeling, also motivates individual giving. It is closely associated with pride of association: If donors feel like they're part of your charity's work, they are less likely to feel lonely. You might even have gatherings for donors, which could further dispel loneliness.

Guilt for having more than others motivates people like no other emotion. Whenever we show the prospective donor in words or pictures those less fortunate and ask for their help, we play on their guilt.

Desire for continuity comes into play when asking for renewal of a past gift. Human nature prefers that things remain constant. Change is disconcerting. After a donor has given you a substantial gift, they very likely will continue giving so as not to let the work done with their previous gift be wasted.

Philanthropy Facts

Individuals donated $160.72 billion in 2001, but a mere 20 percent of those donors contributed around $128 million of that total (based on information in *Giving USA 2002*). This is also a typical ratio for any individual giving program: 20 percent of donors give 80 percent of the cash.

By discussing these insecurities and fears I'm not suggesting you write in a proposal, "If you make a contribution to my charity, you won't be lonely anymore." I am asking you to keep in mind that your charity has something to offer the donor in exchange for their gift, and it's something that is completely tax deductible, affectionately referred to in the fundraising biz as the "warm and fuzzies."

Propose to Me and See What Happens

So when should you send a grant proposal instead of a simple letter to an individual donor?

When You Are Asking for the Big Bucks

If you plan to ask an individual for a major gift (and by that, I mean a gift that the donor would consider major and is significant for your charity), a proposal that lays out all the aspects of your program might be necessary to help the donor decide to make a large gift.

A very large individual gift can affect a donor's family by reducing current spendable income or decreasing what heirs will inherit. The donor will want to discuss the gift with his or her family and financial advisors. The proposal will give the donor the details so that their questions can be easily answered. Proposals to individuals should also include a project budget. The donor will want to understand how the amount you've asked for fits into the project's total budget and how his or her gift will relate to those from others. A well-prepared budget should inspire confidence that the gift will be well spent.

Words to the Wise

Don't make proposals to individuals as long as those to institutions. A four- to six-page letter works best in most cases. If you need to give additional background or testimonials, do so as attachments. Keep the tone personal, using "I" and "you" and avoiding "we" and "one."

Because the donor's family will probably be involved in the decision, any long-term benefits (a parking place near the auditorium entrance) or long-term recognition (their family name over the door) should be included in the proposal. Take a look at the following example from a proposal for a major individual gift.

> To acknowledge your gift of $500,000 to the County Library, we would like to name the reference section "The Smith Family Reference Room." In this way, we can acknowledge your and your family's commitment to the library for generations to come. You spent so much time in the reference section working on your last novel, we already think of it as your room. Of course, if you would prefer to remain anonymous, we will honor that request, but we hope we will be able to honor you in this way, both to express our thanks and to inspire others to become major supporters.

Note that I wrote "we would like to name the reference section," and not "we will name the reference section." Although you want to acknowledge the gift as publicly as the donor will allow, he or she might prefer anonymity, and you should allow for that from the beginning. Public acknowledgement of major gifts does inspire additional giving. (Just ask anyone at a charity that has a wall of honor or similar recognition method.) Also note that I've given a reason why the reference section was chosen. Tying the gift to donor interests is key in any proposal.

Words to the Wise

Don't give away the store! There are a few donors who will want to get as much recognition of their contribution as they can. Be clear and specific about what you will offer and stick to it. Especially in a capital campaign, you don't want to undersell a prominent naming opportunity early in the campaign.

Here is another example, from another proposal:

> We would like to provide you with a reserved parking space near the entrance to the theatre to recognize the importance of your $10,000 gift to the Hometown Theatre Company. We reserve these few spaces for those who have made the most significant gifts to the HTC. (Because the parking garage charges $10 for evening parking, the IRS requires that we tell you that $1,000 of your gift will not be tax deductible, based on your attending an average of ten performances a year for ten years.)

In this example, the wording is trickier because the entire gift is not deductible (see the discussion later in this chapter on tax deductibility). Telling the donor about it certainly makes the whole paragraph sound less gracious, but you have to include this some-where. I've also indicated that the free parking will not last forever.

Now let's look at a full proposal seeking a major gift from a philanthropic couple for a new animal shelter. I've noted in the margins the important points.

> Jane and Henry Bucks
> 456 Walnut Street
> Anywhere, CA 90000
>
> Dear Jane and Henry:
>
> Your many contributions over the years have made a significant dif-ference in how many orphaned dogs and cats the Community Animal Society has helped. Not only have we been able to place more pets in homes with loving families, but the neuter/spay program has been much more successful because of the advertisements we placed in neighborhood newspapers.
>
> I appreciated your speaking with Nancy Thomas and me last week about the Society and its future needs. It was great to learn that you have shared in our dream for a new home for some time, and I hope you will now help us make it a reality.
>
> Community Animal Society is at a critical turning point. The number of homeless animals that are brought to us far exceeds the capacity of our aging building to house and care for them. In examining the options open to us, the board of directors has given the go ahead to begin a capital campaign for a new building on the vacant lot adjacent to our current home.
>
> The new building is necessary for a number of reasons:
>
> ◆ The present building dates to 1938, and its mechanical sys-tems continually fail, making costly repairs necessary. In the last six months alone, $9,000 has been spent on various

I refer to their contin-ued commitment.

You will never ask for a major gift in a letter without first meeting with the donor. Reminding them of their friend who came to the meeting with you reinforces the per-sonal connections they have to the organization.

repairs, and $100,000 would be needed to replace the ailing heating and air conditioning system.

◆ The animal residence area is totally inadequate for today's needs. Cages are almost all too small, as well as too few. As we have become better known, more animals have been brought to us.

◆ The medical facility does not meet the standards for a modern animal surgery. The old materials are nearly impossible to clean any more. We collectively hold our breaths every time the health department makes an inspection.

◆ The adoption area is small and uninviting. When people come in to adopt a pet, they have limited room to get to know the dog or cat before making their decision.

We estimate the cost for such a new facility at $2.5 million. At last night's board meeting, Nancy pledged $100,000 toward the new shelter, which provoked pledges from other board members of an additional $400,000. I hope you will consider matching the board's pledges with a $500,000 leadership gift.

I know that a major gift from you will inspire others in the community to become part of the campaign for a new Community Animal Society building. If you can help us with such a generous gift, we would like to name the new building the Bucks Family Animal Center in honor not only of your gift to this campaign, but also in honor of the many gifts you and your family have made over the years. If, of course, you prefer to make your gift anonymously, we will honor that request, but we know that your name connected with the facility would bring increased support from many people in the community, now and in the future.

The new animal center would provide ...

◆ A modern facility with state-of-the-art mechanical systems. Our engineer tells us that we'll save $20,000 to $25,000 a year in utility bills as a result of more efficient mechanical systems in a better-insulated building.

◆ Five separate suites for housing our animals. Large and small dogs would have separate sections, and the cats and rabbits would be given their own room acoustically isolated from the noise made by the dogs. There would even be a small suite for the exotic pets (such as snakes and ferrets),

---

Clearly express the need for the gift with a sense of urgency. This could have been the place for some tragic or dramatic pet stories to work the emotions. I judged that was not necessary with these donors.

I mention their friend's gift first so they can judge their own gift accordingly, and let them know the entire board backs the project.

Solutions to all the problems in the present facility.

whose numbers increase yearly. And animals with medical problems could be isolated from the healthy pets and from each other in a special ICU—the first of its kind in this part of the state.

♦ New surgery and examination rooms that will make it easier for our vets to treat the animals with the respect and care they deserve. It will also make it easier for us to attract young vets to work at the Society by offering high quality medical facilities.

♦ Six rooms of varying sizes adjacent to the waiting room in which prospective families could interact with the animal they are considering adopting. By having different sized rooms, a family considering a German Shepard could be given enough room for the dog to move around, but the family looking at a kitten could be in a more intimate space. Studies have shown that having better adoption rooms leads to more adoptions.

The prospect of having this new facility has energized the board and staff. You are the first ones outside the board we have asked to take part in the campaign. And by "take part," I do mean more than making an important donation. I know how committed you are to the care of our community's unwanted pets (and to making them wanted pets). Your active participation in inspiring others in the business community with your example (and possibly through your solicitations) surely will ensure the campaign's success.

If you have any questions about the plans for the new facility, please give me a call. Dr. Shepards will lead the committee that will work with the architects, and I know she would value your input.

Thank you for your kind consideration of this request. Together, I know we can create an animal shelter of which the entire community will be proud.

Sincerely yours,

Betty Lapsa

Betty Lapsa
President

Emphasize how important their active participation is—you need them, not just their money.

It can be dangerous to invite major donors to take part in the execution of the project. They might feel too much ownership and want to dictate the design. In this case, knowing these donors, there was minimal risk of that.

When Your Prospect is a Corporate Big Shot

When I have a meeting with a corporate funder (especially if he or she is on the corporate rather than the foundation side of the company), I dress in my gray suit with a white shirt and power tie. By going in (what feels to me like) a disguise, I blend in and the corporate funder feels more comfortable with me than if I went in my typically casual nonprofit attire.

So when you want to get a major gift from someone who is a corporate big shot, you want your request to look as much as possible like something he or she sees on a daily basis. Familiarity breeds comfort. You want to craft your proposal to look something like a business plan, which is not so unlike a grant proposal when you see how the jargon translates, as I've shown in the following table.

Translation of a Business Plan into a Grant Proposal

Business Plan	Grant Proposal
Description of business	Project description
Marketing plan	Outreach plan
Competition	Others working on the same problem
Personnel	People who will work on the project
Financial data	Project and operating budgets
Metrics	Project evaluation

The Small Business Administration gives a sample business plan on its website (www.sba.gov/starting/indexbusplans.html) that you might find useful.

Now let's look at a proposal for that same animal shelter, this time addressed to a CEO. Note that the letter was sent the day after the meeting (and probably hand-delivered). CEOs will expect a quick follow up. This letter would have been written before Betty and Nancy went to meet with Mrs. Banks, and then quickly edited the next day to incorporate notes they took in the meeting.

I've made comments in the margins here only when they differ from those to the philanthropic couple. Please note: I would not offer naming of the facility to two people at the same time. Solicitations at this level must be done one-by-one. (Both this and the previous letter appear on the CD-ROM.)

Grant Talk

Metrics is a term common in the corporate world to mean the measurable outcomes of a project. Will the kids in your after-school program spend more time with their mentor? Will more seniors be able to attend free concerts? How many new books will be purchased for the library? How much will attendance increase if you print a new subscription brochure?

Mrs. Marjorie Banks
President and CEO
Community Trust Company
123 Main Street
Anywhere, CA 90000

Dear Mrs. Banks:

Thank you for meeting with Nancy Thomas and me yesterday to discuss the need for a new facility for Community Animal Society. We're writing to ask you to make a major financial commitment to this project.

Your many contributions over the years have made a significant difference in how many orphaned dogs and cats we helped. We have been able to place more pets in homes with loving families as a result of the new marketing campaign, 200 in last year. Two years ago, the neuter/spay program performed only 150 operations; thanks to the new marketing initiative funded by Community Trust Company, 477 operations were performed in the last twelve months.

Due in part to the success of the recent marketing campaigns, Community Animal Society finds itself at a critical turning point: The number of homeless animals that are brought to us far exceeds the capacity of our aging building to house and care for them. In examining the options presented to us by architectural and fundraising consultants, the board of directors has given the go ahead to begin a capital campaign for a new building on the vacant lot adjacent to our current home.

The new building is necessary for a number of reasons:

♦ The present building dates to 1938, and its mechanical systems continually fail. In the last six months alone, $9,000 has been spent on various repairs, and $100,000 would be needed to replace the ailing heating and air conditioning system. We cannot afford to continue throwing good money at bad systems.

♦ The animal residence area is totally inadequate for today's needs. We operate at 110 percent capacity now and need at minimum 50 additional cages, which means at least an additional 1,750 square feet.

This letter comes to the point in the first paragraph, but the personal friend involved in the solicitation remains very important.

Note that results are quantified and "outreach" has become "marketing."

A just-the-facts approach usually works best. Depending on the CEO, an emotional pitch might work, but I've avoided it here.

- The medical facility does not meet modern standards. So far, health department inspections have brought only warnings, but it is only a matter of time before we are fined due to the impossibility of maintaining antiquated facilities to present-day codes.

- The adoption area is small and uninviting. When people come in to adopt a pet, there is limited room for them to get to know the dog or cat before making their decision. As much as 5,000 sq. feet are needed for this area.

We estimate the cost for such a new facility at $2.5 million. At last night's board meeting, Nancy pledged $100,000 toward the new shelter, which provoked pledges from other board members of an additional $400,000. I hope you will consider matching the board's pledges with a $500,000 leadership gift. I've enclosed our preliminary plan for raising the remaining $1.5 million, prepared with the help of David Smarts, a respected capital campaign consultant.

A major gift from you will inspire others in the community to become part of the campaign for a new Community Animal Society building. If you can help us with such a generous gift, we would like to name the new building the Banks Animal Center in honor not only of your gift to this campaign, but also those you have made over the years. If, of course, you prefer to make your gift anonymously, we will honor that request, but we know that your name connected with the facility would bring increased support from many people in the business community, now and in the future.

The new animal center would provide ...

- A modern facility with state-of-the-art mechanical systems. Our engineer tells us that we'll save $20,000 to $25,000 a year in utility bills as a result of more efficient mechanical systems in a better-insulated building.

- Improved living conditions for our animals. Separate housing suites will accommodate the different needs of dogs, cats, exotic animals, and those with medical problems (isolated in a special ICU—the first of its kind in this part of the state). Calmer animals are more likely to be adopted, thus decreasing our boarding costs in the long term.

> The CEO will be reassured by your sharing the marketing and fundraising plans.

> Same solutions, but descriptions are more focused on results of the new facility in terms of efficiency.

♦ New surgery and examination rooms that will make it easier for our vets to treat the animals with the respect and care they deserve. It will also make it easier for us to attract young vets to work at the Society by offering high quality medical facilities.

♦ Six adoption rooms of varying sizes adjacent to the waiting room, in which prospective families could interact with the animal they are considering adopting. Studies have shown that having better adoption rooms leads to more adoptions.

The prospect of having this new facility has energized the board and staff. You are the first person outside the board we have asked to take part in the campaign for a new shelter. And by "take part," I do mean more than making an important donation. I know how committed you are to the care of our community's unwanted pets (and to making them wanted pets). Your active participation in inspiring others in the business community with your example (and possibility through your solicitations) will ensure the campaign's success.

If you have any questions about the plans for the new facility, please give me a call. Dr. Shepards is leading the committee and works with the architects, and I know she would value your input.

Thank you for your kind consideration of this request. Together, I know we can create an animal shelter of which the entire community will be proud.

Sincerely yours,

Betty Lapsa

Betty Lapsa
President

Note that I provide metrics throughout this proposal, as well as references to consultants involved with the project. A fundraising plan would be attached, as well as a budget.

When Your Prospect Is a Family Foundation Trustee

As I discussed in Chapter 3, when your individual donor serves as a trustee of a family foundation, they might have the power to get your grant approved. Chances are, they will still ask you for a proposal. No matter how committed they are to your charity, they might have to get their siblings or other relatives to agree to do it. These proposals should be big on bullet points that give your advocate good talking points. A strong executive summary might be all you need to prep your advocate, but give him or her a full proposal so that he or she has additional information if needed.

The Cost of Giving

In the charity business we make a big deal about contributions being tax deductible, but does it matter? In surveys too numerous to count over the years, donors constantly say that tax deductibility is not their first concern when deciding to make a donation. Belief in the cause remains the top priority. So why make a big production about contributions being tax deductible?

Well, first of all, the federal government requires us to state if all or part of a contribution is tax deductible. Secondly, people do like to know that they will get a little benefit from making their donation. And finally, donors need to know this so they can stay on the right side of the IRS.

The IRS says that if donors receive anything that has more than a nominal fair market value, the amount of that benefit must be subtracted from the tax-deductible amount. For instance, if someone buys a $1,000 ticket to your benefit, they get dinner, wine, and maybe even some entertainment when they attend. Those things would all have a value if the donor were to get them at a local restaurant. If a restaurant in your area would charge $80 per person for the same thing, then only $920 is tax deductible ($1,000 – $80 = $920). But if you only give them a baseball cap (which falls within the IRS guidelines of a nominal benefit), the gift is 100 percent deductible.

IRS regulations are fairly complex on what does and does not have more than a "nominal" value. If you feel so inclined, you can read the details for yourself on the IRS site at www.irs.gov/charities/article/0,,id=96102,00.html.

When writing grant proposals to individuals, always state very carefully whether you plan to give anything that has a value. If so, you should also offer them the opportunity to decline that benefit. If they want the goodie, they may send you two checks: one from their foundation for the tax-deductible amount and one from their personal checking account to pay for the dinner and dancing.

Tax deductibility is not the prime motivator, but it is an important part of any request for money. Handle it carefully and with respect, and your donors will appreciate your thinking of their best interest.

> **Words to the Wise**
>
> Save your charity money by letting donors decline benefits with value. When I worked for a museum, we had been spending more than $100,000 a year to send exhibition catalogs to members as part of their membership benefits. When we gave them the option to decline the catalogs and increase the tax-deductibility of their membership, our catalog costs went down $40,000.

It seldom is necessary to offer anything that affects the tax-deductibility for a major gift. In general, major donors expect not goodies but information and access when they make an important commitment to your charity. These things meet the IRS's definition of having a nominal value, and they fortunately are just what major donors want. The following are examples of things with a nominal value:

- A visit to your hospital to talk with doctors about how a new CT Scan machine will benefit the community

- A backstage tour at your theatre to see how the stage machinery works

- A visit to the studio of an artist who received a grant from your charity to see her work and hear her speak about it

- A donor newsletter that tells about research to develop a new vaccine

- A lecture for major donors to hear a field researcher tell of her findings

- Advance notice and reservations for popular public programs

And then there are also the warm and fuzzy things like your pet's picture printed in the animal shelter's newsletter or putting the donor's name on your building.

The Least You Need to Know

- Pride of association, fear of being alone, guilt for having more than others, and a desire for continuity motivate people to give.

- Provide major donors with all the information you would provide in a formal proposal, even if it is in letter form.

- Corporate CEO types will appreciate a proposal that shows respect for their business knowledge.

- Trustees of a family foundation might need a proposal from you for the record, even if your grant is a sure thing.

- Being meticulous about what is and isn't tax-deductible respects the donor and keeps everyone on the right side of the IRS.

Part 3

Research, or Just How Nosy Are You?

You can't be a successful grant writer without a healthy, even overactive, curiosity about people and the institutions they create. Being nosy is a virtue in this business. The amount of information available to you is staggering. This part shows you how to be at your "nosy best" by looking at the best the Internet and your local library or bookstore have to offer you to find the information you'll need to succeed.

This part also looks at how you'll whittle your list down to the best prospects, avoid common mistakes, and focus on the funder's interests.

Chapter 7

You Can Find It Online

In This Chapter

- How to discover what foundations really fund
- Where to find clues to corporate giving
- How to read a foundation's IRS return
- Research tools already at your fingertips
- How to discover people's contributions and affiliations

Your writing style might combine the sophistication of John Updike and the warmth and humor of Susan Isaacs, but if you haven't done your research you might as well unplug the computer. Research is the most important thing a grant writer does. Really.

Funders find it insulting if you send them an inappropriate grant proposal. Wouldn't you? And it's just too hard raising money to waste your time crafting a proposal only to have it fall flat because you didn't research the funder thoroughly.

That means making sure you have the most recent information. There was one foundation I had written off as a prospect. When I researched it several years ago, it had a small endowment and made only small grants to small arts organizations. Was I surprised when I recently visited their new website. One of their founders had died a year ago, leaving a major bequest to the foundation. Typical grants were now 10 times what they were eight years ago and there were new program areas as well.

The Internet has revolutionized research for grants, just as it has everything else. You really cannot do grant writing or any kind of fundraising well today without utilizing the Internet. In this chapter, I'll introduce you to my favorite places to get the scoop on just about anyone and any funder. (The next chapter reviews the offline research tools you might also use, some of which duplicate online resources and others you'll find only in print.)

Links to all the websites mentioned in this chapter can be found on the CD-ROM that comes with this book, where you can click through from the listing to the websites.

A word of warning: Websites change every day. In the course of my research for this chapter, I found that some sites I had read about no longer existed. Others were still there, but the URL had changed. If you are unable to find a page where I have given an address for an inner page (such as www.cfda.gov/public/granttopics.asp), try searching again by taking off the letters after one or more backslashes (for example, try www.cfda.gov/public or www.cfda.gov) until you get the correct website, and then use the site search or site map to locate the topic you need. Of course, you can also use any general web search site like Google or AllTheWeb to find the organization if all else fails.

Foundations

Your research on foundations—private, public, corporate, and others—will usually start with a directory, then proceed to the foundation's own website, and on to look at their IRS informational return. Websites maintained by associations of grantmakers and others offer an alternative to directories, with the advantage of having already screened out foundations that, for example, don't fund your type of charity or don't make grants in your geographic area. Let's take a look at each resource.

Directories

Grant writers acknowledge the Foundation Center as one of the most important sources of information on foundations (private, public, and corporate) in the United States. You'll find the addresses of their five offices across the United States in Appendix A. There are also more than 100 collections in public and private libraries and at community foundations that make available their publications and other reference works. These addresses can be found on the Center's website (www.fdncenter.org).

> **Words to the Wise**
>
> To stay on top of the news about funders and the latest RFPs, sign up for a free e-mail subscription to Philanthropy News Digest, which is found on the Foundation Center's navigation bar. They also have a free weekly jobs listing.

The Foundation Center issues reports on different issues in philanthropy, provides access to a wide range of information on grantmaking, offers classes in grant writing, and publishes directories of foundations in print and electronic forms.

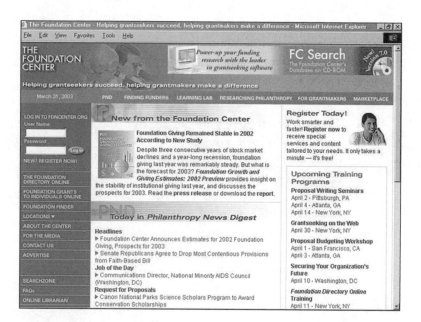

The Foundation Center's home page will be your first stop for many foundation research projects.

The directories published by the Foundation Center are considered the standard in the business. Their signature publication is the *Foundation Directory*, which they offer in a variety of formats: hard copy (paperback and hard-bound), CD-ROM (workstation and network versions), and web-based. I'll discuss the hard copy versions in Chapter 8, and although the CD-ROM versions are technically "offline," using them is closer to using the online version, so I'll discuss those here as well.

The Foundation Center's Database on CD-ROM

FC Search: The Foundation Center's Database on CD-ROM is the deluxe version of four CD-ROM editions; the others contain information on fewer foundations. Some 70,000 foundations, corporate givers, and grantmaking public charities are included on this CD-ROM. Here you'll find contact information, areas of interest, geographic restrictions, abbreviated application procedures, a list of trustees, basic financial statistics, and sometimes sample grants of $10,000 or more. The information is organized much like the print version, but contains around seven times as many foundations. The searchable indices correspond roughly to those in the print copy. The CD-ROM provides 21 fields to use in your searches.

My favorite feature of using the Foundation Center's CD-ROM is the ability to search by grant

---

Philanthropy Facts

The Canadian Centre for Philanthropy (CCP) offers similar services to the U.S. Foundation Center, including publications on philanthropy and funder directories. Its online directory (www.ccp.ca) includes 1,200 Canadian foundations. In addition to the types of searches offered by the Foundation Center, the CCP service enables you to narrow your search by the type of foundation and total grants made—a very useful enhancement.

recipient. Seeing what foundations funded a similar organization often reveals your best prospects. You can also search by trustee name to find out if a helpful trustee at one foundation serves on another foundation board that could also be a supporter of your program.

The links to funder websites are live (meaning clicking on them will open your browser and take you straight to the funder's site). Being able to create and save lists of prospects and to save notes in each foundation's record are handy features unique to the CD-ROM version. Both the CD-ROM and print versions are updated every six months, which, allowing for research and publication, means the data was probably collected a year or more before your receive it.

The Foundation Directory Online

The *Foundation Directory Online* functions much like the CD-ROM, but it is updated biweekly. This is a crucial difference, because foundations change their priorities and guidelines with some frequency, especially in unstable economic times. And of course, because you're already online, clicking through to a funder's website is seconds quicker.

The CD-ROM will cost you a few hundred dollars, which is equivalent to a year's subscription of one version of the online edition. You can, however, get the online edition for a month at a time, which might be just right for you if you are researching only one program rather than performing research on an ongoing basis.

Other Foundation Center Resources

The Foundation Center also offers a good deal of information on its website for free. The most important free resource for you is the Foundation Finder. This database contains the most up-to-date information you can find in one place on the Internet for foundation addresses and contact names. If a foundation has a website, there will be a link to it, and like GuideStar, the Foundation Center provides links to the foundation's IRS return. This is a great free resource.

The Foundation Center also provides a page with links to foundation websites broken down by private, corporate, and community foundations, plus grantmaking public charities. These lists of links are useful for browsing, which is a good way to jog your memory about potential, current, and past funders.

Not sure what foundation might be interested in your program? The Foundation Center also offers a free search engine with which you can search by key words (such as "at-risk youth" or "music") and limit your search to private foundations, community foundations, grantmaking public charities, government agencies, or some or all of these.

In addition to the foundation databases, the Foundation Center also offers tutorials on writing grants, preparing budgets, and researching funders. These are all fairly succinct, touching on every aspect of grant writing and going into a few aspects in some depth.

GrantStation Online

Another good online resource is GrantStation (www.grantstation.com). Fewer foundations are included in GrantStation's database (only around 5,000), but look at what it has left out: foundations that do not accept unsolicited proposals, foundations that give out less than $10,000 annually, and foundations that fund only research and scholarships. Most of the foundations left out are ones that wouldn't have been of use to you anyway (unless, of course, you are looking for research or scholarship funds).

GrantStation's approach is to provide you with detailed information on what the foundation will support, leaving information such as trustee names and extensive lists of grants for you to find on the foundations' websites—links to which are always provided. This practical approach can save you from becoming bogged down in information that is only of interest later in the grant writing and research process.

GrantStation's "area of interest" database search provides, to me, more useful choices than the Foundation Center's (which can be too general like "program support" or too specific such as "art therapy" while not providing a search on "art").

Words to the Wise

You'll undoubtedly discover information that doesn't fit with any grant you're working on now, but save it—it may just be what you need for a proposal you'll work on a year from now. Be sure to note where and when you found the information in case you need to consult that source for additional facts or check that the information remains correct.

More than a database, GrantStation also provides a free weekly funding update newsletter; a very thorough grant writing tutorial that includes many examples, how-tos, and worksheets; links to funders nationally; and a grant deadlines listing. GrantStation's basic membership fee is a bit more than the Foundation Center's cheapest rate for an annual subscription, but this is a site definitely worth looking into.

The Taft Group

The Taft Group, part of the Gale Publishing Company, offers another useful database, *Prospector's Choice*, but only on CD-ROM. The number of foundations it includes lies between GrantStation and the Foundation Center (at around 10,000), but it has in compensation biographical information on trustees and directors of these organizations and also provides much longer lists of sample grants. The biographical information can be a real time-saver in discovering connections that you might be able to make between someone at your charity and a foundation trustee.

Funders' Websites

Funders' websites run the gamut from nonexistent to a few static pages to beautiful Flash presentations that elaborate on their funding philosophy, list all grantees with hyperlinks, and give you complete financial information. I would never prepare a grant without first checking a foundation's website.

Here are a few addresses of some really good foundation websites for you to explore:

♦ **Arthur M. Blank Foundation (www.blankfoundation.org).** The visuals tell you a lot—no matter what the focus area, the real focus is on kids. You'll find a good explanations of programs and helpful grant lists.

♦ **Joyce Foundation (www.joycefdn.org).** Not only do they list their grants, but they give a short statement of what the grants were for—information every grantwriter wants to know but seldom finds so easily.

♦ **The William Randolph Hearst Foundations (www.hearstfdn.org).** The site gives the details on all their grants going back several years and links to each grantee's website. It also provides clear directions on how to apply and what kinds of projects they look for.

♦ **W.K. Kellogg Foundation (www.wkkf.org).** This is a real techie website. An interactive database gives you access to the details on grants going back more than ten years. You can then use links to find grants to the same organization or to groups in the same city, and on and on. It also provides access to a number of studies and helpful publications for nonprofits. You can also apply for a grant online.

♦ **Verizon (foundation.verizon.com).** Verizon was the first company to accept grant applications online exclusively. The forms are easy to complete, and a quick online "eligibility test" will prevent you from wasting time if you don't fit their guidelines.

> **Words to the Wise**
>
> Before exploring the byways of a foundation's site, look for a Frequently Asked Questions (FAQs) section. It will prevent you from spending a lot of time reading about their programs and application procedures only to discover you've already missed the deadline or don't fit their requirements.

GuideStar

Only five or ten years ago, a request for a foundation's or nonprofit's IRS return would have been met with stony silence. Nonprofits were required by law to make them available, but few did so without a struggle. Several charity scandals created a call for greater accountability and transparency, which resulted in the IRS returns and other financial information being much more readily available. That's good news for you, because there's a lot to be learned from the IRS returns.

The best thing that ever happened to transparency in the nonprofit world is the GuideStar website (www.guidestar.org). It has in its database information on every 501(c)(3) organization in the United States, including all 80,000-odd foundations. Foundations tend not to complete the optional information sections GuideStar provides (list of trustees, for instance), but this information and much more can be found in the IRS returns (the 990-PF form, where "PF" stands for "private foundation"), which are available here.

Words to the Wise

Each nonprofit organization in the GuideStar database has the option to add a full report, including a list of its board of directors, goals for the year, accomplishments of last year, and even a newsletter. If your charity has not created a full report, do so. It's free marketing and, for an increasing number of individual funders, GuideStar serves as a charity marketplace. Do it today.

Why do you want to look at their IRS returns? After all, they pay no taxes and it's just an "informational" return. Are you kidding? There is gold in those forms. For instance, you can find ...

♦ If the foundation received any contributions during the year (which is not uncommon for young foundations and for corporate foundations).

♦ The foundation's total assets, five percent of which they must spend on programs, including grants, each year.

♦ Salaries of the top level staff and/or board. (Okay, this is interesting just because I'm nosey, but aren't you curious, too?)

♦ A complete list of trustees (occasionally with home or business addresses).

♦ A list of each and every grant they made.

♦ And sometimes, a statement of what they give grants for.

The information in the IRS returns might be more complete and up-to-date than in the listings in some directories, even though the IRS return might be 18 months old.

Philanthropy Facts

Every foundation must file an IRS informational return (990-PF), but some nonprofits do not have to do so. Nonprofits with income of $25,000 or less and most religious organizations are not required to file the 990 form. Also, foundations must reveal the names of their donors and how much was given, but other nonprofits are allowed to keep this information confidential.

Because looking at the 990-PF is such an important part of research, you'll find parts of several pages of one reproduced in this chapter, and we'll take some time now to go through it together. (I've blacked-out the name and other identifiers of this large foundation. Even through the 990s are part of the public record, some foundations still get sensitive about revealing themselves, and who knows, I might send them a proposal one day.)

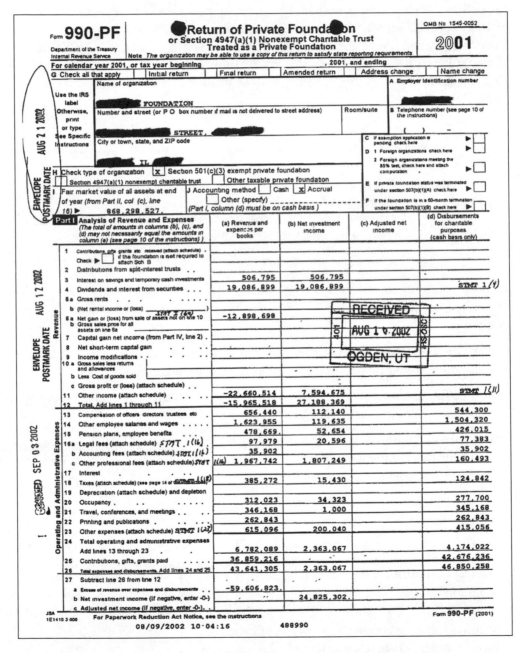

This foundation's 990-PF is typical of those for most foundations. This is a large foundation, and the complete return contains more than 700 pages, most of which report on its investments.

Form 990-PF (2001) Page 7

Part IX-B Summary of Program-Related Investments (see page 21 of the instructions)

Describe the two largest program-related investments made by the foundation during the tax year on lines 1 and 2 | Amount

1 NON APPLICABLE

2

All other program-related investments See page 22 of the instructions

3 NONE

Total Add lines 1 through 3 ▶

Form 990-PF (2001) Page 6

Part VIII Information About Officers, Directors, Trustees, Foundation Managers, Highly Paid Employees, and Contractors

1 List all officers, directors, trustees, foundation managers and their compensation (see page 20 of the instructions).

(a) Name and address	(b) Title and average hours per week devoted to position	(c) Compensation (if not paid, enter -0-)	(d) Contributions to employee benefit plans and deferred compensation	(e) Expense account, other allowances
SEE STATEMENT VIII (1)		656,440.	-0-	-0-

2 Compensation of five highest-paid employees (other than those included on line 1 - see page 21 of the instructions). If none, enter "NONE."

(a) Name and address of each employee paid more than $50,000	(b) Title and average hours per week devoted to position	(c) Compensation	(d) Contributions to employee benefit plans and deferred compensation	(e) Expense account, other allowances
SEE STATEMENT VIII (2)		489,424.		

Form 990-PF (2001) Page 10

Part XV Supplementary Information (continued)

3 Grants and Contributions Paid During the Year or Approved for Future Payment

Recipient Name and address (home or business)	If recipient is an individual show any relationship to any foundation manager or substantial contributor	Foundation status of recipient	Purpose of grant or contribution	Amount
a *Paid during the year* SEE STATEMENT XV (3)				42,676,236.

The first page resembles your own IRS return. It starts out asking for name, address, and tax ID number. The address here will be the foundation's legal address, which might be different from the address used for grant applications. Cross-check with other references before mailing anything to this address.

On the first line below the heading, the foundation will fill in dates if its fiscal year does not equal the calendar year. This foundation apparently uses the calendar year, because no dates appear here. Knowing the fiscal year can guide you as to when to apply. Frequently, foundations (especially corporate ones) budget a set amount for grants for the year (and most do operate on a calendar year). If you apply in their last round of grant making, there might be less money available.

> **Philanthropy Facts**
>
> The bulk of the return will consist of various schedules. One of these will give the trustees' names (and possibly addresses) and note any compensation they receive. A lengthy one will detail the foundation's investments. The schedule of grants therefore can be many hundreds of pages further into the report.

Next, the form asks for any income received during the past year. A number of foundations will receive additional income from their donor(s), and corporate foundations frequently will receive a major donation from the company each year. This explains how (as noted in Foundation Center directory summaries) it's possible for a foundation with $100,000 in assets to make $2,000,000 in grants. The page ends with net income, after detailing income from investments and expenses.

The rest of the form definitely does not resemble your IRS return. Section VIII asks for a list of their board of trustees and for how much anyone was paid. This, too, will probably be on an attached schedule. This foundation gave a total amount paid to all trustees on the form, but in the listing (which was just a page from their brochure), they only gave the names, so you'll never know who received this salary. Part IX will let you know if this foundation makes Program Related Investments (PRIs).

Part XV should contain a list of the grants they have made, but usually these appear in an attached schedule, because most foundations make more grants than would fit on the page. Part XV should also tell you the purposes for which the foundation exists, its grantmaking programs, and other information. This, unfortunately, is frequently the least complete section of the 990-PF. You'll probably have to go to their website for this. This foundation just enclosed a copy of its brochure.

Sometimes, trustee addresses will be given (business and even home addresses). The addresses will help you identify if the John Jones who is a trustee is the same one as on your mailing list or the one who went to college with your board president. A business address can help you discover connections; for instance, if one of your board members works at the same law firm, or knows someone who does, you've found your connection.

Words to the Wise

Although some foundations will give the trustees' home addresses, don't use this information to contact them or even send them a newsletter. You don't want them to feel you have invaded their privacy, especially as you will soon be asking them for money. And mail sent to a trustee at his or her business address will probably be treated as junk mail, so don't waste your stamp.

Sector Websites

Grantmakers apparently never miss an opportunity to join an association of colleagues. There are associations of grantmakers by region, by state, by area of funding, by type (such as family foundations and a different one for small family foundations), by region and type …. Well, you get the idea.

Although intended for the grantmakers, the websites of grantmaker associations offer information for the grant seeker, as well. Many of the regional associations accept a standardized application form, which can save you some time. (But you will still customize each application, right?). Publications and notices of conventions (and they all have conventions) can give you clues to the hot topics with that group of funders and what jargon is currently popular.

Here is a list of grantmaker association websites of interest:

♦ **Regional Associations of Grantmakers (www.rag.org).** This site provides you with links to the numerous regional associations and their standardized application forms.

♦ **The Council on Foundations (www.cof.org).** Check out these links to many foundations and other associations. Convention information is worth a quick scan for buzzwords of the moment.

♦ **Canadian Environmental Grantmakers Network (www.cegn.org).** This is a database of funders to environmental causes in Canada, with links to their websites. Membership in the Network gives you access to additional information.

♦ **Grantmakers in the Arts (www.giarts. org).** This site has all types of funders, fromfoundations to corporate giving programs and grantmaking public charities, in a listing with links.

♦ **Grantmakers Concerned with Immigrants and Refugees (gcir.org).** This site includes links to foundations and tips on grant writing.

♦ **Grantmakers in Health (www.gih.org).** This site includes no links to foundations, but it has lots of links to studies that might provide backup for your proposal's assertions.

> **Words to the Wise**
>
> The sector sites narrow the playing field for you. Just don't let the funders on these sites be the only ones you investigate. Your organization is different in some way from every other organization performing the same services, and there are undoubtedly funders out there uniquely for you.

Corporations

The Foundation Center's resources also include information on corporate foundations, as do GrantStation and Prospector's Choice. Everything I said previously about using these tools in researching private foundations applies equally to corporate foundations and corporate giving programs.

On one corporate site that seemed to have no obvious links to its foundation, putting "grants" into its site search took me right to the foundation. Be aware that some companies, especially those that sell merchandise on the web, keep their corporate information in a separate place. For example, www.TheGap.com is where you can find the nearest store, but you need to go to www.GapInc.com to find corporate information, including the foundation.

Because corporate foundations are connected to corporations, however, even more information exists on the Internet to help you determine how to get a grant from them. Knowledge is power, especially in the corporate world, so don't leave any stone unturned when seeking corporate funding. The more you know about the company and its principal officers, the better you can focus your proposal.

Today's News (And Yesterday's)

The business section of your local newspaper and business publications such as *The Wall Street Journal*, *Crain's*, and *Fortune* are important sources of information on corporations (whose stock is up, whose is down) and corporate officers (who's in, who's out). These all can be found online, mostly for free for at least some articles, except for *The Wall Street Journal*, which is one of the few pay-only web news sites.

Most periodicals maintain an archive of past stories as well. Although many charge a modest fee for accessing the archived news, it's worth it if the story provides the key to your proposal.

EDGAR and His Friends

You should be aware that you can gain access to all filings with the Securities and Exchange Commission through the EDGAR database (www.sec.gov/edgar.shmtl), although the information is probably more esoteric than you will need. If your prospect is a top corporate CEO and you heard that he or she has just received a major stock package, you can get the details from EDGAR, and then decide how much to ask for. More user-friendly is the related Edgar Online (www.edgar-online.com). A lot of this site is only available to subscribers, but the people profiles might provide just the information you need. Another subscription site you should be aware of is Hoover's (www.hoovers.com), a compiler of corporate information owned by Dun and Bradstreet.

Government Funders

Chapter 5 included a number of websites where you can find information on government funders. Here are a few more. (These and the ones from Chapter 5 are all included in Appendix B and on the CD-ROM.)

- **Environmental Protection Agency (www.epa.gov/seahome/grants.html).** This section of the EPA site offers a free tutorial on how to write a grant for the EPA. It takes you through each part of the application, offering tips on what to include and how to say it along the way.

- **GovSpot (www.govspot.com).** This site has an exhaustive set of links to state agencies plus subject listings for federal agencies.

- **Catalog of Federal and Domestic Assistance Grant Topics (www.cfda.gov/public/granttopics.asp).** I discussed this resource in Chapter 5, but this particular section merits a special mention. Here you'll find the federal government's most user-friendly interface for searching for grants by topic.

People

The more you know about the people at the grantmakers, the better you can write your proposal. In finding information about individuals you'll use the same techniques as for institutions.

Google 'Em

To state the obvious, start your research by looking up the person in a general search engine. Both Google (www.google.com) and AllTheWeb (www.alltheweb.com) give excellent results for researching individuals. In a small unscientific test I conducted, searching for information on several people (well-known and fairly unknown, like me) returned about 80 to 90 percent identical returns. Try both search engines, because the differences usually show up in the first page and that way you won't miss any important information.

If you know or suspect that the subject is a civic or corporate leader, also use newspapers' and trade

Words to the Wise

Unless the subject of your research has an amazingly unique name, you'll find a lot of "imposters" along with your subject. To even the odds, always put the subject's name in quotation marks so that you at least get only the Paul Simons, and not all the Pauls plus all the Simons.

magazines' site searches to locate recent articles. The aptly named Find Articles (www.findarticles.com) enables you to search on all periodicals (which will usually give you too many hits) or by sector (arts, business, science, and so on). Newspapers and magazines are both included.

The Directory of Directors (www.directoryofdirectors.com) is another valuable research tool, although you'll have to pay for this one. (Use the print version at your library instead of paying the online fees.) You can search here by person or organization for information on both nonprofit and corporate affiliations. This shortcut will save you valuable time by establishing all kinds of connections.

> **Words to the Wise**
>
> Need information on lawyers? Martindale (www.martindale.com) will give you their business address, area of practice, and what law school they graduated from. After you know what firm they work for, you might find that one of your board members knows someone in that firm even if they don't know the subject. An introduction can be made, and you've got a contact with a funder.
>
> Need information on a doctor? A search engine for doctors can be found on the American Medical Association's website (www.ama-assn.org).

Who's Who has a long history of compiling biographical data on (according to their website) millions of people worldwide. Marquis is the publisher of the most comprehensive Who's Who (www.marquiswhoswho.com). Use of their database is expensive, so this is another case where using the printed book at the library might be a better solution. If you're really lucky, your library will subscribe to the online version.

The Cadillac of Internet search engines (for people and businesses) is LexisNexis (www.lexis-nexis.com). This is a very expensive tool, but it does give you access, for example, to a database with information on some 200 million households and 700 million phone numbers. You might be able to gain free access at some business and academic libraries.

Public Knowledge

Don't forget the telephone directory. Many years ago in one of my first jobs, I was given an intern's project to complete. The intern had spent the entire summer looking for home addresses for a large number of prominent people. She had found most of them, but a dozen or so remained elusive. I found half of them listed in the Manhattan telephone directory. Just because they're rich and famous doesn't mean they aren't listed.

AnyWho.com (based on AT&T information), Yahoo!, and other search engines offer free national online telephone directories. Search results will usually return a complete address as well as the phone number.

If an address is in the telephone book (online or offline), you should feel free to use it for your mailing list. This is very public knowledge, after all. But you'll want to tread carefully least you end up alienating rather than cultivating.

Other charities offer prospect information for you online in the form of donor acknowledgements. Occasionally, someone's name in a donor list will come up in a general search engine search. Check out the competition's websites for program and GOS funders. Comparing lists of two or more charities will reveal those funders supporting more than one—an excellent indication that they might support your charity, too.

Research Portals

Internet Prospector (www.internet-prospector.org) is a website that has been put together by a number of fundraising researchers. It provides dozens of links to other sites where you can research almost everything you'll need information on.

Universities often maintain lists of research grants as a service to their students, but after the listings are on the web, they are there for you, too. Researchers at Princeton have developed an excellent resource page for researching individuals (www.princeton. edu/Giving/devres/researchlinks.html). A few more of these are noted in the following section as resources for individuals seeking grants.

The TechFoundation (www.techfoundation.org) makes technology grants as its name implies, but also offers information on other funders and a newsletter about grants for technology.

Portals for Individual Grant Seekers

Individuals seeking grants have the added obstacle that few institutional funders will make a grant to them. The majority of grants to individuals are made as *regrants* by grantmaking public charities, that is, nonprofits that have raised money from the institutional funders to give to individuals.

Fortunately, there are a few places online for individuals seeking grants. The Foundation Center offers a directory of grants to individuals, both online (gtionline.fdncenter.org) and in book form that covers scholarships, research grants, and other means of support in all areas. The online version is less than ten dollars for a month, which may be all you need to research a project.

Grant Talk

Regrants are grants made by a charity with funds it has raised for that purpose. When seeking a grant to support regrants, be sure the funder allows this—many don't, including many federal grants.

Researchers at Michigan State University (www.lib.msu.edu/harris23/grants/3subject. htm) have compiled this extensive list of websites, interactive databases, and books pertaining to grants for individuals. Because it is a university, it's not surprising that they have concentrated on scholarships.

In the arts, NYFA Source (www.nyfa.org/source) is the one-stop resource for artists in all disciplines. Created and maintained by the New York Foundation for the Arts, this database contains information on nearly 2,700 organizations and more than 7,000 opportunities for artists. And it is free and updated daily.

The Medical University of South Carolina (research.musc.edu/ord/granttips.htm) has compiled a page of links to grant writing guides, focusing on medical research proposals. The University of Texas (www.lib.utexas.edu/subject/ss/grants.html) maintains a links page for researchers in the social sciences.

The Least You Need to Know

◆ The Foundation Center, GrantStation, and Taft Group's Prospector's Choice are the three top places to begin your research online or by using one of their CD-ROMs.

◆ Make sure your information is current by cross-checking resources and noting when websites were last updated.

◆ GuideStar.org provides an easy link to websites of all kinds of foundations and nonprofits, including each funder's IRS return.

◆ Foundation IRS returns offer a wealth of information, including assets, grants made, and trustee names (and possibly addresses).

◆ Don't overlook the obvious sources of information, including general search engines and online telephone directories.

◆ Individuals seeking grants should start with service organizations in their area of interest.

Chapter 8

You Can Find It Offline

In This Chapter

- ◆ How to do research without the Internet
- ◆ The best directories for institutional and individual donor research
- ◆ How to gather information in the course of your everyday life
- ◆ The research library in your mailbox
- ◆ Where to find grant opportunities for individuals

The Internet has transformed research of all kinds, including funder and donor research. But you can still do valuable research offline, and there are some resources you'll only find offline. There's also something to be said for using a printed directory of funders and letting the eye scan listings adjacent to the one you looked up. Serendipity can play a role in research, just don't depend on it.

Of necessity, print directories can focus on only one approach to a subject at a time: who's giving money away (funder directories), or who's receiving grants (grant guides), or what's the money being given away for (topic guides). You'll find trying to cross-reference this information quite interactive, as you furiously flip pages in several books.

Because most of the online and CD-ROM directories owe their existence to printed directories, you'll find much the same information in both. The key difference will be the freshness of the data. In this chapter, I'll look at some of the print equivalents of a few of the resources discussed in the previous chapter, as well as some that can only be found offline.

You can find complete bibliographical entries for all the books mentioned in this chapter in Appendix A.

Directories

You will want to make the Foundation Center your first stop offline as well as online when researching foundation and corporate funders. They started out publishing their funder directories in printed form, and they've continued to do so even with the expansion of their electronic resources.

The Foundation Center operates offices in New York, San Francisco, Atlanta, Cleveland, and Washington, D.C. You'll find their addresses in Appendix A. More than 100 collections in public and private libraries and at community foundations make available Foundation Center publications and other reference works. These addresses can be found in the front of directories published by the Foundation Center and on its website.

The Foundation Center's *The Foundation Directory* contains several indexes that will make your research much easier and more fruitful:

◆ **Donor, officers, and trustees index**. Has a trustee at one of your current funders been particularly supportive? Look here to see what other foundations he or she serves as a trustee.

Words to the Wise

Both the Foundation Center's *The Foundation Directory* and Taft Group's *The Foundation Reporter* are offered on CD-ROM (Taft calls their CD version *Prospectors Choice*). You'll need a computer, but not Internet access. Both offer searches on many different fields, the same types of information as in their print versions, and the ability to print out prospect lists and individual records. The CD-ROM versions are discussed in Chapter 7.

◆ **Geographic restrictions index.** Note here in particular funders outside your state that fund your area. You might easily overlook these if you stick to the state-by-state listing. Note the foundations are numbered 1 to 10,000, so knowing that you state encompasses number 451 to 997 makes it possible to spot the out-of-state funders represented by numbers lower or higher.

◆ **Subject index.** Quickly find out which funders make grants in your sector: children, health, culture, and so on. These categories are broad, so you'll still have to read all the listings carefully.

The Foundation Center's *Grants Guides* offer indices of grants divided by sector, including grants for arts and culture, children, education, the environment, libraries, mental health, minorities, women and girls, and other topics. Here you look up grants, and then find out the information on the funders. These are very helpful for finding out which funders support charities similar to yours.

By only including grants of $10,000 or more, however, they exclude funders who might make many smaller grants that would be perfect for your charity. As good as these books are, they reveal the truth of the maxim that no one book (or website) will answer all your research questions.

Philanthropy Facts

Several publishers offer dozens of directories on funders based on subject (mental health, education, children services, performing arts, and so on). I've never found these directories very helpful. For example, one directory claims to be a directory of technology funders. On closer examination, the vast majority of the funders provide funding for the use of computers in schools K–12. That's not much help if you're raising money for a seniors' center or arts organization. These books appear to be very specific, but to get to be book length, end up being quite general.

The Foundation Center's *National Directory of Corporate Giving* contains information on more than 3,000 corporate grantmakers, including both foundations and company giving programs. The listings are particularly informative because they also give you information on the sponsoring company. This makes it possible for you to compare and contrast the funding interests of each, as well as noting all the names that might help you if you can find a contact within your charity.

The Taft Group, part of the Gale Publishing Company, also offers directories of foundations and corporate giving.

◆ *The Foundation Reporter* gives information on funder interests, guidelines, restrictions, and contact information, but also provides biographical data on foundation trustees. This information can save you several steps in your research in establishing connections between foundation trustees and people connected with your charity. This directory has 13 indices. (Note that the CD-ROM version of this directory has a different name, *Prospector's Choice*.)

◆ *The Corporate Giving Directory* likewise includes biographical data on the corporate leaders of these giving programs along with the standard contact, guidelines, interests, and restrictions entries. It includes the 1,000 largest corporate foundations and giving programs. It also gives you information on corporate volunteer programs and branch locations, valuable information not included in the Foundation Center's publication (although Taft covers only a third as many corporations).

Your Personal Assistant

If your organization has $695 to spare, you can get the staff at the Foundation Center to do some of your research for you. By joining their Associates Program, you receive the right to call them ten times a month with research questions. If you have limited reference sources and very limited time, it might pay to have an expert help you. I've found this service to be very good at getting biographical information or answering a specific research question, but less so in developing a prospect list. Other grant writers might have had different experiences.

Words to the Wise

When collecting research material, be sure to note where and when you found the information in case you need to consult that source for additional facts or for a citation in the proposal you're working on now, or one you work on a year from now.

Don't have $695 to spare? Remember that your local librarians can be one of your greatest resources. If they aren't used to doing the kind of research you need, they'll probably welcome the challenge.

People Information

Never overlook the obvious sources for information. Case in point: the telephone book. People you'd think would have unlisted numbers can be found right there.

The *Directory of Directors* provides the kind of information researchers most value—it shows connections. You can look up a person and discover his or her nonprofit and corporate affiliations. There is also an index by organization. Not to be outdone, The Foundation Center publishes *Guide to U.S. Foundations, Their Trustees, Officers, and Donors*, a two-volume directory.

Words to the Wise

To research individuals in professional directories, you have two choices: online or the library. These directories are—for the most part—prohibitively expensive for most nonprofits to own.

The Who's Who directories provide basic biographical information. Marquis is the publisher of the oldest and most comprehensive editions of Who's Who. They also publish directories by profession and region. These might be of some use to you.

The social register might seem antiquated, but it, too, will give you addresses of potential major donors. It is particularly good for finding vacation home addresses and tracing family relationships. The membership lists of private clubs also offer addresses you'll find nowhere else. Although clubs won't give them to nonmembers and restrict members from anything other than personal use, you might impose on a board member or volunteer to give you one or two hard-to-find addresses.

Periodicals

The *Chronicle of Philanthropy* is the nonprofit world's newspaper of record. Issued bi-weekly, it includes articles on trends in philanthropy. It also reports on recent grants by foundations and companies. Skimming this listing is a great way to pick up some prospects for further research. Much of its content is available online (www. philanthropy.com), but some is reserved for subscribers to the paper edition.

The *NonProfit Times* offers articles for nonprofits beyond fundraising to include management issues. It can be had for free if you are a full-time nonprofit executive. It, too, offers much of its content free online (www.nptimes.com).

The Stuff You Used to Throw Away

Believe it or not, a lot of information probably exists in your home and office right now that will assist your funder research. If you pay attention, everyday contacts with nonprofits will yield valuable information on their donors and board members.

Programs, Brochures, Annual Reports

Being a fundraiser changes the way you experience the world. Attending a concert is great, but it's also an opportunity to obtain a list of the orchestra's donors, conveniently listed in the program. What restraint it takes to not read the donor list during the performance! Going to see the latest museum exhibition? Be sure to pick up the brochure to see who funded it (and don't forget to check the labels on the paintings to see who donated them).

Philanthropy Facts
If someone has given to two charities similar to yours, the chances of their giving to your charity are excellent. Some people tend to be "joiners," who like to be associated with as many groups as possible. Membership officers at the three largest New York City art museums estimate that a third or more of their members overlap. Foundations behave similarly. Comparing the donor lists of three New York City nonprofit theatres, I quickly found seven foundations that supported all three.

It's not just arts organizations that offer this valuable information to the public. Brochures describing any type of service will likely credit the funders. But annual reports offer the greatest insight into who pays for what. Annual reports cost a lot to produce, so not every organization will have one, but even the simplest report will contain a list of the charity's most important donors.

How do you get hold of the competition's annual reports? Ask. Smart fundraisers know that a new grant to your charity will not result in a decrease in funding for their charity. After all, they hold the stronger position as a current grantee. I have had colleagues call to ask me what my experience has been with a particular foundation, and I've made those calls, too.

Words to the Wise

If your colleagues aren't willing to share information, make a small contribution to get on their charities' mailing lists, then call as a donor to request a copy of the annual report.

Don't, however, ask a colleague for his or her donor list, which implies a listing containing addresses and other possibly confidential information.

After you've assembled a number of programs, brochures, and annual reports, it's time to cross-check names. You'll find that individual donors and foundations tend to support a limited number of causes. If the prospective funder appears in the listings of two organizations, definitely put them on your prospect list. If they turn up on three or more lists, put them at the top.

This can be somewhat tedious work, but it shows that there is some research that still needs to be done offline.

Your Mail Box

Without even asking, you're probably receiving prospecting information in your mailbox every day. Benefit invitations carry lists of donors. Plain old requests for donations might include board lists. As a grant writer, you do not have the luxury of throwing away unsolicited mail from any charity. Add these mailings to your offline research file for cross-checking and mining.

Books for Individuals

Few foundations make grants to individuals, making most foundation directories of little use to the individual grant seeker. The Foundation Center publishes a useful one, but it covers all possible sectors including scholarships, which makes it impossible for it to go into depth in any one area.

Service organizations and grantmaking public charities make many more grants to individuals than do foundations. There are helpful books and newsletters for discovering what these organizations can offer you. Here are a few of them.

The following publications cover individual grants in the arts:

- *Grants and Awards Available to American Writers, PEN American Center,* 2002–03 Edition.

  PEN's directory is widely recognized as the most comprehensive resource for opportunities of all kinds for writers, from grants to writing contests to artist colonies. It is updated biennially.

- *Dramatists Sourcebook 2002–03 Edition: Complete Opportunities for Playwrights, Trans-lators, Composers, Lyricists, and Librettists,* Kathy Sova, Gretchen Von Lerte and Todd Miller (eds.), Theatre Communications Group.

This comprehensive guide lists more than 1,100 opportunities, including 150 prizes. It also offers a guide to submitting scripts and other helpful information.

◆ *Opportunities in New Music, 2002 edition*, Lyn Listen, ed. American Music Center.

This directory of ongoing grants, awards, and competitions for composers is supplemented by the monthly newsletter, *Opportunity Updates*, which mostly lists competitions and calls for scores, but other opportunities and grants do appear.

◆ *Poets & Writers Magazine*, Poets & Writers.

This bimonthly magazine lists both recipients of recent grants and awards as well as upcoming opportunities. It includes many advertisements of additional opportunities.

◆ *The Artist's Resource Handbook*, Allworth Press, 1996.

Visual artists will find in this book a guide to organizations that can assist them along with information on legal and health and safety issues and other topics.

◆ *Directory of Grants for Crafts and How to Write a Winning Proposal*, James Dillehay. W. Snow Publishers, 2000.

The author has brought together a directory of grant resources and a guide to writing grants, all with the crafts artist in mind.

Words to the Wise

Newsletters and magazines published by sector service organizations provide more useful information than books for grants for individuals. These periodicals have the advantage of always being up-to-date. The only disadvantages are that you cannot get an overview of what's available, and you might not find out about a grant until one or two months before the deadline.

The following publications cover individual grants in the sciences:

◆ *Directory of Biomedical Health Care Grants, 2003*, Lynne and Jeremy T. Miner, Oryx Press, 2002.

Some 2,500 programs are listed in this directory to support work in the health sciences from laboratory studies to health-care delivery systems. It also includes a short guide to proposal planning and writing.

◆ *Financial Aid for Research and Creative Activities Abroad*, Gail Ann Schlachter, Service Press, 2002–2004.

This guide covers more than 1,200 opportunities for Americans seeking funds to study abroad (from high school to postgraduate levels). It's organized by the country or area for which the grant allows you to study.

◆ Michigan State University offers a bibliography of books on grants for individuals in various sectors, but you'll have to go online to get it at www.lib.msu.edu/harris23/grants/3subject.htm. It concentrates on scholarships, but includes books in other areas, as well.

◆ The Internet offers many more resources in the sciences, which are covered in the previous chapter and appear on this book's CD-ROM.

Although the most current information can usually be found only online, directories, books, newsletters, and a wide variety of materials from nonprofits still appear in print. If you lack easy Internet access, you'll do well working with the print resources to get started, but you'll want to check the Internet for the latest information.

The Least You Need to Know

◆ Many online directories are available in print form with indices that mimic online search capabilities.

◆ The Foundation Center and Taft Group publish the best print directories of funders.

◆ Seemingly antiquated publications such as the social register can be useful in locating hard-to-find addresses of individuals.

◆ Concert programs, service program brochures, benefit invitations, and direct mail appeals all contain useful funder information.

◆ Most fundraisers will share their publications that list their donors with you (but not their actual donor list).

◆ Newsletters of professional associations offer timely listings of grants for individuals.

Chapter 9

Narrowing Your Prospects

In This Chapter

◆ Determining funder interest through published materials and grant lists

◆ When a past gift is not an indication of foundation interest

◆ How to address funder interests and avoid common mistakes

Sending off a grant proposal without tying it to a funder's interests wastes everyone's time. Yet many grant writers make this mistake, even though they think that by reading the funder's mission statement they have done their homework. Because a funder supports K-12 education does not mean it will necessarily support technology education or an artist in the schools, for example. Support of libraries could include book purchase, technology upgrades, or programs for the public.

Each funder will have its niche interest, and it's up to you to find it. In this chapter, you'll learn how to avoid common pitfalls, find the information that will help you focus your proposals, and thoughtfully address the funder's interests.

Get the Details

Before you put fingers to keyboard on a grant proposal, you must carefully read the funder's mission statement, guidelines, lists of recent grants made, and program descriptions, which you can find online, in annual reports, or other publications. All of this information will not be available for every foundation, but use as much as you can gather as your starting point.

Sometimes, the information a funder makes public is general and of limited use, but even if the funder provides detailed information, you'll want to go further by checking into the recent actual grants they have made.

Many foundations' annual reports simply list the names of their grant recipients and the amount. In their 990-PF forms, this is almost always the case. Although that information will help you, it doesn't tell the whole story. For example, was the $10,000 grant to the after-school program for teacher training, operating support, or equipment? Unless you know, you're at a disadvantage in preparing your proposal.

Words to the Wise

A good prospect list for a program should have no more than ten prospects (and even as few as three) by the time you're ready to write the grant. I have seen grant writers with dozens of prospects. That's not a prospect list; that's a directory. Research potential funders thoroughly so you don't waste time preparing fruitless proposals.

Thankfully, a number of foundations do provide that kind of information. The ones I listed in Chapter 7 as having good websites all give you details on their grants online. Guides to funding in particular areas are worth briefly examining in a library (rather than buying), because they might provide that level of detail. You can also look for funding credits and donor listings published by the grant recipients to discover the purpose of the grant.

There's enough to know about and do in preparing a successful grant proposal without following a false lead. By cross-checking funders' grant lists with reference books and recipients' listings, you will narrow down your prospect list to the few foundations that will truly be good prospects for your charity.

Avoid False Leads

A popular European guidebook series refers to words that appear to be cognates but aren't (the Italian "caldo" looks like it would mean "cold," when it really means "hot") as "false friends." Funders make a lot of grants that are the grant writer's false friends. These sometimes come under the heading of *discretionary grants* in their annual report.

Grant Talk

Discretionary grants enable trustees to support charities that they care about but that lie outside the funders' guidelines. It's sometimes seen as a perk for trustees. In family foundations, it can be a means of keeping the peace when family members' interests vary.

Don't be misled by discretionary grants. They do not indicate an area of interest for the foundation. Unless you know which trustee made the discretionary grant and have a connection to him or her, this will be a dead end in your grant search.

False leads also show up in donor listings. I once noticed a familiar foundation in an opera company's donor list in the $25,000 category. But while checking out the foundation's guidelines I saw that this was the only opera company the funder supported and it seldom made grants over $5,000. How can this be explained? Checking the trustee lists revealed a common person on both the foundation and opera boards. This was a discretionary grant, not a new direction for the foundation.

Well-intentioned volunteers and your board of trustees might be good at feeding you false leads. When periodicals from *Forbes* to the *Chronicle of Philanthropy* publish their lists of the richest and/or most generous people, people who are not professional fundraisers are apt to suggest you target some of these people.

If your charity already has a relationship with one of the people on the list, or one of them has a foundation that supports organizations like yours in your geographic location, they might well be a very good prospect—otherwise, pursuing them will be a waste of time. Wealth is not an indication of a good prospect, but involvement with your charity (or a similar one) is.

Funders Have Needs, Too

Now we'll look at how to express your knowledge of a funder's interests and tie it to your program in a proposal. In a full proposal, each of the following examples would be the first or second paragraph in the cover letter or the proposal (or both).

Although most of the examples are based on good and bad proposals I have seen, no foundation or charity names are real (although the performing arts venues are very real). Read each of them, make your own notes, and then see my comments that follow.

Example #1: Knowing of your interest in education, we respectively submit this proposal for a $5,000 grant to provide new computers for the Community Children's Center.

Example #2: The Rose Foundation's support of writers through its fellowship program has helped many novelists complete their works. At Fiction Writers' Center, we, too, provide fellowships to writers, and we request a $15,000 grant from the Rose Foundation to support this program.

Example #3: The Wolf Foundation's dedication to the performing arts is well known through its support of the Metropolitan Opera and Carnegie Hall. Our organization supports composers early in their careers so that they one day will be presented by these institutions.

Example #4: The Downtown Foundation's dedication to all that is new in the performing arts has been well demonstrated through its support of The Kitchen, P.S. 122, and the Bang on a Can Festival. Our organization supports composers early in their careers so that they one day will be presented by these institutions.

> **Words to the Wise**
>
> Check to see if the funder issues RFPs. Even past ones will give you detailed information on the types of projects the funder prefers.

Example #5: We are writing to request a $10,000 grant from the Downstate Community Foundation to support education for inmates at the Big Prison upstate. The success of the program for inmates you supported through I&P Services locally is a model program we hope to emulate.

Example #6: Like the Hometown Community Foundation, our organization seeks to improve the lives of all the people of Hometown. We request a $20,000 grant to provide counseling services for at-risk youth, who are among the most disadvantaged of our citizens.

Example #7: We request a $5,000 grant to bring literary programming into community settings through readings by both authors and actors. The spoken word is a powerful force in involving people, in particular young people, in literature. When great writing is combined with a persuasive performance, magic can happen in people's lives.

Example #8: We would like to applaud the Leotard Company's support of performances of dance in all its forms in New York City. The field can easily become very fragmented, and your enlightened support offers one common element to tie the dance community together. At Dancers Plus Association, we also embrace a wide variety of dance forms, from tap to flamenco, ballet to modern. We hope that you will become a supporter of Dancers Plus Association with a $20,000 grant as we strive to provide services to the same dancers you support in other ways.

Example number one is so vague, it's obvious the grant writer didn't read past the "interests" listing in the Foundation Center directory. (Has the foundation funded technology before? If so, that should have been mentioned.) Beginner grant writers make this their most common mistake.

In the second example, the right research was done but the wrong conclusion was reached. If a foundation makes grants directly to writers, they probably have a good idea of the kinds of writers they want to support and would be unlikely to support a similar program over which they would have no control.

The third example also illustrates wasted research. Both the Met and Carnegie Hall are first and foremost presenters and maintainers of the status quo with minimal interest in living composers. (I know they would both disagree, but that's my opinion.) A funder's support of these two organizations is no indication of an interest in new art and artists. They might, of course, be supporting a particular program at these institutions dedicated to

Words to the Wise

GuideStar offers more than 990 forms. They also provide a few articles such as the excellent "What Grantmakers Want Applicants to Know." The 15 tips range from "Do your homework" to advice on what to send and not to send with your proposal. You can find it at www.guidestar.org/news/features/grantadvice.stm.

How to Say It

Never quote verbatim from a funder's mission statement or program guide in a grant proposal. They won't take you seriously unless you can express in your own words what your program will do and how it relates to their interests on more than a superficial level.

new composers, which would be a totally different case, which the grant writer would no doubt have mentioned it had it been true.

The fourth example is almost an exact repeat except that this foundation supports groups that are known for their interest in new art and artists. This one stands a very good chance of funding.

Remember geographic restrictions? The fifth example asks a local community foundation (that only makes grants in its service area) to fund a program many miles away. Even through they have shown an interest in this specific type of program, this proposal won't get very far.

The sixth example hits the nail on the head by asking for a project that meets the interests and geographic restrictions of the community foundation. "At-risk youth" is even one of the foundation's favorite buzzwords.

Number seven doesn't directly compare the charity's program to the funder's, but the points that it makes about the spoken word are exactly parallel to (but don't quote) the funder's stated interests "to develop an appreciation of spoken English." If you can make your point without an obvious "mine and yours" statement, do so.

The last example begins by praising the funder for giving money to other people, and in doing so reveals that they know who the funder supports and what form that support takes (in this case, for performances). The grant writer then ties his or her program directly to the funder's interest.

The good examples came about through careful research and cross-checking. Some of the negative examples contain mistakes that are obvious, some subtle, but all the mistakes would result in an immediate rejection.

In most of the examples, the grant writer has asked for an amount right up front. You don't have to do this, but it's good to get it out of the way. Another common mistake is to omit a request for a specific grant amount. You certainly don't want the funder to have to wonder about how much you are seeking.

The Least You Need to Know

- Detailed research will eliminate funders in your sector who have shown no interest in your specific kind of program.

- Avoid being misled by false leads by checking the grants list against foundation interests and trustee connections.

- Use common sense to eliminate funders with competing programs.

- When concentrating on funder subject and program interests, don't forget about geographic restrictions.

◆ Express your charity's connection to the funder's interest without parroting back the funder's own language.

◆ Show your knowledge of the funders' interests by referring to another grant they have given or a public position they have taken whenever possible.

Part 4

Strategies for Success

No grant proposal is an island. It exists in a busy world where funders' program officers are overwhelmed with proposals, nearly all of which deserve a grant. You can tip the odds in your favor by building bridges to funders before asking for their money. Here, you'll learn how to do just that.

The funder courtship is as fraught with possibilities for false steps and detours as is a personal relationship. This part examines how to introduce your charity to a funder and cultivate the beginnings of a relationship to move you toward success.

With all the information you've accumulated by this point in the grant-making process, you'll be wondering what to do with it all. I'll help you organize it into a plan that will coordinate your research and cultivation of funders with the actual proposal writing.

Chapter **10**

Sow Before You Reap

In This Chapter

- ◆ How and when to use newsletters to build knowledge of your charity

- ◆ Advantages and disadvantages of print and e-mail newsletters

- ◆ Elements of a good donor newsletter

- ◆ How to create a cultivation event that will appeal to funders

Looking back at the letter from Jack to his parents in the first chapter, how successful do you think the identical letter would have been if his parents had received it from a total stranger? Right. So why would you send a proposal to a funder that has never heard of your charity?

By educating a foundation staff member (and hopefully one or more trustees) about your charity before submitting a grant proposal, you will greatly increase your chances of success. Occasionally, a cold proposal will get funded, but by warming funders up, you'll definitely increase your success rate. In the fundraising biz we call this cultivation.

Newsletters

Newsletters designed for those your charity serves can be an effective means of educating funders about your activities. These newsletters show firsthand exactly what services you are providing, how you provide them, and how you interact with your clients. Consider putting program officers at key funders on this mailing list in time for them to receive two to three issues before your proposal arrives. With political contacts, remember to send them to their local as well as legislative offices when possible.

Newsletters written specifically for your donors can be even more effective tools for cultivating institutional funder contacts. Your donor newsletter should give your spin on what you have done, reporting on program accomplishments, giving news of past clients who have gone on to great accomplishments, and reporting on your fundraising successes.

> **" "** **Words to the Wise**
>
> If you don't have the name of someone at the funder, don't waste your stamps. After all, you know what happens to "Resident" mail that shows up in your mailbox. Check the funder's website and call to find out who would be the best person to receive your mailings.

I like to put all of my funder contacts on the mailing list for the donor newsletter, and a smaller group who have a real interest in the field on the list for the client newsletter.

Just as you don't want your proposal to come out of the blue, your first newsletter shouldn't arrive out of context either. Always include a cover letter similar to the one following when adding a funder contact to a mailing list.

Dear Mr. White:

I have enclosed a copy of the Service Organization's recent newsletter, which contains information that might be of interest to you as the program officer for arts and culture. This issue has an article by Steven Critic on the Venice Biennale and a complementary one from Sara Painter on the artists that represented the United States in that exhibition.

This newsletter is published bimonthly and enjoys a readership of 50,000. You'll note that in the back we provide information on a wide variety of opportunities for artists, including many offered by other agencies.

We hope you will find our newsletter of interest. If, however, you would prefer not to receive future issues, please let me know by calling me at 212-555-1234 or by e-mail at smith@service.org.

Sincerely,

Sandra Smith

Sandra Smith
Director of Development

Note that the emphasis in the first paragraph is on the information Mr. White can use, not on the charity itself. Although this letter introduces a client newsletter, when sending a donor newsletter for the first time, you'll also want to point out an article that the funder might find useful for something other than learning about your charity.

If you mail out a couple dozen of these letters, you can expect to hear from one or two people that they don't want to receive any future issues. This might be a good indication that your proposal will meet with the same reaction, or it could just be an overworked program officer. If an individual phones you to ask to be removed from your mailing list, try to find out which is the case by asking if there is anyone else at his or her foundation that might be interested in your newsletter.

If yours is an e-mail newsletter, it is just as important to send a "cover letter." I'd send an e-mail (one at a time) a day to two before the first newsletter issue with language just like the sample snail-mail letter. Be sure to include something in the subject line that identifies your organization. Don't repeat words or use all uppercase (both typical of spam) in the subject line (or in your message).

> **Words to the Wise**
>
> As long as you're preparing an introductory letter for your client newsletter, why not share it with whomever handles public relations at your charity? A similar approach works well at educating the press about what your charity does. (Your donor newsletter, however, will be of little interest to the press.)

Because we all receive so much spam every day, you might also send a printed letter by regular mail to introduce the forthcoming e-mail. Otherwise, the funder might automatically delete your introductory letter if he or she doesn't recognize your address or your organization's name.

> **Philanthropy Facts**
>
> A number of vendors provide the means to both manage your e-mail lists and create impressive e-mail newsletters for as little as $50 a month (or for several thousands of dollars a month). Most allow you to create fully designed (HTML) newsletters concurrently with a plain text version for people using older e-mail software. It's well worth the cost to present your charity in the best possible light.

Actually mailing a newsletter is becoming almost quaint in these days of increased electronic communications. A printed copy gives you complete control over how your story is presented. But with HTML e-mails becoming more common, you can distribute electronic newsletters that are just as attractive as printed ones. Plain text newsletters are quickly becoming obsolete. Long ones won't get read.

Hopefully, the program officers on your list will share your newsletters with others. This is really easy with e-mail newsletters. But printed newsletters, especially if they are attractive and graphically interesting, will likely get circulated, too.

If your charity doesn't have a donor newsletter, seriously consider creating one using e-mail to keep costs down. As a grant writer you're already familiar with your charity's current programs and those in the planning stages. Knocking out the text for a two-page newsletter should be easy.

Two medium-length articles are all you'll need to give your newsletter substance. You'll be surprised at how easy it is to do and what a positive response you'll get. Just keep everyone in your charity (including key board members) up-to-date on what you are doing. Here are examples of content found in donor newsletters:

◆ Pictures of your staff helping clients. Pictures of people on the front page of the newsletter are particularly important at drawing people in.

◆ News of accomplishments of clients (current and past).

◆ Pictures of your supporters at benefits or cultivation events. People like to see other people.

◆ A report on a major grant recently received, including how it will be used and why the donor decided to make it to your charity.

◆ A report on successful programs, including comparison to past programs and prominent funder credits.

◆ Articles on giving that offer practical advice to donors, such as articles on bequests or charitable trusts that have benefited your charity.

Words to the Wise

E-mail newsletters (and printed newsletters) should also be posted on your website to give them a longer shelf life and increase readership. More and more, e-mail newsletters consist of short summaries of articles with hypertext links to the full articles on the website.

You'll find that some of the most successful articles (in terms of donor response and appreciation) will be on resources outside your charity. The article could be on a crisis in your sector (Funding for Libraries Slashed Statewide!) or about issues affecting your sector (Early AIDS Vaccine Trials Offer Little Hope). You could also review a book on wise giving or profile the local community foundation. By including articles that lie outside your charity, you show a broader perspective that funders appreciate while offering them information that they will find useful in several ways.

Events

Using benefits and other special events to cultivate funder contacts can be difficult. You'll find that program officers and trustees can be hesitant to accept complimentary tickets for events everyone else is paying for, especially if they are expensive. They rightly don't want to send the wrong message to you as a potential grantee by allowing you to think that they owe you a favorable review of your proposal.

Instead of depending on fundraising events (or ticketed performances or exhibitions) to acquaint funders with your charity, develop events specifically to cultivate them. This is not the place to ask for money. You want to cultivate them before you solicit them (and not all in the same night). Cultivation events should not cost you much money and

should require a small fraction of the time to produce that a benefit would. Some of the cultivation
events I think you'll find successful include …

Words to the Wise

Developing and organizing
cultivation events lies well outside
your responsibilities as a grant
writer, but you should encourage
the fundraisers at your charity to
plan them and be ready to give
them names from your prospect
list to invite.

- A cocktail party at a prominent trustee's
  home. People love to see how others live,
  and the trustee should foot the bill for the
  refreshments.

- A talk by a curator about an upcoming exhibition that promises to be controversial. Those
  who attend can "dine out" on the advance
  knowledge they receive for weeks. If you can
  hold it in someone's home, they'll have two
  reasons to attend.

- A preview of the work of regrant recipients, with some in attendance to speak
  about their work and others represented by slides or reports.

- A simple luncheon that mixes scholarship recipients with current and potential
  scholarship donors. There's nothing like a kid's first-hand testimonial to open
  those pockets.

- A more formal luncheon at which a prominent scholar speaks about issues con-
  fronting the charity's sector, but not necessarily about the charity itself. Although
  this might take your charity out of the spotlight, those who attend will remember
  that you were the one who provided the insights they gained from the talk.

Basically, any event that provides knowledge that is not readily available to the public
will work. People love to know more than their friends and neighbors. And be sure to
give them something to take home with them, whether it is just a brochure or a complete packet of information on your charity.

Newsletters and events represent the cultivation you do before you apply for a grant. In
Chapter 20, I'll discuss what needs to be done after you receive a grant to set the stage
for a renewal grant. And while the grant is under consideration … I'd keep a respectful
distance as far as cultivation is concerned and restrict myself to answering the funder's
questions.

The Least You Need to Know

- Client newsletters and donor newsletters provide different means of educating
  funders about your charity.

- Never put a funder on any newsletter list without sending an introductory letter.

- Both e-mail and printed newsletters work well to cultivate funders.

- The best newsletters include information on more than your charity.

- Paid, ticketed events are not always ideal for funder cultivation.

- Cultivation events that impart inside knowledge or provide contact with clients engage funders best.

Chapter 11

Testing the Waters

In This Chapter

◆ Why and how to write an inquiry letter

◆ When and how to make an inquiry call

◆ Handling a meeting with a funder

◆ How to pull strings without getting tangled up

You've done all your research, cross-checking and checking again. You've warmed up the program officers at least to the point where they recognize the name of your charity. One additional step remains before you can start on the proposal—the inquiry. Some fundraisers suggest that a pre-proposal personal contact with a funder can triple your chances of getting a grant. I'm not sure about that statistic, but it definitely is important to test the waters and, whenever possible, to make a personal connection.

Inquiries, by their very nature, almost invite a "no." The very fact that you are inquiring might presume you have some doubt about the appropriateness of your proposal. The challenge is to banish all reservations and doubt and make the initial contact in a way that doesn't necessarily prompt a yes or no response, but gives you information to use in your proposal. (Of course, if the funder wants to say "yes" at this point, that would be fine.)

In this chapter, I'll take a look at the different ways of gathering information to further prepare the funder to receive your proposal in a positive light. I'll also discuss how and when to use board contacts.

Inquiry Letters

An inquiry letter lies somewhere between a request for guidelines and a full proposal. In the inquiry letter, you want to describe your project well enough that the funder can give you the information you require, but you also want to avoid making it appear too much like a proposal. You may ask for a meeting in your inquiry letter, too. (I discuss meetings later in this chapter.)

Peer-to-peer contact usually works best. Inquiry letters should, when possible, be addressed to a program officer, not the head of the foundation. At smaller funders, there might not be program officers, so you'll have to start at the top.

- If the letter is to a program officer, you or your director of development should sign it.

- If the letter is to go to the head of the foundation, your director of development or executive director should sign it.

An inquiry letter should include …

- A reference to the newsletters and other materials you have been sending.

- A clear request for information about *their* programs.

- A general description of your project that shows a connection to and your understanding of the funder's interests (see Chapter 9).

- Easy ways to contact you, especially an e-mail address.

- A list of your board only if one or more names might be recognizable by the funder (having the board list as part of your letterhead design works better than an attachment).

- A request for a meeting to discuss the project (optional).

- A copy of your organization's general brochure if you believe your previous cultivation might not have sufficiently paved the way (optional).

- If available, one (and only one) short press clipping to show the prominence your charity has achieved.

An inquiry letter should *not* include …

- ◆ A request for money, not even in general terms.
- ◆ A budget.
- ◆ Supporting materials, such as your tax-exempt letter.
- ◆ Annual reports or other bulky items.

Your inquiry letter might be something like the following example.

Ms. Sara Brown
Program Officer, Health and Human Services
White Family Foundation
456 Broadway
Anytown, IL 60000

Dear Ms. Brown:

I hope you have found the clinicians' newsletter from the Counseling Center of Broome County (CCBC) informative about the need for psychiatric counseling to the disadvantaged citizens of Broome County. The CCBC has provided these services for more than twenty years.

The CCBC has made great strides in reaching more people through its mobile facility, reaching clients in the most remote reaches of the county. As you probably know, state funding has been drastically reduced for next year, and we must replace that funding in the next six months to continue this service. We would welcome the opportunity to speak with you to discuss how this project operates and how the White Family Foundation might become involved with it.

The speech Dr. Phelps, who I understand is your health advisor, gave at the Illinois Association of Psychiatry on just-in-time services certainly spoke to the types of situations we at the CCBC deal with daily and that the mobile facility helps so much in meeting.

If you could possibly meet with us to discuss our current programs, we would greatly appreciate it, but I understand the limitations you have on your time. I'll call you next week to see if we can arrange a meeting, or failing that perhaps we can speak then about how we might develop a proposal to the White Foundation. In the meantime, I can be reached at 312-555-1222 or ssmith@ccbcounty.org. I look forward to speaking with you.

Sincerely,

Susan Smith

Susan Smith
Director of Development

Procedures differ slightly for a current or past funder.

◆ For a renewal grant for the same program from a current funder, you would probably just send in the renewal proposal (after making the necessary reports). An inquiry letter would serve no purpose because you know the funder likes your charity and its programs.

◆ For a grant for a new program from a current funder, you would probably phone your contact at the funder to discuss the new program rather than write an inquiry letter, which might seem too formal given the current relationship.

◆ If the past funder has not given you a grant in more than a year, you might skip the inquiry letter, and instead phone before sending the proposal, even if the grant would be for the program they supported previously.

An inquiry letter might be answered with a letter telling you to look elsewhere. In these cases, it's unlikely that a full proposal would have done any better, but when this happens you can't help but wonder what would have happened if you had been able to state your case directly. For this reason, many grant writers prefer to take the bull by the horns and make an inquiry call.

Inquiry Calls

The peer-to-peer principle applies equally if not more so when making an inquiry phone call. It's unlikely that the grant writer will be able to get through to a foundation head of a large foundation. Also, it might be interpreted as a lack of seriousness for the grant writer rather than an executive director to call a foundation head about a proposal.

Words to the Wise

Be strategic about when you place an inquiry call. The day applications are due or the day before a board meeting will probably be particularly hectic for the program officer. Determine, if you can, when these events occur and avoid them. If you must leave a voicemail message, do state you name clearly, why you are calling, and repeat your phone number. Make it as easy as possible for them to pay attention to you.

Before you call, have all your facts lined up and put them down as a series of bullet points you can refer to easily. Go over what you plan to say with a colleague, asking him or her to try to anticipate what questions the program officer might ask. If someone else will make the call, give that person your bullet points and review them to make sure any questions that might come up can be quickly answered.

You don't, of course, have to have the answers to every question—you can always say you'll get back to them with that information, but you should be prepared to respond to the obvious ones, such as who will run the program or what's the total budget.

When you have the program officer on the phone, be professional at all times. Don't try for a breezy or too informal manner, and don't address the program officer by first name unless you actually know them. Keep in mind the things that should and should not appear in an inquiry letter and try to stick to those topics in your call. Take notes on everything discussed. It will all come in handy at some point.

If your main purpose in calling is to arrange a meeting, be clear about that before you get into describing your project. The program officer might prefer to hear about it over the phone rather than in person, but give him or her that option.

If you have been sending your newsletter to the funder, I'd start by asking if it had been received and, if so, if he or she had found it informative. If your inquiry call is following up an introductory letter (that accompanied a newsletter, for example) or an inquiry letter, state that right away to make a connection between what they should have seen and know about your charity and you.

CAUTION

How to Say It

Prepare for your inquiry call with bullet points you want to cover in the call, but have additional information on the project organized and at hand to respond to any questions that arise. Stick to the point and work to come away with some positive result, even if that means just keeping the door open for the future.

Work to keep the conversation positive and general. You want to peak their interest in your proposal in hopes of gaining insight into how to best pitch it to the funder's specific interests. If you are told that the funder would not consider your project, ask if you can continue to send your newsletter and if you can call again when a different project requires funding. Try to get some positive action out of the call.

Informational Meetings

With the huge number of applications funders receive, it becomes more and more rare for them to agree to an *informational meeting*. Many funders include in their guidelines a request that you not ask for a meeting before submitting an application, after which they will determine if a meeting is warranted. If the funder you plan to approach says this, don't ask for a meeting.

Grant Talk

Informational meetings with funders are no different from those advised by many books for job seekers. In both cases, you're asking someone to meet with you to gather information when in reality you're hoping they'll be so impressed they'll give you money (as a paycheck or a grant). In both cases no one is fooled by the pretense, but it allows both parties to learn about the other.

On the other hand, if your charity and the project you want funding for fall clearly within the funder's interests (and their guidelines don't preclude meetings beforehand), they might be willing to meet with you. A meeting with a funder offers you your very best chance to make a good impression: You establish a personal connection, you get instant feedback on your projects, and you learn about the funder's current priorities.

If you are fortunate enough to get a meeting, here are some points to remember:

- You are there to listen as much as to talk.

- Be precise and stay on point. Don't give a complete blow-by-blow history of your charity's last 20 years in response to the what's-new-at-your-charity question.

- If you have had a grant previously from this funder, report on how that project went (or continues to go), stressing its accomplishments. Talk about its challenges only if you're there for funding the same project again.

- Don't give the funder any materials at the beginning of the meeting. It will only distract them, and you want to maintain eye contact. If you have materials for them, present them as you're saying your good-byes (and make sure all materials are directly to the point of your program).

- It's much better not to have to refer to notes, but if it's absolutely necessary, have your list of bullet points to remind you of the topics you need to cover and the questions you need to ask.

- Do take notes when the funder speaks (on the pad you brought with you), even if you know you'll remember every word. Taking notes shows interest.

> **Words to the Wise**
>
> In Chapter 4, I advise that you should do everything you can to blend in when visiting a corporate funder. Preparing a PowerPoint slide show might be tempting in this situation—what could be more corporate? Only do this if you know you'll be speaking to a number of people. Eye contact will serve you better than slick graphics if meeting with one or two people. Let the funder know if you plan to make a formal presentation, then keep it short, making sure you have time to get to know the corporate representatives before you turn down the lights.

- Don't doodle instead of (or in addition to) taking notes.

- Ask questions about the funder's interests that show you have done your research.

- If the funder has been in the news recently, comment on it to show your interest.

- If you feel like your project pitch is getting nowhere, have a fall-back project to offer. You're not going to get a second meeting anytime soon, so make the most of this one.

◆ Call or send a note the day after your meeting—not two days, the next day—thanking the funder for meeting with you and highlighting points from the meeting needing amplification or emphasis, or making a point you forgot to make in the meeting.

You want to make sure that the funder understands not only the details of your program, but also your charity's passion for it. If possible, a program person directly involved in the program should go along with your executive director or development director. Although you'll want to be there, too, don't send so many people as to outnumber the funder staff attending.

Only occasionally have I had meetings with funders that did not result in a grant. If they take that kind of time with you, they are probably serious about funding you. Program officers can be very helpful in coaching you in the forms and buzzwords their board looks for, so it pays to take notes and follow them to the letter.

When to Pull Strings

So you've had a really positive meeting with the program officer and you know just how to pitch your proposal. Now you discover that one of your board members went to college with one of the funder's trustees. So you call your board member and ask him or her to phone their old school chum to recommend your charity.

That's all well and good, but you've skipped an important step. The program officer who you have worked so hard to cultivate might feel blindsided if word comes from above to take special care of you. Instead, upon discovering your connection, phone the program officer and tell him or her of your discovery and ask for the program officer's advice on using this knowledge, or at the very least, let the program officer know that you're planning to use your connection.

> **Words to the Wise**
>
> Circulate a list to your board at least twice a year giving the names of trustees at the foundations on your prospect lists, asking that they note anyone they know (and how well) and return it to you. Keep careful track of these contacts for when you begin preparing the various proposals.

If, of course, you had discovered the board connection earlier, an inquiry letter might not have been necessary. If one of the funder's trustees has invited you to apply, you'd state that in the very first sentence of the proposal's cover letter. Knowing someone on the inside with the authority to ensure your proposal receives serious consideration separates yours from the masses of proposals received by the funder every day. Just be upfront with your contact at the foundation about what strings you plan to pull.

When you have discovered a personal contact between your charity and a funder (usually through one of your board members), ask that board member if he or she will contact the foundation on your behalf. In the case of foundations that do not accept unsolicited proposals, this will be the only way you can get your proposal read. In others it can make yours stand out from the many other proposals.

Your board member's contact with the funder could take several forms, listed here in the order of decreasing effectiveness:

- ◆ A phone call to the foundation trustee.

- ◆ A letter followed by a phone call to the trustee.

- ◆ A letter sent well ahead of your proposal to the trustee.

- ◆ A letter that you can use as your cover letter or include as a support letter with your proposal.

Whichever method your board member is most comfortable with is the one you'll have to use, but you can certainly encourage the phone call.

Chances are that if a letter is involved, you'll be asked to write it. If this is the case, be sure to use a different tone and don't repeat phrases from your cover letter or the proposal. Indent the paragraphs of the board member's letter to make it look more personal, and be sure to use the correct salutation (first name, nickname, whatever). Letters from a board member ideally will be on their personal or business stationary, not that of your charity.

Managing Your Contacts

After all your hard work developing contacts at funders through cultivation activities, mailings, phone calls, and meetings, you'll want to keep track of everything relating to your new relationship. Some donor software or calendar programs include a "contact manager" that enables you to note every piece of mail sent and phone call made. By tracking this information, you'll avoid contacting funders too often or not often enough. More importantly, you can set up reminders for yourself to follow through on mailings and phone calls.

How often is too often to contact a funder? During the courtship/cultivation phase, once a month is probably the most you'll want to do. After you've had the first date/ informational meeting, the all-important follow-up note should set the stage for the proposal. Basically, your instincts on how the program officer responds to you are more important than any guidelines I can give you. Don't be a pest, but don't wait so long between contacts that they forget who you are.

> **CAUTION**
>
> **How to Say It**
>
> As time goes by, you'll probably become very friendly, if not actually friends, with program officers at funders. Remember, however, that this is an unequal relationship, because you will be the one asking for something 98 percent of the time. Remaining somewhat circumspect in talking about your charity even off the record will serve you well.

The Least You Need to Know

◆ Inquiry letters and phone calls are essential parts of the grant process.

◆ Use the inquiry process to gather information about the funder's specific interests.

◆ Avoid anything that appears to be "an ask" when making an inquiry.

◆ Prepare carefully for both inquiry calls and meetings.

◆ Make the most of any meeting, including having an alternate project to discuss if necessary.

◆ Use trustee connections in a way that will not alienate or undermine program officers.

Chapter 12

Planning for Success, Now and Tomorrow

In This Chapter

♦ Why create a grant writing plan

♦ The elements in a plan

♦ Meeting deadlines

♦ Using a schedule to create success

You're not quite halfway through this book and already there seems to be a lot to remember. Well, there is a lot, but through planning and scheduling (and good record keeping) you can make it work. This chapter's title refers to "Now and Tomorrow" because no grant exists in a vacuum.

♦ Research for one program will turn up leads for a different one.

♦ Your contacts at funders will come and go.

♦ Sometimes you'll discover the perfect funder the day after the grant application deadline.

♦ Good grant proposals are based on knowledge of a program's long-term plans.

I'll use this chapter to discuss how to manage all the information you gather through research, manage input from program staff, and chart your way through the grant-writing process.

Developing a Grant-Writing Plan

What could possibly sound more boring than developing a grant-writing plan? Plenty! (How about writing a summary of the C.P.A. association's changes in accounting rules?) You'll be surprised at how helpful it will be to assimilate all the information you've gathered into a plan: Your ideas about a proposal will coalesce, and any omissions in research, program descriptions, or budgets will become obvious.

Forming a plan also provides a mechanism for the program staff to work with you. They will appreciate knowing what's expected of them and when. A grant-writing plan will also involve working with finance and executive staff and possibly board members. You are the glue that holds all this together.

Articulating the Program

Before you can do anything else, you must know what you need to raise the money for, and this means working with program staff. Schedule time with the senior people involved with a program to discuss what they have in mind. Come prepared with a list of questions that you'll have to address in any proposal, such as …

- ◆ The program's mission (or purpose) and goals.
- ◆ Your charity's history with similar programs and how it fits with your charity's mission.
- ◆ Why the program is needed.
- ◆ Whom the program will serve.
- ◆ How the program will be run.
- ◆ Who will run it.
- ◆ How the program will be evaluated.
- ◆ How you will know if the program has been a success.

Words to the Wise

Most program people will not understand how you work, what you do, or what a grant proposal represents. It's a fact of nonprofit life, and if development and program staff are working at odds, the charity will suffer. Do your best to educate them, but be prepared for misunderstandings. Although you certainly want your proposals to be an accurate depiction of what the program will finally be, details will undoubtedly change and funders understand this. Make sure program staff also understand that there is flexibility with any funding request.

When seeking answers for these questions, don't be content with hearing about what will happen over the next year. Get the program staff to lay it out for you for three years. Even though they will probably not be able to give you very specific information about subsequent years, by forcing them to think in longer terms, you will get a clearer idea about how the program will function in the short term. And besides, the next step in this process is …

Developing a Three-Year Funding Plan

Funders commonly ask you to address how the program will be paid for after their funding ends. If you don't know what will happen programmatically in the second and third years, you can't know how much it will cost, and therefore cannot know how it will be funded. Asking for a three-year budget will probably throw program staff for a loop, but if they have given you a clear direction, you might be able to construct a rough budget with help from the finance staff. Just be sure the program staff have a chance to review what you end up with if you intend to use it in a proposal. I'll discuss budgets in detail in Chapter 15, including multi-year budgets.

Following is an outline to use when developing your funding plan. You'll want to create a separate page for each program. The plan will contain broad strokes as to the program and budget, but funding sources and deadlines will be detailed. (A plan created by the program staff would contain information in reverse proportions.) The funding plan isn't intended to be the outline for your proposal, just the facts on which you'll later base the proposal. If the program is expected to grow in subsequent years, note that here for future reference.

The most important costs to note in a funding plan are the total project costs. Creating a budget is part of the proposal process. You don't have to come up with one at this point. If, however, one or two activities or items make up the majority of the expenses for this program, include those details in your plan, because they will influence which funders you can approach. For example, if the main program expense will be making regrants, your funder list should consist of those that allow regranting.

Finally, you'll include important deadlines for all activities associated with the program, beginning

Words to the Wise

A discussion of future funding plans presents a good opportunity to get information from program staff for any outstanding reports. If activities included in the original grant proposals were not completed, be certain to find out why and what, if anything, was done instead. You don't want to reiterate something in a new proposal that didn't work the first time.

How to Say It

It's never too early to start developing the language that will help you focus your proposal for each funder. For example, corporations and venture capitalists will appreciate your adult education program more if you are developing "artist entrepreneurs" or "social entrepreneurs" rather than just teaching these people how to make a buck from their art or develop a new means of reaching disadvantaged children.

with grant deadlines, but also including reports, cultivation activities, and any related public programming. When you have completed a funding plan for each program, the deadlines from the funding plan sheets will feed into your grant schedule. (The accompanying CD-ROM includes a Funding Plan Worksheet template that you can use and adapt for your purposes.)

Sample Funding Plan for Evergreen Conservation Society

Program #1

Forest land acquisition

Program staff contact: Henry

Purpose

To preserve native forests through acquisition of extensive first- and second-growth tracts, focusing on land adjacent to the nearby National Forest. Benefits to the community include preserved watershed and recreation. Additional benefits include wildlife habitat preservation. Goal is to acquire at least 1,000 acres each year for ten years.

Relationship to past programs

In the early 1990s, Evergreen purchased 2,500 acres south of the city, establishing it as a nature reserve for teaching and passive recreation. That land remains largely in its natural state through Evergreen's management. Funders from this project will be approached for the new one.

Cost

$100,000 to $500,000 each year, depending on the land that is acquired, in direct costs plus $15,000 to $22,000 in personnel and indirect costs each year.

Funders for the first year

$20,000	John Bunyan Foundation (renewal)
$100,000	E.P.A. (requires 2 to 1 match)
$50,000	Wildfowl Society
$ unknown	Major individual donors, including direct land donations (coordinate with major gifts officer)

Funders for subsequent years

Renewals from Bunyan and Wildfowl

Need to find five additional prospects by end of September. Look for capital funders as well as other environmental funders.

Important deadlines and other dates

9/5	Boilerplate proposal completed
9/24	John Bunyan Foundation
10/16	E.P.A application
11/1	Report to Baumlieber Trust on last year's grant for a feasibility study and legal research

Program #2

Environmental education on the secondary level county wide

Program staff contact: Mary

Purpose

To provide instructors to work with teachers in public and private secondary schools to integrate environmental awareness and knowledge into secondary school curricula. A model curriculum will be made available and the instructors will assist teachers in adapting it for use in various courses. Instructors will also be available to give special lectures during or after school hours.

Relationship to past programs

Evergreen has offered evening classes in environmental studies to an adult lay audience for more than 15 years. Nature talks have been offered at Evergreen's nature preserve to groups of mixed ages since 1998. Last year, a grant from the Smith Family Foun-dation made possible the creation of a curriculum for secondary schools, which will serve as the basis for this program.

Cost

$65,000 for instructor fees, coordination by Evergreen's education department, and printing of curriculum materials.

Funders for the first year

$50,000	Community Foundation
$25,000	Frances P. Jones Charitable Trust
$5,000	Local fuel oil distributor
$10,000	Commercial Bank and Trust
$ unknown	Other banks

Funders for subsequent years

Smith Family Foundation: $25,000. Although they paid for the curriculum development, they made it clear that they wanted to see other funders make a commitment to the program and would not make another grant this year.

State Department of Education: $50,000 over two years. We just missed this year's deadline due to a delay in completing the curriculum. (They have an 18-month time lag from application to start of grant period.)

Renewals from some first-year funders.

Important deadlines and other dates

9/15	Boilerplate proposal completed
9/8 and 9/15	Presentations of curriculum at Board of Education program—good education/cultivation opportunity for all potential funders to attend.
9/15	Report to Smith Family Foundation
9/20	Community Foundation. They have no set deadline, but next board meeting is in late October, after which they don't meet again until February.
10/1	Meeting with fuel oil distributor. Follow up immediately with grant request.
10/3	Frances P. Jones Charitable Trust

You might not have all the prospects you need for a program (especially for the second and third years) when developing your plan. That's fine, but note the number of funding sources you will need to approach and a date when you expect to complete the research to find them. The amounts you will request from your prospects should add up to much more than the program cost—all of your proposals will not be successful, no matter how good a job you do.

Also note which funders have supported each program or another program at your charity in the past. Remember to include funders for every sector: foundation, corporate, government, and individual major gifts.

Live by Your Schedule

Deadlines are one means by which funders separate serious proposals from those prepared by amateurs. Serious grant writers will be acutely aware of any deadlines and submit their proposals on time, and, whenever possible, early.

All too often, grant writers create a schedule that targets proposal completion to the funders' deadlines, getting them in only in the nick of time. Doing this makes it impossible for the program officer to give you any feedback and invite you to revise your proposal. Also, if you have to use an expensive messenger service or next-day mail delivery, the funder might see that as a waste of money. At best, it can look amateurish.

Many program officers at all kinds of funders (even government agencies) will look at a draft proposal and offer suggestions. They can't do this if you send it to them the week applications are due when they are the busiest. Ideally, you should time your applications to arrive one to two months before the deadline, possibly even earlier. This will allow plenty of time for review. If you miss a deadline, your proposal is dead. Don't call and ask that an exception be made if you can help it.

Words to the Wise

If your proposal will be delivered at the last minute and the funder has strict deadlines (and especially if the funder receives hundreds of proposals), ask for a receipt when the proposal is delivered. They won't mind giving you one, and it will protect you against a slip-up at the funder.

A lot of funders have a rolling deadline, which means they will accept an application at any time. What this really means is they have no published deadlines. These funders, too, have board meetings at which proposals are considered. Try to find out when the program officer would ideally like to receive your proposal so as to present it at the earliest possible board meeting.

It's equally important that grant reports be submitted on time. If your reports to a funder are late, that can put your next proposal in jeopardy. If it looks as if the program staff will need additional time to complete the project, request an extension of the grant period. This will require a progress report, including a budget showing how the funder's grant has been spent so far and what remains to be spent. Extensions should be requested at least two months before the end of the original grant period.

If you are a full-time grant writer, you will have dozens of deadlines for proposals and reports to meet during the course of a year. A schedule committed to a calendar will be a lifesaver. The following table presents an example of just such a schedule. Your grant schedule should include all important dates and basic program information organized by kind of activity. (Note that foundations listed here, amounts, and programs they give to are for illustration only and are not meant to reflect any real funding interests.)

The September calendar includes dates in October and even November. Keeping your eye on what's next will help you manage your time, prepare for each activity, and anticipate conflicts.

Grants Schedule for Evergreen Conservation Society: September

Date	Foundation	Purpose	Grant Amt.	Staff
Proposals Due				
9/15	Geese Unlimited	Wetland preservation	$25K	Polly
9/24	John Bunyan Foundation	Land acquisition	$20K	Henry
9/27	F.P. Jones Charit. Trust	Environ. education	$5K	Mary
9/30	Community Foundation	Environ. education	$10K	Mary
10/5	E.P.A.	Land acquisition	$100K	Henry
	(real deadline is 10/16; get all info from Henry by 10/5)			
10/12	Thomas Family Foundation	GOS	$8K	N/A
Looking Ahead				
11/1	Ford Foundation	Wetland preservation	$100K	Polly
Reports Due				
9/15	Smith Family Foundation	Environ. education	$35K	Mary
10/1	Baumlieber Trust	Land acquisition	$50K	N/A
Research				
Five new prospects for E.P.A. matching requirement				
Two new GOS prospects				
New education funder (talk to program officer at Smith Family Foundation for suggestions)				
Review periodicals for current environmental issues to use as background in various proposals				
Cultivation				
9/8 & 9/15	Presentations of curriculum at Board of Education program			
9/9	Funder tour of forest land under consideration (RSVPs by 9/3); Henry			
9/16	Exec. Director to lunch with Thomas Family Foundation chairman			
10/1	Fall donor newsletter (check with major gifts office on actual availability)			

To Win Friends and Manipulate People

Program people are usually caught up in managing their programs, giving little thought to when new funding proposals need to be submitted and when reports are due. By adhering to your schedule and helping others to do so, too, you'll be more likely to keep the money flowing in, which should make everyone happy.

To Save Your Sanity

This isn't college—there should never be a need for an all-nighter to complete a proposal if you have a clear and accurate schedule. Keeping to your schedule will help you avoid ever having to tell your boss you missed a deadline. Insisting that everyone involved in the grant development and review process stick to the schedule will garner respect and make them appreciate you as a professional. A complete schedule also brings peace of mind, knowing you have everything under control.

> **Words to the Wise**
>
> If your program people tend to be slow in responding to requests for information, you will want to create artificial deadlines for them well in advance of the real ones. Having a cushion of time will save you all a lot of panic. Be sure to include a second cushion to allow for internal review before you can mail the proposal.

The Least You Need to Know

◆ A funding plan lays out for each program its goals, budget, funding prospects, and significant dates.

◆ Developing a funding plan requires collaboration between development and program staff.

◆ A grant schedule includes, in calendar form, proposal and report deadlines as well as research and cultivation activities.

◆ Sharing the grant schedule with program staff will enhance cooperation and information sharing.

◆ Program staff will respect your sticking to a schedule.

◆ Strive to submit proposals well in advance of the deadline.

◆ Early proposals invite helpful comments from funder program officers that can result in a revised and stronger proposal.

◆ If necessary, create artificially early deadlines for program staff to ensure you have information in time to create a successful proposal or grant report.

Part 5

Writing the Proposal

It's been a long journey, but you're finally ready to write a proposal. I'll go through each part of a grant proposal in the order you'll need to create them.

Along the way, I'll point out different ways you can continue to sell your program, driving home your most important points at every opportunity. We'll even get down to the dollars and cents to make sure they make sense with the rest of your proposal.

13

The Parts of a Grant Proposal

In This Chapter

♦ What goes into a program description

♦ How program staff and the grant writer collaborate

♦ The parts of a program description

When you use the word *proposal*, the program (or project) description is probably what comes to mind. It is the heart and soul of your proposal—the place where you go into all the details about the program's execution as well as its underlying philosophy. Although the pitch you will make in the cover letter might be more obviously like selling, don't forget that the program description must reinforce everything you put in the cover letter, continuing to sell the funder on your program and your charity's ability to perform it.

To write a program description that sells your program, you'll have to keep in mind what the funder wants to support and balance that against what program staff expect to see in the proposal. You'll have to preserve both perspectives through the numerous stages in editing. I'll take you through how to do that, as well as the many elements that go into a proposal.

Getting the Facts Straight

Ideally, the program person at your charity will write the first draft of the project description. He or she should possess the greatest knowledge about the program and—just as important—the greatest passion for the project. If you work for a small non-profit, you might very well be both program person and grant writer, which will make this process easier.

After reading the program person's first draft, meet with him or her and talk about what you understand the project to be. After you're sure you both have the same understanding about the project, you're ready for the second draft, which you will always write. (Count on two to five drafts in all to get the language worked out that will form your basic proposal.)

In some cases, you'll have to write the first draft by interviewing the program staff. In this case, the tables are turned. The program person will then read what you have written and alert you to any discrepancies between your draft and what he or she intended.

Before beginning the second draft, you have one intermediary step to do. Create a one-sentence summary that describes the project's essence in a way that makes a case for the funding. (That means it should be a really good sentence.) If you can't do this, you don't understand the project well enough to write the second draft. Go back to the program staff and talk some more.

For an idea of what a summary sentence would look like, the new animal shelter project described in the two letters in Chapter 6 could be summed up as "The new shelter will promote increased pet adoptions, provide state-of-the-art medical facilities, and increase the number of animals that can be housed at one time."

> **CAUTION**
> **How to Say It**
>
> Nothing in the project description should deviate from the sole purpose of generating interest and enthusiasm for the project. In the cover letter, you'll want to include a reference to any past support from the funder to keep the reader interested, but in the project description, you'll only mention past programs that relate *directly* to the one you now want funded.

> **Words to the Wise**
>
> You should be able to describe any program in one strong sentence. Don't move on to a second draft until you can do this. It will serve you well in many parts of the proposal.

Parts of a Program Description

Some funders specify the order in which they want you to present the information contained in a project or program description. Follow their instructions to the letter. Whatever their order or specific instructions, in some way each will want you to include …

- **Purpose of the program.** What will the project accomplish? (Hint: You can use your one sentence summary here.)

- **Why you are doing this project.** Why is the program needed? Is the program being performed by any other organization? How does it fit with your charity's mission?

- **How you will make it happen.** What resources are needed to carry out the program? What are the steps you will take to prepare for and to execute the program?

- **Who will do what.** Who will run the program? What staff will be involved and how much of each person's time will be devoted to this project? Will consultants be used? A combination of staff and consultants? What will the roles of each be?

- **Who will benefit.** How many people will the program serve and who are they? Why is it important to serve these people?

- **How you will know that you have done well.** What results are expected from the program? What are its *goals* and *objectives*? How will the program be evaluated?

- **Summing it all up.** Can you sum up the proposal into two to three sentences to leave them with a simple picture they can really remember?

The ability to weave together the answers to these questions into a seamless readable narrative represents the grant writer's primary skill. In large organizations, there will be different people who do research and others who prepare the budgets. Writing the project description will, however, remain the province of the grant writer.

Purpose of the Program

So what is the "purpose" of your program? You might be able to answer that question in one or two words: alleviate hunger; purchase library books; vaccinate children; find a cure; make a film. Unfortunately, you can't stop there. Because the funder will know that any number of organizations have programs that work toward the same purpose, you must show why your charity should receive a grant to pursue this goal.

A strong (even bold) statement of purpose at the beginning of a proposal can grab the reader's attention and set an ambitious tone for the rest of the proposal. For example ...

> **Grant Talk** _____
>
> **Goals** and **objectives** are often spoken about as if they are the same thing, but they actually are quite different. Goals represent what we want to have achieved at the end of a program. Objectives are the measurable steps we will need to take to get there. Goals are about the outcome; objectives are about the process.

> **How to Say It** _____
>
> Beginning grant writers often hesitate to make bold, sweeping statements, having been taught in college to avoid generalizations and not to make any unsubstantiated statements. Sweeping statements are a means of getting the reader's attention, and although your assertions should be supported somewhere in the proposal, the substantiation doesn't necessarily have to immediately follow your bold declaration.

- Community Food Bank will provide two meals daily to one hundred homeless people, none of whom are now reached by any other agency.

- Nonprofit managers attending the Managing Your Board workshops will come away with the knowledge and skills to transform their relationships with their boards, resulting in more productive nonprofits throughout the city.

- The forgotten children in the city's homeless shelters will be given a new sense of identity through the music workshops we propose.

That one strong sentence summing up the program I asked you to write earlier in this chapter has, you see, multiple uses. Note that in each case I have used the helper verb "will" instead of "would." "Will" makes a more positive statement, implying that the project will go forward no matter what. "Would" is weaker, implying that the project is not only conditional on this grant coming through, but perhaps on other factors as well.

Many grant writing guides (and some funders) will recommend a catchy title for your project. If you'll need eventually to market your program to a wide constituency, a good title will definitely help, but try to keep it short and make it connect to your charity. You don't want a program title to stand a chance of having an identity separate from your charity. People need to know immediately who is responsible for a program.

Why You Are Doing This Project

One of the critical points you will have to make concerns the *need* for your program. The funder will want to know that you have a thorough knowledge of the issue you seek to address and how what you propose to do fits in with what others are doing or have done. Is your approach different? Complementary? Why is it needed? In what way will the program aid the program's clients? What would they do if your program did not exist?

Grant Talk

Need is one of those nonprofit words that gets bandied about in many guises. Every project must fulfill some need, but every grant award is not "need-based." Need-based grants use the need of the applicant as the primary or sole criteria in deciding on the award. Disaster relief grants are an example of this. Your proposals will mostly be for merit-based awards. You'll not only have to demonstrate your clients' needs, but also why your charity merits the award.

The need for the program should resonate with your charity's mission. Just because you are a good organization and the community has a need doesn't mean that your charity is the best one to address a particular issue. Explain how this program fits in with everything else you do. Proposals that are too inward looking (that is, concentrate too much on what your charity needs) are doomed to failure in most cases. Proposals that focus on clients' needs—the people you will help—stand a much better chance of success.

Never trash the competition in your proposal. Today's competition is tomorrow's panelist deciding on the fate of your grant proposal. It's also not polite or necessary. That is not to say that you shouldn't contrast your approach to that of other organizations, but you should do so in a way that will offend no one. For example, you'll say …

> The Community Food Bank will provide meals to 100 people daily who are now being missed by other social service providers.

Or:

> The Community Food Bank will provide meals to 100 people daily who are unable to get transportation to food services offered by other social service providers.

Either version is a lot more positive than "The Community Food Bank will provide meals to 100 people daily who Food for People do not reach because of their unwillingness to look outside their immediate neighborhood."

Words to the Wise

Be sure to check to see if any funder you're approaching has done a study that relates to your proposal. Using their own data (or that of another funder) to justify the need for your program is as strong a needs statement as you can possibly make. Some foundations (Pew Charitable Trusts and W.K. Kellogg Foundation, among others) make a practice of commissioning studies that might be useful to you.

You can make your need statement stronger by bringing into your proposal statements from neutral third parties that express or reinforce the need you seek to address. These could be stories in the press or studies that have been done by groups other than your charity. This not only gives greater credence to your cause, it also shows that your charity sees itself as part of the larger issue and that it keeps abreast of the latest thought on the issue. Here are a couple of examples:

> The *Daily Times* reported that Mayor Thomas stated in his speech to the Rotary Club last week that "hunger remains one of the city's most pressing problems, especially among the transient population that lives on the fringes of the industrial area." Community Food Bank agrees, which is why we approach the distribution of meals through a mobile facility rather than depending on our main office to handle all clients.

> Social Think Tank, Inc., in its report issued last month, drew attention to the difficulty that traditional place-based food banks have in reaching the most needy populations,

which tend to exist outside central urban areas where most of these agencies are located. Community Food Bank agrees, which is why ...

How You Will Make It Happen

You will have to give the funder an idea of how the program will work. Only in rare cases will this be a "first we do this and then we do that" kind of narrative. Instead you'll want to give an outline of how the program will proceed. Here are a couple of short examples.

How to Say It

Your strategy on how much detail to give is just like giving answers on *Jeopardy!:* Give enough to let them understand you know what you're talking about but not too much lest you trip yourself up with the details. (Answer: "North American water bird with long legs." Question: "What is a heron?" (No need to risk making a mistake by saying "gray heron" when it's really a "blue heron" they were looking for.)

The Managing Your Board workshop series will consist of four weekly sessions, each lasting two hours. Workshops will begin with a lecture by an expert in board/executive director issues followed by a question-and-answer period. During the final half-hour of each session, participants will break down into groups of 10 or less to discuss what they have learned in practical terms that relate to their organizations. The themes of the workshops will be Avoiding Micromanagement, Helping a Board Fundraise, Making the Executive Director's Performance Review Work for You, and Building the Board You Need.

The Music for Kids program will provide musical instruction to young people living in the city's largest homeless shelter. Transportation will be provided to our partner's recreational facility after school two days each week. The emphasis will be on rhythm and simple songs, rather than trying to teach them how to read music. This remains a transient population requiring short-term goals that can be met by each of the young people. Most of the 90-minute sessions will be devoted to working all together, but there will be time each day for more personalized attention from the teaching assistants.

Note that both paragraphs briefly describe the format of the sessions, give information on the content, and give the time participants will be involved in the programs. A real proposal would go into additional detail.

Deciding on which details to give should be done strategically based on who will be reading your proposal. You will want to give details and examples that will resonate with the reader.

In the case of a proposal that will be reviewed by the funder's staff and board, you should take into consideration other grantees of the funder and any other nonprofit connections the funder's trustees might have. If you'll be hiring a consultant, find out if the funder has hired any consultants in the same area and use them as examples. If you plan to hire a particular consultant, don't state that you will do so without contacting the consultant first.

An online service for which I was raising funds might, on face value, have appeared to compete with services offered by other grantees of a particular funder. I was careful in both the cover letter and the proposal to describe in detail how our new service will drive people to the websites of the other grantees rather than taking business away from them.

CAUTION

How to Say It

Don't let too many details take away the flexibility the program staff will need to run the program. Don't say "We will hire John Jones as our management consultant." Instead say, "We will hire a management consultant such as John Jones, Mary Chin, or Thomas Brown."

If a peer panel will evaluate your proposal, keep in mind who those people might be. Even if you don't know their names, each nonprofit sector offers a relatively small universe of potential panelists. Be especially sure that you don't denigrate any other organization. If your proposal will call for your working with other organizations (or even just using their mailing lists), give examples that include some of the people you think might be on the panel if possible.

Who Will Do What?

The funder will also want to know who will conduct the program. Will it be done entirely by your staff, or will outside consultants be used? It is critical that the staffing described in this section match exactly the staffing detailed in your program budget. You needn't get too detailed, but give them an idea of where the responsibilities will lie.

Words to the Wise

Use the names of staff or consultants when they are well-known or are included in a "key staff" attachment. Otherwise, you're just as well off using more general descriptions like "program staff" or "clinicians" to allow greater flexibility in the program's execution and make it clear to the reader who is doing what.

You will want to build in the case for participation by staff members at various levels. Will the executive director be involved in program development or execution in any way? If so, you can allocate a small part of his or her salary to this project. After you've done that for enough programs, you've gotten your boss' salary paid for through restricted grants!

The staffing sections of the two programs described previously might read like this:

◆ The director of programs will select the consultants who will lead the workshops in consultation with other members of the program staff and from referrals from colleagues at other service organizations. Program staff will manage the enrollment of the workshop sessions and be present at each workshop to assist with the breakout groups. Each of the first three workshops will be led by one consultant, with two consultants jointly leading the final session.

◆ Our education staff will provide the musical instruction throughout the program. They will be supervised by the director of programming and the director of education, both of whom will assist in creating the lesson plans and review progress with the instructors weekly. We will be paying a fee to our partner organization for the use of their bus and bus driver. The custodial staff at the partner facility will also be paid from program funds.

Who Will Benefit

Who will benefit from the program is, of course, an obvious part of a program description. But it's not just who, but how many and how well. If you can give an estimate of any measurable results of the program, the funder will appreciate it. To corporate and some other funders, the numbers will make a huge difference in judging the worthiness of your proposal. Giving exact numbers before the program even begins will be impossible, but you can give ranges.

> **Philanthropy Facts**
>
> Foundations and other funders seek to solve some social problem, whether it's hunger, literacy, access to the arts, or helping nonprofits work better. In submitting a proposal, you are volunteering to help them solve one of their problems. Focusing on the needs of the ultimate beneficiaries of the program (rather than on your charity) will resonate more strongly with the funder's "problems."

You might feel like you need to inflate the number of people who will be served to make the funder feel like it will be getting its money's worth. Don't! Those numbers will come back to haunt you when it's time to report on your results. But don't give numbers that are too low either, or funders might think the program is not cost effective.

Funders realize that different kinds of projects are more efficient than others and that efficiency is not the sole judge of worthiness. A website might cost $50,000 to make and reach 250,000 people or 20 cents per person, whereas a workshop series might cost $50,000 and serve 100 people or $500 per person. The value of the program is not in the math—it's in the ability of your charity to deliver a program that accomplishes its goals and serves a worthy purpose.

How You Will Know You've Done Well

Program evaluation should be an integral part of everything your charity does. How else will you be able to analyze how good a job you have done, if people benefit enough to justify the expense, and if the program should continue? A lot of charities coast along with only anecdotal evidence of program success. These charities will eventually get an unwelcome surprise when a new board member or funder starts asking hard questions.

Don't let your charity be one of the ones getting caught short. Talk to the program staff about evaluating their programs at various stages. It can be as simple as a survey given to each participant or as complicated as a multimonth study by an outside evaluator. Find the appropriate solution that will best suit your program (and fundraising) needs.

How to Say It

Funders will not judge your program solely on the numbers—the ability of your charity to deliver a program that accomplishes its goals and serves a worthy purpose is much more important. But do supply whatever *realistic* numbers you can to provide an idea of the scope of your program.

Just as your program evaluation needs to be thought through, so does the way you describe it in the proposal. Don't say you'll use an outside evaluator (which is usually very expensive) unless you know your charity will do it. Outside evaluators are frequently used with pilot programs, although they can certainly be effective for long-running programs, too.

Don't try to hide the lack of evaluative procedures by giving some vague statement of your charity's belief in evaluation like "Our charity follows a rigorous evaluative process to assess the efficacy of all programs through surveys, interviews with participants, focus groups, and independent evaluators."

That's all well and good, but how will you evaluate *this* program? A sound evaluation will provide excellent material for all future proposals.

For the workshop series on How to Manage Your Board described earlier in this chapter, an evaluation plan might read like this:

> Short surveys will be provided to participants at the end of each session in which they will be asked to grade the speaker, the content, and the overall workshop on a five-point scale. They will also be asked for information about themselves and the organizations for which they work so that *cross-tab* reports can be prepared to assess the program from many angles. Workshop leaders will be interviewed to gain insights from their point of view. Subsequent workshop series will be modified should the analysis of this data indicate a need for a different approach or different instructors. The cross-tab reports will also help focus the marketing and outreach for future programs.

Given the ages of the participants in the music workshops for homeless children (also described in this chapter), surveys would not be as effective a method of evaluation. In this case, an evaluation from the charity's director of education might be best, especially if you can show that she has a background that allows her to do this objectively.

Grant Talk _____

Cross-tabs are tabulations of one set of data in terms of another set of data. In the example here, that might mean counting the number of people from large charities rating the workshop excellent and comparing it to the number from small charities giving it an excellent rating to see which group was better served by the workshops. You should familiarize yourself with some of the jargon of the evaluation world before getting too deeply involved in describing evaluations in your proposals. The Management Assistance Program for Nonprofits offers a free guide to program evaluation and more at www.mapnp.org.

Summing It All Up

At the end of your proposal, you'll want to sum it all up for the reader. The summary should usually be no more than one or two paragraphs and should include ...

1. A moving argument for funding your proposal stated differently than elsewhere in the proposal (which includes both needs and the results).

2. A restatement of the amount of the grant you are requesting.

3. A thank you for considering your proposal.

This is where you want the reader to hear the violins soar and see the cowboy ride off into the sunset. This is your big ending. Make it a good one. Here's an example.

> Life in a shelter for homeless families is especially hard on the children. Going to school provides some respite, but often the school day simply exchanges one institutional environment for another. Music for Kids will ensure that for at least three hours each week, as many as 60 kids living in these shelters will be taken out of the institutional environment and out of themselves through music.
>
> Individual and small group instruction will provide much needed personal attention and the group singing will encourage community and cooperation. Such simple activities have an enormous potential to assist these young people, as has been shown in the recent study by Urban Educators Conference. Your $20,000 grant will make all this possible for these lost citizens of our city.

A common question is "how long should the proposal be?" Without being facetious, the answer is "as long as it needs to be." Some funders will impose limits on length (as little as three pages), but I've written 15-page proposals that (at least to me) didn't seem long. The important thing is to stay focused on the project, avoiding any tangents. If the proposal will be more than five pages, you might want to make a table of contents, and you'll definitely want section headers that will help the funder's staff skim through to find particular information.

The Least You Need to Know

- First drafts of proposals should be either written by program staff or by you based on an interview with program staff.

- If you can't sum up the project in one persuasive sentence, you don't understand it well enough to write a proposal.

- Express the need for a program as it relates to your charity's mission as well as to what it will do for your clients.

- Take into consideration who will be reading your proposal when deciding how technical to be in describing how it will be executed.

- Use concrete methods for evaluating a program that you know you will be able to include in your report to the funder.

- Use a moving closing section to reinforce the key points in the proposal and repeat the ask.

Chapter 14

Selling Your Project

In This Chapter

◆ Identifying with funders' interests

◆ Writing a jargon-free proposal

◆ Different methods to structure a proposal

◆ The special case of the operating support proposal

In Chapter 9, I touched on customizing your proposal to match a funder's interests. In this chapter, I'll provide more in-depth examples to show how you can move beyond parroting back the funder's language to make a more convincing case.

In the preceding chapter, I took you through the different parts of a proposal. Now I'll show you how to use one of two different methods to give a point of view to the proposal while incorporating all of those parts. One method concentrates on the process by which a program is carried out, and the other stresses the results. I'll also help you decide which method is right for your proposal.

The preceding chapter and most of this one will help you write program proposals, but what about proposals for general operating support? These are a special case, which is why they receive their own section in this chapter. The other special case I present for your consideration is the use of jargon, which can take the life right out of an otherwise excellent proposal.

Making a Persuasive Argument for Each Funder

Making the proposal fit the funder is where you really turn a project description into a grant proposal. Using the description you and the program staff have agreed on, you'll bring into play all you learned during your research to create a new description that expresses the project in a way that will get funded.

You'll modify your base description for each funder to appeal to each funder's specific interests. You'll also include references to any past funding of similar projects and anything else that will build recognition on the part of each reader.

Words to the Wise

Don't sink your proposal with a word-processing error. There's no excuse for sending out a proposal to one funder with a different funder's name appearing in the project description. Keep a clean, unmodified version of your project description free of any funder's name or specific interests to begin work on each proposal.

Before going any further, make a checklist of all the elements each funder requires, both in the proposal and as attachments. You will refer to these lists as you develop each proposal and use it again for your final sign-off.

Let's look at a few examples of customization based on the slightly differing interests of three funders. (You might also want to review the examples in Chapter 9 as illustrations of how to tie your proposal to grantmakers' interests.)

First, take a look at the main section from a proposal for a literacy program that has been reviewed by all concerned at the charity and is ready to go.

The Ralph Goodson Literacy Project works with young people and their families in the inner city to promote literacy and the pursuit of knowledge. We do this through three initiatives.

(1) To develop a love of reading in the early years, we sponsor story times at day-care centers. Volunteers read to the two- to five-year olds twice a week. Art projects based on the stories extend the children's interests. Older children can take home copies of the stories they have heard to share with their families.

(2) We also work with children in grades K-3 to develop reading skills to further learning in all subjects. After-school tutoring ensures that each child will reach or exceed their grade-appropriate reading level. Students are encouraged to complete writing exercises about what they have read to further develop skills and learn to express themselves in writing.

(3) Studies have found that reading skills must be cultivated at home to become engrained. Too often, parents lack good reading skills themselves. Volunteer tutors work with entire families on reading skills in one of our four centers or, in some cases, make "house calls" for the more difficult-to-reach families.

We have found that this holistic approach provides the best environment over a sustained period to develop advanced reading skills in children from any background.

Following are excerpts from the guidelines of three real foundations, after which you'll find the preceding program description modified to match those interests. I've italicized passages that have been changed and used ellipses (…) to indicate that the remainder of a paragraph would be repeated unchanged from the basic description.

Foundation 1. "Helping children and youth develop the skills and experiences they need to reach their full potential."

The Ralph Goodson Literacy Project works with young people and their families in the inner city to promote literacy and the pursuit of knowledge. We do this through three initiatives.

(1) *For each child to have the opportunity to develop into the best person and citizen he or she can be, a love of reading must be established in the earliest years. The Literacy Project sponsors* story times at day-care centers *to achieve this.* Volunteers read to the two- to five-year olds twice a week. […]

(2) We also work with children in grades K-3 to develop reading skills to further learning in all subjects *and ensure continued development.* […]

(3) […]

We have found that this holistic approach provides the best environment over a sustained period to develop advanced reading skills in children from any background. *After being equipped with the marvelous skill to read anything put before them, the students participating in this program have unlimited opportunities available to them, no matter what their field of endeavor.*

Foundation 2. "Development of a broader knowledge base … so that students make the transition from learning to read to reading to learn."

The Ralph Goodson Literacy Project works with young people and their families in the inner city to promote literacy and the pursuit of knowledge. We do this through three initiatives.

(1) To develop a love of reading in the early years, we sponsor story times at day-care centers. Volunteers read to the two- to five-year olds twice a week. [The balance of this paragraph was omitted for this funder.]

(2) We also work with children in grades K-3 to develop reading skills to *help them move from simply learning to read to applying their reading skills to every subject they study.* After-school tutoring ensures that each child will reach or exceed their grade-appropriate reading level, *working with them to read and comprehend texts in many subject areas.* […]

(3) [...]

We have found that this holistic approach provides the best environment over a sustained period to develop advanced reading skills in children from any background. *After being equipped with the marvelous skill to read anything put before them, the students participating in this program have unlimited opportunities available to them, no matter what their field of endeavor.*

Foundation 3. "Stimulate personal development and encourage commitment to social equity ... through writing, literacy, and the promotion of the voices of youth."

The Ralph Goodson Literacy Project works with young people and their families in the inner city to promote literacy and the pursuit of knowledge. We do this through three initiatives.

(1) To develop a love of reading in the early years, we sponsor story times at day-care centers. Volunteers read to the two- to five-year olds twice a week. Art projects based on the stories extend the children's interests *and encourage them to tell their own stories.* Older children can take home copies of the stories they have heard to share with their families.

(2) We also work with children in grades K-3 to develop reading skills to further learning in all subjects. After-school tutoring ensures that each child will reach or exceed their grade-appropriate reading level. Students are encouraged to complete writing exercises about what they have read to further develop skills and learn to express themselves *creatively* in writing.

(3) Studies have found that reading skills must be cultivated at home to become engrained. Too often, parents lack good reading skills themselves. Volunteer tutors work with entire families on reading skills in one of our four centers or, in some cases, make "house calls" for the more difficult to reach families. *By working to improve the reading skills of the entire family, the program makes it possible for the adults to participate more equitably in society, and ensures that their children will have opportunities to do so as well.*

We have found that this holistic approach provides the best environment over a sustained period to develop advanced reading skills in children from any background *and to bring more children and families into the mainstream of American society.*

Each version speaks to the funder's interests without parroting back the same language. Some points get expanded for one funder; other points get condensed for another. The actual program, however, remains the same.

Buzz, Buzz, Buzzwords

I couldn't write this chapter without addressing the scourge of grant writing—jargon. A few years ago, Tony Proscio of the Edna McConnell Clark Foundation wrote a much-discussed booklet about the use of jargon in grant proposals. He took particular exception to terms such as "at-risk" for its vagueness (at risk of what?); "capacity" for its overuse, especially when not referring to something measurable; "proactive" when "preparatory" or "pre-emptive" would be more precise, and many other buzzwords.

His booklet points out how using buzzwords weakens your proposal. It's always best if you can describe your project in your own words. Some people advise throwing the funder's jargon back at them in your proposal. I think this just shows a lack of imagination and a superficial understanding at best. The more you can get beyond buzzwords and to the heart of what the funder wants to support, the more successful you will be.

> **Philanthropy Facts**
>
> You can download *In Other Words* and its sequel, *Bad Words for Good*, at the Edna McConnell Clark Foundation's website (www.emcf.org). You'll find they breathe fresh air into your writing.

If a funder's guidelines state that their interests lie in "pedagogical initiatives designed to stimulate systemic change" it's fine for you to write that your project "seeks to develop new teaching methods that will transform the way teachers relate to their students." The funder will see that you understood their jargon-filled interest statement but have a mind of your own.

Even though you'll want to avoid funder buzzwords whenever possible, it is even more important that you avoid your charity's internal jargon. Nonprofits become mired in program names and acronyms along with technical language peculiar to each of them. Don't use any of this in your proposals. I know you'll probably be stuck with whatever name your charity calls a program, but after first stating that name, you can thereafter refer to it in simpler terms.

Acronyms can be off-putting to someone trying to understand your organization. Even if your charity uses acronyms, try to stay away from them in your grant proposals. If you need a shorthand term for a long program title, use one or two words from the title rather than the acronym, and the reader will understand what you mean. For example, "Ecology Education for Tomorrow's Leaders" could easily be referred to as "Ecology Education" and is more understandable than "EETL." Never sacrifice clarity for insiders' lingo.

> **Words to the Wise**
>
> Chances are, your charity, like mine, loves using acronyms for program names, but acronyms are the worst form of jargon. They attempt to give those in the know a special feeling of inclusion, but they also give those not in the know a feeling of exclusion.

Your teacher-training course might be known within your charity as Training Talented Teachers to Teach Better or T4B (ugh), but you don't have to use the cute acronym, and you could also refer to it simply as "our teacher training program."

Process Versus Outcomes

Chances are, the first draft you received from the program staff was all about the *process*, that is, how they would carry out the program. The *outcomes* method, in contrast, focuses on the results that are anticipated at the end of the program. I usually prefer to use the outcomes method because it makes it possible for me to grab the reader's attention with the anticipated results and express my enthusiasm for the project right up front. When I later describe the steps leading to the glorious outcome, the reader has a reference point for each step in the process.

Outcome-focused proposals are particularly effective when you are seeking a grant to continue an existing program. All the accomplishments of the program thus far can be used to bolster your case for the grant. Preparing a proposal this way is similar to the general operating support proposal described later in this chapter.

Grant Talk

Process and outcomes are the macro versions of goals and objectives, which we discussed in Chapter 13. To decide which method to use to organize your proposal, ask yourself what will be more interesting to the reader: the process by which you will carry out the program or the results (outcomes) that will be achieved.

There will be cases where the process method is best, especially if you are developing a new method of performing a service or one where the outcomes might not be dramatic. For example, a project description for a program that works with severely disabled children might concentrate on the process. The outcomes might not be dramatic in themselves, but the ways the clinicians work with the kids day after day to effect incremental changes over a very long period might well make a moving story.

A process-focused proposal can also be effective with a relatively new program for which measurable outcomes are not yet available. Here's an abbreviated program description for just such a program using the process method.

Program Description Using the Process Method

The Curatorial Internship program seeks to increase opportunities for minority art historians to become curators with major museums. Art museums have been perceived as bastions of WASP culture and the preserve of the wealthy. The old saying goes that the first qualification to become a curator is an independent income. At City Art Museum, we believe this represents outmoded thinking that is out of step not only with our times, but also with the art we collect.

City Art Museum will recruit candidates for this program through outreach to universities with large minority student bodies and through referrals from a wide variety of galleries and alternative art spaces. Interns will work closely with a number of departments within the Museum to gain practical experience in the range of activities in which professional curators must be proficient.

Learning by Observation

Interns will assist Museum curators in mounting at least one major exhibition each year. The interns will be part of the entire process, from assembling the exhibition checklist to hanging the art works. In addition, they will be involved in the research that goes into planning exhibitions for future years. The research will encompass working with the Development Department to craft grant proposals, visiting private collections, and providing detailed research working with the Museum's registrar and librarian.

Learning by Teaching

Today's curator must also be an educator. The modern museum expects curators to be able to communicate with a variety of audiences to engage them with the art on view. The interns will actively participate in the Museum's education program for young people and adults under the supervision of the Curator for Education. We believe the interns will be particularly effective in working with the pre-teens that form a large part of our arts-in-the-schools programming. Being nearer in age to the students than typical docents and in many cases more closely matching the ethnic makeup of the schools, the interns will have a unique opportunity to engage the students with the mostly Western art we collect. Interns will, however, also lead some special tours for Museum members.

Learning by Doing

All the preparation in the world will not build an intern's resumé as much as credit for curating an exhibition. Using our new alternative space for twenty-first century art, each intern will curate an exhibition at the end of his or her second year using works from the Museum's permanent collection along with contemporary works the intern has selected from artists in our studio program.

By thoroughly immersing the interns in the workings of the Museum, we will help them build a resumé that will get the notice of any museum director to whom they apply for work. The curators for whom the interns work will serve as their mentors for at least two years after they leave our program to help them in their career development, offering advice and making personal connections when possible.

The actual proposal covering the previous material would be about four pages, which would be filled out with background on past programs and on the curatorial process, specific examples of work that would be done, and quotes from past participants and curators. The proposal gives the reader a feeling for how the interns would work, but the specific outcomes of each section are left pretty much to the imagination.

This is very similar to a proposal I once wrote that received a major grant, so the approach worked. But now let's look at a condensed proposal for the same program using the outcomes method.

Program Description Using the Outcomes Method

The Curatorial Internship program seeks to increase opportunities for minority art historians to become curators with major museums. Art museums have been perceived as bastions of WASP culture and the preserve of the wealthy. The old saying goes that the first qualification to become a curator is an independent income. At City Art Museum, we believe this represents outmoded thinking that is out of step not only with our times, but also with the art we collect.

City Art Museum will recruit candidates for this program through outreach to universities with large minority student bodies and through referrals from a wide variety of galleries and alternative art spaces. Three interns will be chosen each year to work closely with a number of departments within the Museum to gain practical experience in the range of activities in which professional curators must be proficient.

Interns will sharpen the research, communication, organization, and diplomacy skills needed to be a modern curator. Coming up with the concept for an exhibition can be the easy part. Curators must also be prepared to articulate the exhibition for use in grant proposals and press releases. The laborious process of piecing together works of art from many public and private sources requires in-depth knowledge of how to conduct scholarly research into the location of the works and their provenance. Curators also must exhibit diplomatic skills in working with the owners of the art works. Interns will make contacts through this process that will benefit them throughout their careers. Interns will assist curators as they go about these tasks and others in the mounting of one exhibition each year.

Interns will curate an exhibition at the Museum's alternative space for twenty-first century art in their second year, gaining a major resumé credit and putting to use all they have learned by assisting. Until one has actually received credit for curating an exhibition, the only positions open will be those of assistants. When curating an exhibition, an intern will have the full resources of the Museum behind them, as well as their curator mentor to turn to for advice and assistance. The curators will, in fact, continue to mentor the interns for at least two years after they leave the program, providing advice and entree into a wide variety of museum and gallery opportunities. *The effect of this program will only be evident over a period of years. For this reason, we will maintain contact with the interns for at least five years to assess their professional success.*

> *Interns will gain advanced skills in imparting their knowledge to a variety of audiences.* Modern curators must be willing and able to engage a number of different audiences with the art they love. Interns will visit classes in the schools and guide the pre-teen students through exhibitions. Just as a curator must be prepared to cajole a reluctant art owner to part with a painting for an exhibition, a curator must also be skilled in speaking to groups of art collectors and museum donors. By giving exhibition tours to membership groups, interns will gain these skills as well.
>
> Interns who complete this two-year program will have gained significant experience that will make them more employable, as well as connections with curators and art collectors that will benefit them for years to come.

Whichever approach you determine is best for your proposal, you'll still need to cover all the parts of a proposal described earlier in this chapter.

Operating Support Proposals

The project description for a proposal seeking general operating support (GOS) would technically include everything your agency does. If your charity does only one or two things, it may be possible to use the process method to describe each of them in a GOS proposal. Otherwise, the outcomes method is your only practical choice. The project description for a GOS proposal will frequently read much like a report on the previous year's activities. A list of notable accomplishments from the previous year can be used as a starting point for briefly describing how similar outcomes will be achieved in the current year. The following are examples:

♦ Information Services provided assistance to some 380,000 artists in all disciplines last year through publications, Internet resources, and a toll-free hotline. In the coming year, we expect the number of artists served to increase significantly through the introduction of a new database of opportunities for artists that will be promoted nationally through announcements on National Public Radio stations.

♦ Public school students had the opportunity to work with artists in their classrooms through the Arts in Education Program last year. Some 3,000 students were served through 20 residencies in 18 cities. We have modified this program for next year to allow the residences to expand beyond the schools to involve members of the local community. By creating interactions among the students, community residents, and the artist, we seek to effect a more long-lasting change on how art and artists are perceived by members of the public.

Words to the Wise

Don't neglect the bold opening statement in your GOS proposal. This is not the place to be shy. State clearly and succinctly what good your charity does at the beginning of the proposal (and in the cover letter) to get their attention and provide a focus for your GOS proposal.

" " **Words to the Wise**

Using boilerplate text is more common for GOS proposals, but your charity will be better served if you customize each one. This might just involve changing the order so that the program of greatest interest to the funder comes first.

Create a paragraph such as one of the preceding for each of your programs, add a strong introduction and closing, and you've got yourself a GOS proposal. This approach is a lot more interesting than operating support proposals I've seen that consist of an organization's history with a few recent statistics sprinkled in. Don't confuse your charity's history with a GOS proposal. A GOS proposal is about the present and future, *not* the past.

Even if the GOS proposal seeks support for everything you do, you don't have to describe every single program and activity. Keep the proposal focused on what will be of interest to the funder. And just because it's a GOS proposal doesn't mean you won't customize it for each funder. If the funder makes a lot of education grants and one of your programs involves education, move that section up to the top. In some cases, you might expand on some sections to suit the funder's primary area of interest or add statistics that correspond with the funder's geographic target area.

One GOS funder I deal with has a three-county area as its primary service area, even though it provides funding much more widely. They ask for, and I give them, the numbers of people in their primary service area we have assisted at the end of each program's description in the GOS proposal.

Last Call

By this point, program and executive staff have edited the basic proposal, including the executive and development directors, or whoever is in charge of your charity, whether that's the soccer coach or the choral director. Before putting it into the mail, it's a very good idea to have someone read over it one last time. If there is someone at your charity who has not yet read it but understands the program for which you're seeking funding, that person would be ideal. A fresh pair of eyes can catch jargon and those fatal word-processing errors that allow language from past proposals to creep into the new ones.

The Least You Need to Know

- Every proposal should be customized for every funder.
- Organize proposals using the outcomes method whenever possible to stress the effect the project will have.
- Organize proposals using the process method when the outcomes might be small in comparison with the process needed to achieve them.

◆ General operating support proposals can use a list of resent accomplishments as starting points for present and future program descriptions.

◆ Give everyone involved in the program (including executive staff) a chance to review the final draft of your first completed proposal on a project.

◆ Avoid buzzwords—both the funder's and those of your charity—and acronyms that might confuse the reader.

Dollars and Cents

In This Chapter

- ◆ What to include in a budget
- ◆ How administrative personnel costs fit into a program budget
- ◆ Telling your story in numbers
- ◆ Explaining the big numbers

A budget is an integral part of a grant proposal. Many funders go right from the cover letter to the budget to see how it fits with what you propose to do. Program officers and others working for funders might see hundreds of budgets for programs similar to yours. They can usually spot an inconsistency pretty quickly, so don't take the budget casually.

The way you present a budget is just as important as what's in it. Jargon is as out of place here as it is anywhere else in your proposal. You'll want each expense labeled as clearly as possible. Large amounts listed as "miscellaneous" or "other costs" will send up red flags, so don't use these terms.

Words to the Wise

Remember that your budget will be an integral part of the contract that results from a successful grant proposal. You will eventually report on the finances as well as what happened programmatically.

Similar expenses grouped together and subtotaled make it easier to evaluate the relationship between aspects of the budget. At minimum, subtotals should be used for personnel, direct expenses, and indirect expenses. Depending on the nature of the program, you might further group expenses to show mailing and distribution costs (if your program involves a publication, a marketing campaign, or some similar project) or different types of consultant fees (if a number of different kinds of consultants will be used).

You'll find many budget examples throughout this chapter and in Chapter 21, where I cover grant reports. I've also provided you with a Program Budget Worksheet on this book's CD-ROM that includes formulas for allocating personnel costs and determining indirect expenses.

Personnel

Many nonprofit employees don't realize that the salaries of the five most highly paid employees making $50,000 or more are listed in their charity's 990 IRS information form. What your top people make is part of the public record (and available for all to see on the Internet on sites such as GuideStar), but people remain naturally sensitive about having their salaries revealed. For small nonprofits that don't file the 990 form, executive salaries remain private, but some funders will ask you to include them as part of your proposal.

Philanthropy Facts

Salaries at nonprofits became headline news several years ago when the exorbitant salaries of a very few executives were made public. Since then, the public perception has seemed to be guilty until proven innocent. There is a much greater expectation today that charities will make this information readily available, however uncomfortable it might make the nonprofit executives.

As a grant writer, you are privy to information on salaries and other costs. It's part of your responsibilities to maintain the confidentiality of this information. If you need to circulate the budget for review by program staff, black out the salary details, leaving only the total personnel amount visible. You might also put a blacked-out version in your files as part of the final proposal.

I'll Take 75 Percent of a Program Officer and ...

Seldom will you actually give any employee's full salary in a program budget. It's a fact of nonprofit life that most of us have a variety of duties that cross a number of program areas. More typically, you'll have a listing such as the following:

Executive director (10%)	$12,000
Program director (30%)	$29,000
Program officer (75%)	$32,000

The percentages reflect the amount of each employee's time spent on the program. Always include them to help the funder understand how the program will be staffed. You'll need to consult with the person in charge of the program to get an idea of what percentages to use. If they have trouble coming up with a percentage, ask them how many days a week they will spend on the program. You can use that to determine the percentage (one day a week = 20 percent).

Fringe Benefits

The bane of nonprofit budgets these days is fringe benefits. Insurance rates of all types seem to go up and up, so it's only fair that a funder that is paying part of someone's salary cover a proportionate amount of their fringe benefits. Your charity probably has an average number to use for fringe benefits (possibly 20 percent or even more). Get this from your finance staff and use it consistently in all applications. (You don't need to worry about who signed up for the dental plan and who didn't, an average rate will do.)

Words to the Wise

If your fringe rate is very low because your charity offers few employee benefits, you might footnote that fact in your budget presentation so it doesn't look like a mistake. In a GOS proposal, this may bolster an argument for increased funding to provide support for expanded benefits.

The Full Personnel Budget

Your proposal will need a detailed personnel budget, showing how the program will be staffed, including all consultants.

Personnel Budget	
Executive director (10%)	$ 12,000
Program director (30%)	$ 29,000
Program officer (75%)	$ 35,000
Program assistants (2 @ 50%)	$ 40,000
Subtotal	$116,000
Fringe (@ 20%)	$ 24,200
Total salaried personnel	**$140,200**
Part-time instructors (3)	$ 60,000
Evaluator	$ 45,000
Total consultants	**$105,000**
TOTAL PERSONNEL	**$245,200**

This presentation clearly shows how much time the charity's staff will spend on the program and what parts of the program will be entrusted to outside contractors (consultants).

Typically, only small portions of higher-level staff members' salaries will be attributed to a single program. Obviously, these are the people with the widest responsibilities. For example, attributing 30 percent of the executive director's time to a program would raise eyebrows at the funder unless yours is a very small agency with few programs and where the executive director actively participates in programs on a daily basis. Including small parts of high-level employees, however, is good budgeting that contributes to your charity's bottom line.

> **Words to the Wise**
>
> Personnel expenses are one of the fuzzier items (or fungible numbers) in a budget. That your executive director has something to do with most programs is obvious; the exact amount of time he or she spends on each program is less clear. The ability to find ways to include operating expenses (such as administrative salaries) in a program budget creatively is a talent highly valued by every executive director.

Unfortunately, you can never include any of your time or that of any other development staff in program budgets. The only exceptions are capital campaign budgets, because raising money is one of the major activities of the campaign. If, of course, fundraising staff perform other functions (such as marketing), you can include their time, but refer to the position according to its function (marketing, for example) rather than fundraising.

How Much Is That Notebook?

The expenses you will itemize are those that relate directly to the program. If you weren't doing the program, you wouldn't have any of these expenses. Typical direct expenses include ...

- Art, laboratory, or other consumable supplies that will be used by program participants.

- Supplies your staff will use beyond what they'd need without this project, including increased use of letterhead, pens, notebooks, tape, and on and on.

- A new computer workstation and even a new desk, if needed, for a new staff position related to a program.

- Travel expenses (including a per diem) to get staff, consultants, or participants to where the program will take place.

- Duplicating and printing costs, including fees paid to designers for creating the printed materials.

- Rental of any additional space for the program.

◆ Postage, freight delivery, and mailing house costs.

◆ Long-distance telephone and a portion of your local telephone use.

◆ Website maintenance. (If you will be posting anything about the program on your website, someone will have to do it. Even if it's a staff member, it's still a direct program expense.)

◆ A small amount (around $200 to $500 or one percent of the total direct expenses) for "contingency," which sounds better than "miscellaneous."

Words to the Wise

Be prepared not only to justify expenses if asked, but also to spend them. Many funders will ask that when reporting to them you compare actual costs line by line with your budget and explain any discrepancies of as little as 10 percent. Everyone at your charity involved with the program should understand that not spending one budget line does not give him or her more money to spend in another one.

If a company will be donating supplies or free travel, you should still include these items in your expense budget (it would look odd if they were missing). You might want to separate out the in-kind expenses so the funder can easily compare them with the corresponding amount you include in the income section of your budget.

And Who Will Pay the Rent?

I've not yet touched on what are probably your charity's largest expenses: rent, utilities, and fundraising and administrative personnel. These items must usually be paid for by including a portion of them as indirect expenses.

In Chapter 5, I discussed the use of indirect rates with many federal government grants. These official indirect rates must be justified and negotiated with a federal agency *before* you apply (many months before, to allow for processing and negotiating). If you don't have an official indirect rate, you can include some of your charity's basic expenses as direct costs in these budgets based on how those relate *directly* to the program's execution. Just be prepared to justify them in the context of your grant if asked.

Words to the Wise

Don't try to double-dip on your basic expenses. If you're using an indirect rate, you cannot also include any of the expenses that go into that indirect rate as direct program expenses.

With funders that do not require a negotiated indirect rate, a modest indirect rate of 10 to 15 percent should be accepted without question. Always include one unless instructed not to by the funder.

Here's a sample calculation for determining how much in indirect expenses to allocate to a program costing $100,000:

$550,000	Total expenses for the charity
− $75,000	Exceptional expenses*
$475,000	Basic expenses
−$400,000	Expenses funded with program grants
$75,000	Nonprogram funded expenses

$75,000/475,000 = .1567 or 16 percent, your indirect rate

$100,000   Cost of program in your proposal

$100,000 × 16 percent = $16,000 indirect costs to be included in your program budget

Such as for regrants or capital expenses for equipment, etc.

If you include a line item for indirect expenses, you cannot also include any of the expenses that go into that indirect rate as direct program expenses. This sounds obvious, but I've seen it done. If your charity has a standard indirect rate, multiply the total personnel and direct costs of the program by that percentage.

Show the indirect rate in your budget on a separate line below the subtotal for the direct costs, stating the percentage as well as the amount. This amount should not be an even number (such as $4,000); it should be something that obviously has been carefully calculated (such as $4,123). You can find examples of this formatting in the complete budgets included on this book's CD-ROM and in the appendixes.

Who Else is Paying?

Many funders do not like to be the only ones contributing to a program. You might not know where all the money is coming from when you apply for a grant. That's okay, but you will need to indicate the possible sources such as in the following example.

Income	
Requested from the Smith Foundation	$10,000
Continental Airlines (in-kind, committed)	$ 2,500
Jones Family Foundation (received)	$10,000
Community Foundation (pending)	$15,000
Participant fees	$ 5,000
Total	**$47,500**

Always list the request from the funder first and label it "request." (You don't want them to think you've counted their money before you even applied.) You might have three other applications pending, but only list enough funders to make the budget balance. If all the other money is "pending," you might give a footnote to explain that you are also submitting applications to additional funders at the same time, whether you name them or not.

Notice that participant fees are included in the income projection in the previous table. If your program will generate several types of earned fees, you might want to subtotal earned *versus* contributed income. Funders love to see earned income, so make the most of it.

Words to the Wise

The total income should always equal the total expenses, exactly. In the real world, this will never happen, but this presentation should show that a balanced program budget is your goal. You might have to adjust a couple of expense lines slightly up or down to get a perfectly balanced budget.

If you are asking the funder to make a matching grant, you will need to give specifics on where you expect to raise the remaining funds both in the budget and in the program description. If you're asking a funder to match another funder's grant, the matching grant should be mentioned in your proposal narrative and cover letter and should, of course, be listed separately as in the following example.

Contributed Income	
Smith Family Foundation (requested)	$ 10,000
Community Trust challenge grant (received)	$ 50,000
Widget Corp. of America (received)	$ 10,000
Jones and Jones Trust (received)	$ 5,000
Benefit dinner income (projected)	$ 25,000
Total Contributed Income	**$100,000**

If you are requesting a funder to make a challenge grant, you would need to devote a substantial part of the program or budget narrative to how you would raise the additional funds and why this funder's making the grant as a challenge would help you raise the balance of the funds.

Always think strategically about which other funders you list, keeping in mind which funders know other funders and which have overlapping trustees. Also, "miscellaneous" or "unknown" are best not used in the income section.

Budget Narrative

Occasionally, a funder will request a budget narrative. This entails a brief discussion of how the expenses relate to the project, explaining in particular the major expenses.

Budget narratives are especially important when you are asked for budgets covering more than one year. In multi-year budgets there inevitably will be variations. The narrative gives you the opportunity to explain them.

Even if you are not asked for a budget narrative, you will want to include footnotes at the bottom of the budget page to explain exceptional costs or to point out ties to the program narrative.

Here's a sample budget that includes all we have discussed so far. (Additional budget examples including a multi-year budget can be found on the accompanying CD-ROM and in the appendixes.) This budget is for a program that makes grants to community arts groups and also provides those groups with management assistance provided by staff and by a fundraising consultant.

Expenses

	Total Budget	Requested from Bank Fdn.
Regranting Activity		
Regrants		
Category I Grants	$ 70,000	$0
Category Ii Grants	$ 30,000	$0
Sub-Total: Regrants[1]	**$100,000**	**$0**
Grantmaking Expenses		
Panelist Fees	$2,000	$0
Panelist Expenses	$ 400	$0
Sub-Total: Grantmaking Expenses	**$2,400**	**$0**
Administration		
Personnel		
Director of Programs (10%	$10,000	$ 7,000
Grants Officer (50%)	$29,000	$20,300
Services Officer (20%)	$ 6,000	$ 4,200
Fringe Benefits @ 18%	$ 8,100	$ 5,670
Sub-Total: Full-Time Staff	**$53,100**	**$37,170**
Program Consultant	$10,000	$ 7,000
Evaluator[2]	$20,000	$14,000
Sub-Total: Consultants	**$30,000**	**$21,000**
Total: Personnel	**$8,100**	**$58,170**

	Total Budget	Requested from Bank Fdn.
Nonpersonnel Direct Expenses		
Telephone	$ 140	$ 138
Travel	$ 600	$ 420
Printing[3]	$2,000	$1,450
Postage & Mail Preparation	$ 600	$ 420
Supplies	$ 260	$ 232
Advertising	$1,000	$ 700
Website	$ 500	$ 350
Delivery/Freight	$ 260	$ 232
Hospitality	$ 500	$ 350
Sub-Total: Nonpersonnel	**$5,860**	**$4,102**
Indirect Costs @ 20%	$17,840	$12,488
Total Expenses	**$209,200**	**$75,000**
Income		
Bank Foundation (requested)	$75,000	$75,000
Smith Family Foundation		
(received for regrants)	$100,000	$0
Other pending proposals[4]	$ 33,000	$0
Sub-total: Contributed Income	**$208,000**	**$75,000**
Application fees[5]	$ 1,200	$0
Sub-total: Earned Income	**$ 1,200**	**$0**
Total Income	**$209,200**	**$75,000**
Surplus/(Deficit)	**$0**	**$0**

(1) The regrants are fully funded by the Smith Family Foundation. No funds from the Bank Foundation will be used for regrants.

(2) An outside evaluator will be hired to review the program and prepare a written report, which we will make available to all program funders.

(3) Includes printing of application forms and a technical assistance booklet.

(4) Five additional proposals have been submitted, all but one to new funders. Several board members are also expected to contribute through their family foundations toward this total.

(5) Application fees of $30/application partly offset the panelists' expense.

From this budget presentation, you can see at a glance that this program will be making $100,000 in grants (nearly half the total budget). Three staff members will work on the program, but two consultants will also be hired: one to work on the program and one to conduct an evaluation.

> **Philanthropy Facts**
>
> Although I've repeatedly pointed out that fundraising costs should not be included in program budgets, some funders will make grants specifically to pay for additional fundraising consultants or staff, usually under the heading of "capacity building."

Because the Bank Foundation does not allow its grants to be regranted to other organizations, I have given a separate column to show how their money will be used. Because the amount requested from the Bank Foundation is about 70 percent of the total expenses (excluding the regrant-related costs), I've taken roughly 70 percent of all remaining costs (with some rounding up or down to make it all come out even).

This two-column presentation is also effective when you are asking a funder for a grant for a particular activity that is part of a larger program. Showing the larger program gives a fuller picture of what your charity is doing to address a problem, but separating out a particular activity allows funders to get a better picture of what they will be paying for.

If instead of footnotes you had wanted to (or been asked to) include a budget narrative, it might have read like the following:

> The $100,000 for regrants has been fully funded by the Smith Family Foundation, but the technical assistance and administrative costs have not yet been funded. Because of the significant technical assistance provided over the course of a year, the personnel costs are the second largest program expense, including a program evaluator. With the program now in its third year, the time has come for someone outside the program to take an objective look at what is being accomplished and how the program is executed.

> Five additional grant proposals have been submitted, all but one to new funders. Several board members are also expected to contribute through their family foundations toward this total. We are confident that we will raise the remaining funds. Should the funds raised fall somewhat short of the goal, the role of the evaluator could be reduced or postponed to the following year.

The income section shows that nearly half of the total cost has already been received, which includes all the money to be given away. This funder and a number of unnamed other outstanding requests will be expected to make up the balance to cover administrative costs. Had there been solid prospects for the additional costs at the time this application was submitted, the names of those prospects would have been given. Too large an amount in "other funders" will, however, cause the funder to doubt your ability to fund the program completely.

In some cases, your project and organizational budget may be the same. For example, if you are raising funds for the Friends of the Hometown Library, virtually your entire budget may be devoted to raising money for the library. Fundraising expenses might appear in this budget, because that's pretty much all the Friends group does. You won't, however, be asking for a grant to cover fundraising costs, but rather to support the library in some specific way. If the Friends organization has its own nonprofit status, its budget might look something like this one.

Expenses	
Fundraising consultant	$ 2,500
Building staff overtime[1]	$ 1,200
Printing[2]	$ 2,000
Postage	$ 500
Volunteer reimbursables	$ 300
Total direct expenses	$ 6,500
New Book Fund donation	$15,000
Total Expenses	**$21,500**
Income	
Thomas Family Foundation (requested)	$ 5,000
Community Foundation (received)[3]	$ 6,000
Membership dues	$ 6,000
Bake sales and other activities	$ 4,500
Total Income	**$21,500**

(1) The Friends must pay overtime for the library's janitor when holding events at the library.
(2) Printing of flyers advertising the various fundraising events.
(3) The Community Foundation matched 1 to 1 the funds raised in membership dues.

Note that if you subtract the cost of the fundraising consultant (that's you!), you'll see that the bake sale and other activities just broke even, which is probably why they hired you to raise the big money.

If the Friends organization were not tax-exempt, you would need to apply using the library's status and would therefore use the library's total budget with your proposal. In this case, you would separate out (and subtotal) the Friends' expenses. You would also highlight the Friends' donations to the library from its various fundraising activities in the income section.

Multi-Year Budgets

Many programs take place over a number of years (such as the curatorial internship program, which I used as an example in Chapter 14). In cases such as this, you'll be seeking a grant to cover the entire time period of the project. Many foundations make such grants, but they usually do as a "$10,000 a year for two years" rather than giving

Organizational budgets represent your charity's total operations, including all personnel (including fundraising staff) and expenses and all sources of income. If you are writing a proposal for general operating support, the *program budget* and your *organizational budget* are one and the same.

you $20,000 up front. This way, they delay payment until they have received a report from you letting them know the program is continuing.

The budget for the two-year curatorial intern program appears in Chapter 21 (where I give it as an example in reporting on grants) and on the CD-ROM. Many of the expenses have simply been allocated equally to each of the two years. Other expenses obviously belong to one year or the other. For example, the exhibition the interns will present takes place only in the second year, and the outreach efforts to find qualified interns takes place only in the first year.

Organizational Budget

Proposals will also require an *organizational budget*, which will include all your charity's expenses for every program as well as general operating expenses. An organizational budget will follow the same general format as the program budget, but you will use a condensed personnel budget rather than list the salaries of every single person who works for your charity. The personnel section could look like either of the following examples.

Example 1	
Personnel	$350,486
Fringe @ 20%	$ 70,922
Total salaried personnel	$421,408
Consultants	$100,000
Total Personnel	**$521,408**

Example 2	
Administrative staff	$156,200
Program staff	$194,286
Fringe @ 20%	$ 70,922
Total salaried personnel	$421,408
Management consultant	$ 40,000
Clinical freelance staff	$ 60,000
Total nonsalaried personnel	$100,000
Total Personnel	**$521,408**

The second example makes clear the relationship between administrative and program personnel costs—in this case, administrative salaries are only around 10 percent less than those for program staff. If accompanying a program proposal, this might look like too little (relatively speaking) was being spent on programs, so you might not want this breakdown. For a GOS proposal, however, the relationship might present a good argument for increased support of general operations.

Your financial officer should prepare the organizational budget for you, but you will probably want to do some additional formatting. Just as you did with the program budget, you will want to group like activities (such as making regrants or running a clinic) and subtotal them so they tell the story you need to reinforce the message in your narrative.

Income in an organization budget is usually broken down by type of funder rather than specifying individual ones. For large organizations, the types might be broken down into subgroups to make a point about your funders. Here are two examples to illustrate what I mean.

CAUTION

How to Say It

One of my pet peeves is the use of the term "unearned income" to categorize donations. What is unearned about it? We fundraisers work very hard to earn it, as does the program staff to create and run programs worthy of donations. A more accurate description is "contributed income."

Words to the Wise

Check your formulas! No matter if you or someone in your finance department prepared a budget, be sure to check and double-check the formulas in your spreadsheet. A mistake in the budget will call into question the veracity of your entire proposal.

Example 1

Contributed Income	
Government	$400,000
Foundations	$190,000
Corporations	$140,000
Individuals	$ 30,000
Subtotal Contributed Income	**$760,000**
Earned Income	
Clinic fees	$ 25,000
Interest and investments	$ 85,000
Subtotal Earned Income	$110,000
Total Income	**$870,000**

Example 2

Contributed Income	
Government	
Federal grants	$370,000
State grants	$ 30,000
Subtotal Government Grants	$400,000
Foundations	$190,000
Corporations	$140,000
Individuals	$ 30,000
Subtotal Private Support	$360,000
Subtotal Contributed Income	$760,000
Earned Income	
Clinic fees	$ 25,000
Interest and investments	$ 85,000
Subtotal Earned Income	$110,000
Total Income	**$870,000**

Whether income is contributed or earned is pretty clear except, perhaps, with corporate contributions. Most charities list corporate grants under contributed income. Corporate sponsorships, however, are usually listed as earned income.

By breaking down the sources of the government support, the charity's significant dependence on federal support becomes clearer, illustrating the need for greater support from other sectors. To dramatize a need for general operating support, the budget narrative might contrast the amount of support received for programs *versus* operating expenses.

Of necessity, budgets are frequently the last part of a grant proposal you will prepare. Don't let your rush to get the proposal in cause you to present a budget that is not in sync with the proposal narrative or one that does not reinforce the narrative's most important points. Get help when you need it from program and finance staff.

The Least You Need to Know

- Your budget should describe in numbers the activities included in your narrative.

- Include part of the salary of everyone who will work on a program and state the percentage of their time next to their title.

- To decide what are direct expenses, ask what expenses you would not have if the program did not exist.

◆ Whenever possible, include a reasonable indirect expense line.

◆ Use footnotes or a budget narrative when your numbers require context and explanations to be effective or when the funder requests an explanation in some form.

Chapter 16

The Cover Letter and Executive Summary

In This Chapter

- ◆ How to grab the reader's attention
- ◆ How to play to your audience
- ◆ Differences between cover letters for new and renewal grants
- ◆ Why a cover letter is no substitute for an executive summary

The cover letter is the most important part of your proposal. It is, after all, what funders see first. If you can capture their attention (or even better, their imagination) with the cover letter, you will immediately separate your proposal from all the others.

Most grant writers create the cover letter last, which makes sense, because it will need to include information from all the other parts of the proposal. Coming last in your writing, however, should not mean it gets done in haste on the day before the proposal deadline. The cover letter is just too important to rush. I like to work on the cover letter while others at my charity review the other parts of the proposal.

A cover letter should ...

- ◆ State the purpose of the proposal in one sentence, including the grant amount requested.
- ◆ Connect personally to the reader whenever possible.

- Relate the proposed program to the funder's stated interests.

- Provide a context for the request, either in the form of background on your charity or a brief report on a previous grant.

- Present clearly the three key arguments why you should receive the grant.

- Include contact information for additional questions (not relying on the phone number on the letterhead but giving a direct line or extension and an e-mail address).

- Thank the funder for considering your request.

I'll look at how to create some of these parts, as well as address tone, personality, and style in this chapter.

> **Words to the Wise**
>
> Don't sink your proposal with a careless cover letter. In addition to covering the necessary points, be sure to use the salutation that reflects the letter signer's relationship to the person receiving it. Don't use first names unless you have a reason to do so.

Know Your Audience

People, not institutions, make grants, and the cover letter gives you an opportunity to show that you understand that. And grants are made to people, not institutions, so your cover letter needs also to reflect the personality and style of the person who signs the letter. If possible, your cover letter should connect with the reader on a personal as well as a professional level.

Address the letter to whomever the funder gives as the contact person, unless your contact at the funder told you to send it to him or her, instead.

If one of your board members knows someone at the foundation other than the contact, you can go one of two ways: Send the original letter to the person with the personal connection and "cc" the official contact person, or send the original to the official contact person and send a "cc" with a hand-written note from your board member to his or her contact.

With either approach, you will cover all the bases and ensure that your proposal will be processed through the usual channels even if your special contact drops the ball. The second method has the advantage of respecting the chain of command at the funder and giving a more personal touch to the personal contact.

It's About the Reader

If your research revealed that the contact person has a background in education and pedagogy and your proposal addresses the training of teachers, you can discuss the subject using terminology appropriate to addressing another expert in the field. If you know the contact has young children, you can address his or her interests as a parent in improved teacher training. If the contact is a young program officer fresh out of college, your discussion of teacher training might connect with the reader's own recent educational experiences.

Whoever the reader is, you want to make that person your advocate when the funder's board meets. You therefore want to include the strongest parts of your rationale for funding in the cover letter and present them in such a way as to make it easy for the reader to remember them when discussing your proposal with others. Bullet points will help the reader find your key points. Good writing will help the reader remember them.

Words to the Wise

Don't get "married" to your prose. It most likely won't be your name at the bottom of the letter, and the letter signer has every right to have the letter reflect his or her style. Just don't let the message get watered down in the interest of personal style.

It's About the Writer

The person who will read the cover letter is, of course, only half of the equation. The letter must also be appropriate for the person who will sign the letter. In larger organizations, this rarely will be you. More likely it will be your charity's executive director, development director, or board president. For simplicity's sake, I'll refer to the writer as the executive director.

If possible, read any letters or speeches the executive director has written (or approved) to get an idea of the degree of formality he or she uses in different situations. Through trial and error, you'll eventually get a good handle on the executive director's personal style. The better you can do this, the more effective the letter will be.

Negotiating the tone of the letter with the executive director is part of the process, but too often the letter's message can get diluted through over-editing. It's your job to make sure that doesn't happen. Executive directors and others I've worked for have usually listened when I objected to one of their edits because it changed the meaning or weakened the argument. Usually we compromised on a third version of the text.

When to push for your language and when to accept the executive director's edits must depend on what will best serve the proposal, taking into account your experience with the particular funder versus the executive director's experience. This applies to the entire proposal, not just the cover letter.

How to Say It

The simple word *draft* at the top of any document you present to others to review will make a world of difference. By thus signaling that you acknowledge that the document is incomplete without their input, you'll not only make friends, you'll make your job easier. Also put a date on each draft to avoid confusion.

One executive director I worked for drove me crazy with repeated changes to a government proposal. (I had started to label the versions of the proposal with the day, hour, and minute to make my not-so-subtle point about all the revisions.) As annoyed as I was, I knew he had more than twice the experience with this particular funder than I had. Trying to keep the language to my prose in this situation would have been foolish and detrimental to the proposal's chances for success. In the end, I learned a lot from his edits that has helped me write proposals for all kinds of funders.

Above all else, make the letter's salutation appropriate for the executive director. If your executive director is on a first-name basis with the reader, using a formal salutation will be a real turn off, but over-familiarity will have the same effect.

Personal Versus Personality

You want your cover letter to be personal and have a personality, by which I mean a distinctive point of view. Don't be afraid to be dramatic:

"The Community Food Bank prevents 1,000 of the community's least fortunate members from going hungry every day."

And don't be afraid to praise your charity's work:

"The Community Food Bank does more than any other agency in the city to prevent hunger."

But avoid blatant overstatements, claims that you could never quantify, and exclamation points.

"The Community Food Bank has transformed the lives of thousands, making them better, more productive citizens!"

How to Say It

We've all received those magazine sweepstakes mailings that repeat our names every few lines in boldface type. That kind of personalization is out of place for grant writing. Avoid over-using the funder's name in the letter and proposal other than when thanking them, referring to past or anticipated support, or possibly referring to something in their guidelines or one of their publications.

The cover letter must have a style, a personality, that makes it human. Never forget that this is a personal communication.

If the executive director knows the recipient well, he or she might want to add a personal note about a recent social occasion or to inquire about a spouse or child. I think these comments are best done in a handwritten note accompanying the proposal rather than making them part of the formal cover letter that will be read by a number of other people.

Handwritten notes on the cover letter itself, however, provide an important personal touch. A note such as "Thanks again for inviting this proposal" or "It was good seeing you at the mayor's awards ceremony last week" warms the letter up without making it overly personal.

For Current and Recent Funders

You can assume the reader has a degree of familiarity with your organization if you are applying for a *renewal grant* or for a new grant from a funder who supported your charity in the recent past. You might therefore be able to leave out (or move to an attachment) background information such as the year you were founded, your mission, and a list of programs. But remember to follow the funder's instructions, and include background in the cover letter if it is asked for.

Grant Talk

"Renewal grant" can be a loaded phrase. On the one hand, it signifies a continuing relationship with your charity, which is a good thing to remind them about. On the other, it might imply to a funder that you expect the funder to continue supporting your charity and maybe even take their continued support for granted. Learn all you can about a funder's attitude toward continuing support before referring to your grant request as a renewal.

With a current or recent funder, you'll stress how its previous grant helped your charity accomplish the program's goals and where that program stands now (even if you're now applying for a different program). Don't waste this opportunity to reinforce the importance of past funding and to thank the funder once more.

With rare exceptions, funders will not accept a new proposal if you haven't reported on their past funding. If the timing of a program makes it necessary to apply before reporting, call the funder before you send anything to see if they will make an exception.

Here's an example of a cover letter to a funder that already supports this charity. (Additional sample cover letters appear as part of the sample proposals in the appendixes and on the accompanying CD-ROM.)

Ms. Sara Silver
Trustee
Silver Foundation
98 Oak Street
Anytown, TX 77000

Dear Ms. Silver:

I want to express my sincere thanks for the Silver Foundation's past support of Countywide Literary Project's services to the community. Your last grant was instrumental in allowing us to maintain all our classes for young people and adults during a perilous economic period. With this letter, I have enclosed a report on Countywide's activities during the past year and also a request for a renewal grant in the increased amount of $40,000.

The past year has been a difficult time for everyone in Butler County, as the recession has reached every corner of the community. Demands on the Literacy Project's services have been higher than any time in memory. Significantly more adults have come to us when they realized that basic English literacy was key to making them more employable.

We have devised a plan for serving the increased demand on our services that calls for decentralizing the teaching facilities and offering classes in English as a second language. The former part of the plan will allow more people to take classes before and after work by holding the classes nearer to where they live. The latter scheme recognizes the large number of non-English speaking immigrants in our community and their need for instruction apart from illiterate English speakers. Specifics on these plans for the coming fiscal year are enclosed.

Expanding services while the community remains in a recession will be particularly challenging. For this reason, we are asking all of our funders to consider a significant increase in support. As you know, few funders are taking on new charities, so we must rely on our old friends to see us (and our clients) through this period.

If you have any questions about the report or the proposal for a renewal grant, I can be reached at (414) 555-1234 or exec@litprod.org. Thank you again for your continued support.

Sincerely,

Kay Lang

Kay Lang
Executive Director

For New Funders

New funders will need to have some background information on your charity in the cover letter (even if you include it in the proposal or an attachment and even if you've been cultivating them for months). You will need to position the program for which you're seeking funding in the context of what your charity is all about.

The following letter to a new funder makes a point of the charity's background as well as its recent accomplishments. This theoretical foundation's primary interest is helping nonprofits develop sources of earned income. They have also been supportive of many minority arts groups.

Mr. Matt Sterling
Chairman
James and Mary Brush Foundation
1 City Plaza
Anytown, FL 33000

Dear Mr. Sterling,

Sheila Burns recommended that I write to introduce you to the African American Literary Council and ask for your support through a $10,000 grant from the James and Mary Brush Foundation. Your grant would be used to support increased marketing of *Black American Voices*, our quarterly journal of fiction and literary criticism. Local writers such as Sheila and Joshua Jefferson were first published in our journal years before their popular and critical successes. Both have been loyal to the journal, allowing us to continue to publish their new works alongside stories by new African American writers. No other African American journal offers this combination of accomplished and emerging talents.

The Council also takes an active role in the local community, providing literary opportunities for adults and students alike. We have concentrated our after-school program on middle school students for the last two years after a study by the state university revealed students at this age to be of particular risk of dropping out of school.

By providing the literary workshops, we encourage the students to express themselves by telling their stories in a supportive environment, which has resulted in greater retention and less truancy.

To continue our tradition of success, we must broaden our base of support. As you might know, the Butler County Community Trust has provided a substantial part of our funding for the last six years. They have informed us that their support must end next year because of their limit on consecutive year funding, and we are writing in hopes that you will help us fill the gap left by their departure.

I've enclosed a copy of the most recent journal along with a proposal outlining the goals and objectives we have set for it in the coming two years. The journal's editor and I would welcome the opportunity to meet with you to answer any questions you might have and to discuss how the Council and the James and Mary Brush Foundation might work together. I can be reached at president@aalitcouncil.org or (904) 555-1234. Your kind consideration of this request is greatly appreciated.

Sincerely,

Mary Adams

Mary Adams
President of the Board

Note in this letter that Sheila Burns, a writer published by this journal, obviously knows Mr. Sterling and allowed the Council to use her name when applying for a grant. Putting the familiar name right up front helped ensure the letter (and the proposal) would get considered.

Cover Letter Checklist

Here are some questions to ask yourself when writing a cover letter:

♦ What do I know about the person who will receive the letter? Is there anything about them personally that could relate to my proposal?

♦ Does the person signing the letter know the contact at the funder? If so, should they be addressed by first name or a nickname?

♦ How can I address the funder's interests and relate them to my program?

♦ What are the key points that are my best argument for funding?

♦ How do I lay these out so that the reader can easily find them?

♦ If the letter is to a current or recent funder, did I thank them for their previous gift and report something about that project?

♦ If the letter is to a new funder, did I include enough background and information on recent accomplishments to place the program in context and give my proposal legitimacy?

♦ Have I slipped into jargon of my charity's or the funder's invention? (If so, see all about buzz words in Chapter 13.)

♦ Did I include contact information prominently for the letter's signer and possibly an additional person at my charity for questions?

♦ Is the letter dated correctly (that is, not still carrying the date of the first draft) and was it signed?

♦ Is the letter two pages or less? (If it's longer, it becomes a letter proposal.)

♦ Did I ask for money?

> **CAUTION**
>
> **How to Say It**
>
> Consider varying your formatting in the cover letter to make it stand apart from the proposal. Indented paragraphs look more personal that those that are flush left. A comma after the salutation also makes a difference but is best used when the recipient is being addressed by their first name. Boldface type immediately looks word-processed and impersonal, underlining looks less so.

An Executive Summary Is Not Another Cover Letter

You might think that an excellent cover letter perfectly summarizes your program and therefore is also an executive summary, but you'd be wrong. These two related parts of a proposal exhibit some key differences.

Whereas your goal was to make the cover letter personal, connecting with the individual and with the institution, the executive summary presents your proposal in a more formal manner. This is not the place to mention that your kids are on the same soccer team.

In the cover letter you highlighted the key reasons they should fund your program. In the executive summary, you should include all the reasons for funding. If it doesn't fit into the summary, you probably don't want it in the proposal. Keep the summary to one page and make it a terrific page. Often the executive summary and the budget are the only parts copied for everyone evaluating your proposal to see.

CAUTION

How to Say It _____

Save the personality for the cover letter. The executive summary should be business-like and straightforward. It should still, however, convey to the reader your passion for the program and its importance for your constituents.

Here's a sample executive summary for the same grant as the cover letter from the African American Literary Council given earlier.

The African American Literary Council requests a $10,000 grant from the James and Mary Brush Foundation to support the publication of *Black American Voices*, a quarterly magazine of fiction and literary criticism focusing on African American writers in northern Florida.

Begun in 1990 as a 16-page unbound photocopied book and circulated largely as a free publication in regional bookstores, *Black American Voices* has since grown into a respected literary journal with 6,600 subscribers, including 220 university libraries throughout the United States. Issues now typically consist of 64 pages, which are saddle stitched and printed in two colors.

Short stories originally published in *Voices* have won O'Henry and other respected awards. Major publishers such as Penguin Putnam have published writers we introduced. Essays in *Voices* have similarly been honored by the African American Journalists Association and others.

Black American Voices has now reached a turning point in its development. The subscription base, although steady, has not grown significantly in the last two years. The grant requested would, in part, make possible additional marketing through a 100,000-piece direct mail campaign, which will result in 900 to 1,100 new subscribers. Fall has traditionally been the best time of year for subscription campaigns, and we expect to mail our offer in early November so as to receive most of the return before the end of the year.

A larger subscription base increases earned income, which will help sustain publication in future years. We must expand the subscription base now, when the Butler County Community Foundation's long-standing support is ending because of their limit on consecutive year funding. The Community Foundation has agreed to make a $15,000 one-time grant specifically to support the subscription campaign. Your funding would complete the funding needed to enable us to take this important step forward.

Our editor, Tanya Mills, oversees the journal's content and works closely with our marketing consultant to make the journal more visually appealing. A consultant, Mark Jacobs, has developed the marketing plan, including the proposed direct mail campaign.

Your grant will allow us to achieve two important goals simultaneously:

1. It will allow us to bring the writers in *Black American Voices* to the wider audience they deserve.

2. It will increase earned income that will help support the publication for years to come.

Sheila Burns, O'Henry winner and one of the first short story writers we published, has written us that "*Black American Voices* believed in me when I wasn't sure if I believed in myself. Seeing my first published story changed everything for me. All I have accomplished since can be traced back to the success of that one story."

Help us introduce more Sheila Burnses to the literary community. Help *Black American Voices* grow.

Note that the executive summary concentrates on the program for which funding is sought. The other programs the charity offers are not mentioned. (They would be covered in an organizational history, which would be one of the attachments.) The executive summary gets more specific about the program, including how the grant would be used.

Executive Summary Checklist

An executive summary should summarize your entire proposal, including ...

♦ A one-sentence statement about the program for which you are applying and the grant amount you seek.

♦ Mention of any grant history with this funder.

♦ A highly condensed context paragraph pointing out your charity's qualifications for carrying out this program.

♦ A one paragraph description of the program, including the program's main activities, who will run it, goals, and anticipated beginning and end dates.

◆ A reference to the budget, noting areas of greatest expense to be covered by the grant and if any other funder has already committed to the program.

◆ A moving closing paragraph stating the difference the grant will make to your constituents and to the community (where applicable).

There will of necessity be some redundancy among the cover letter, executive summary, and proposal. Occasionally you may even repeat some language exactly (but try not to do this). To make an effective proposal, however, each part must reinforce the others and remain consistent in conveying your message. Stay on point and no matter what order the funder reads your material in, he or she will understand why your proposal must be funded.

The Least You Need to Know

◆ Customize every cover letter to reflect what you know about the addressee and who at your charity will sign it.

◆ Your cover letter should grab the reader's attention and point out the key reasons why you should receive the grant.

◆ Use clear language and formatting to make it easy for the reader to find and remember the points in your cover letter to advocate for your proposal.

◆ Use the cover letter to current or past funders to briefly report on their last grant and thank them one more time.

◆ Use the cover letter to new funders to place your program in context within your charity's mission and goals.

◆ Make the executive summary a true summary, touching on all aspects of the proposal, including the budget.

17

Repute and Tribute

In This Chapter

- Why you shouldn't use the same history with every proposal
- How to make your history reinforce your proposal
- How to use testimonials
- Documents to include—and not include—with a proposal

Before the funder decides to make the grant, they will want to know more about your charity than the one program you have described. In the background section you get to tell your charity's history in your own way with tributes from grateful clients and others thrown in to reinforce your claims.

So far in the proposal, you've been the one saying how great and deserving your charity is. You can gain greater credence by the use of quotes or entire letters testifying to your charity's ability to carry out the project. And testimonials from members of the press can carry additional weight. Here's how to put it all together into a package that will help your proposal, rather than just fill pages.

You've Got History with This Issue

Most organizations have a standard history that its grant writers have used so many times they can recite it from memory. You can just drop that old history into your proposal and call it a day, or you can take the time to tweak it to give it a special spin that relates to the rest of the proposal.

For example, your charity is probably known for more than one activity. Rather than treating each equally, condense the areas that don't relate to your proposal and beef up the ones that do. It's a little extra work, but if done well, it will reinforce your proposal rather than drag it down.

For example, my employer, the New York Foundation for the Arts (a grantmaking public charity, not a foundation), is best known for making grants to individual artists, and we usually begin our history with a description of that program:

> The New York Foundation for the Arts provides more fellowship support for artists than any other private organization in the United States. Since 1985, more than $18 million has been awarded to artists practicing in one of 16 artistic disciplines.

We also provide a wide range of information services, which more and more often rely on the Internet. For grant proposals to support these programs, a better spin on our history would begin with the following:

> The New York Foundation for the Arts (NYFA) today provides information to nearly one million artists annually through Internet, telephone, and print resources. NYFA's history with technology extends back to the founding of Arts Wire in 1992 as the nations first electronic network for artists and arts organizations and has been continued with such recent developments as the introduction in 2002 of NYFA Source.

If your history goes for more than a page, you should use bold-faced headings to draw the eye to important sections. Use bullet points to give prominence to listings of accomplishments.

Although a "history" implies a chronological narrative, you will be better able to make your points about the importance of your program if you organize it according to your principal accomplishments instead. Follow a rough chronology only if detailing how your charity has met challenges over time makes a better story.

The process and outcomes methods I discussed in Chapter 14 to organize program descriptions also can be used with organizational histories; only in this case, process almost always involves a chronology. Process, unfortunately, is mainly interesting to historians and management consultants, not funders. Focus instead on accomplishments when you can. Notice the contrast in the following two examples.

Outcomes-Focused History

The Friends of the New Town Public Library makes it possible for the Library to offer services far beyond what can be provided with public funding alone.

Twenty to one hundred new books have been purchased each year by the Friends since 1988—1,200 books so far. These have included multiple copies of best sellers, replacements of popular children's books, and new reference works. The Friends book fund thus touches a wide variety of library users.

Literary readings sponsored by the Friends bring talented but lesser-known writers to the attention of the community. Four hundred people now annually attend these events, begun in 1995, with an average of 45 people attending each event.

The Friends raises the funds for these activities through book sales (of unneeded copies of books and books donated by the community), bake sales, and grants from foundation and corporate sources. Membership dues (now ranging from $25 for individuals to $500 for patrons) paid by the Friends, however, now constitutes the major source of funding. The Friends is an entirely volunteer-run organization made up of 700 citizens that this year contributed $58,000 to New Town Public Library.

Process-Focused History

The Friends of the New Town Public Library makes it possible for the Library to offer services far beyond what can be provided with public funding alone.

Founded in 1988 to supplement the Library's book acquisition fund when city budget cuts were greatest, the activities now identified with the Friends began with a fall bake sale that raised $398. Librarians identified the major areas of book acquisitions needing support as multiple copies of best sellers, replacements of popular children's books, and new reference works.

The response from the community to the 1988 sale and the number of people who asked to get involved led to the founding of a formal Friends group that was incorporated the following year. Membership dues were established at $25 for individuals and $40 for families.

An annual book sale was begun in 1990 using donated books and unneeded copies from the Library. The book sale, bake sale, and dues from the Friends amounted to $2,200 that year, representing a significant growth in only two years of existence.

Success bred success, and in 1995 the Friends were able to provide support for a series of literary readings as well. This program was begun with the first grant the Friends received, from the New Town Community Trust for $6,000.

> The literary events not only introduced lesser-known writers to the community, they also brought the Friends to greater attention, so much so that today membership in the Friends stands at 700. This year a total of $58,000 was raised by the all-volunteer Friends.

Both versions of the history convey the same information, but the outcomes-focused history gives a better picture of the impact the Friends group has on the Library, whereas the process-focused history better conveys how the organization grew dramatically in a short time. I believe the former would make a greater impression on the funder, but either is acceptable.

Testimonials

There's nothing quite like including a quote from a satisfied client to strengthen and personalize your proposal. Your charity probably receives letters like this from time to time. Make sure executive and program staff know to give you copies of any that come in.

Words to the Wise

Always get permission from the person who praised you before printing a quote attributed to them. Otherwise, you could use the quote without attribution, but it won't seem as genuine.

It's great if you can quote exactly what someone said, but frequently he or she will use incorrect grammar or include something personal in the middle of his or her praise for you. Don't use awkward devices common in academic writing such as "[sic]" for misspelled words, ellipses to show that you omitted some words, or "[T]oday" to show that a word did not originally begin the sentence.

Improve the grammar and make the quote shorter. No one, including the person who gave you the quote, will ever notice the difference. But *never* make any changes in the meaning of the quote. Retain as much of the original language as you can to maintain the tone of the original.

Other Endorsements

If your charity is collaborating on a program with another charity (or a business), you should include with your proposal a letter of understanding between your charity and the collaborator stating the roles you will each play in the program, or at least obtain a letter of support stating that the other charity endorses your applying for the grant.

If your charity has been (favorably) in the news, by all means include quotes from articles, or in some cases the entire article, as additional confirmation that yours is a legitimate charity worthy of support. When your charity is in the news is a great time to submit proposals. The funder might already be thinking about you.

Staff and Consultant Bios

Many funders will ask for biographies of key personnel. For general operating proposals, that means your top three to five staff members and possibly your board president as well. For program proposals, key personnel are those who will have some control over the execution of the program, either as supervisors or through doing the actual work involved.

Each bio should be kept short—no more than a half page at the most. Full resumés should never be sent unless requested. They take too much time to read. By converting a resume into a 125- to 150-word paragraph, you save the program officer a lot of time, which he or she will appreciate. Needless to say, there must be experience mentioned in bios that directly applies to the program for which you seek funding.

> **CAUTION**
>
> **How to Say It**
>
> Bios should be written in the third person (not first) and begin by giving the person's relationship to the program and to your charity. The experience detailed should mostly relate to the program. This isn't like a resumé for a job where every year in someone's career must be accounted for.

Are You Legal?

As I discussed in Chapter 2, you must be a recognized nonprofit organization to receive a grant. Proof of nonprofit status should be enclosed with every grant proposal, including renewal proposals. If you have a fiscal sponsor, include proof of the sponsor's tax-exempt status. The only exceptions to this rule are government agencies (such as public libraries and schools) and religious organizations.

A federal recognition as a 501(c)(3) organization trumps every other kind of nonprofit status. If you have it, you don't need to include proof of state exemption.

And Everything Else

Most funders will ask for a list of your charity's board of directors with their professional affiliations, such as "General Manager, Community Bank" or simply as "philanthropist." If someone is retired, give the former occupation and note "retired" after the job title. The board list should be on a separate page. Don't give addresses or phone numbers. Some funders will also want to know how long each board member has served on your board.

Funders also like to know who else supports your charity. Funders seem to be able to come up with an amazing number of ways to ask for your donor list, but mostly they want to know the institutional funders (not individuals) in the last year that have given you $1,000 or more. Occasionally, you'll be asked to include all funders to which you have applications outstanding, which you'll mark "pending" and give the amount you expect to receive.

CAUTION

How to Say It _____

A list of attachments helps the funder by identifying the content and order of the attachments, and it also helps you by serving as a checklist of what you intend to include. You can give the list of attachments at the end of the cover letter (in which case all the parts of the proposal would also be listed), in a table of contents (ditto), or at the end of the proposal narrative (before the budget).

You'll be tempted to include other items to support your proposal, yet too much material can hurt rather than help your application. Usually, send only those attachments that the funder specifically requests. You might, however, also consider including the following materials *if they are germane to the proposal*:

- A general organizational brochure will supplement the background information you have given as part of the proposal. These will be particularly helpful to new funders.

- Two or three press articles (not press releases) that pertain directly to your project (or for general operating support, anything about your charity) will reinforce your charity's reputation.

- Documents that support your claim to have done similar programs in the past, such as a lesson plan, teacher's guide, disease prevention pamphlet, concert program, publication, or flyers announcing your programs are also of interest. Keep these to a minimum unless the funder specifically requested them.

- Annual reports are good for new funders. Current funders should have already received them. Of course, it would be even better if the new funder had received your most recent report as part of your cultivating them.

Never include videotapes, audiotapes, or books unless requested to do so by the funder. With all the materials the funder must already process, these will simply add an awkward bulkiness to your proposal. They won't be seen, heard, or read.

The Least You Need to Know

- Don't rely on the same statement of your history to convey the important points relevant to your proposal. Customize.

- Consider applying the outcomes method of proposal construction to your history to provide a clear picture of your charity's impact.

- Use testimonials from clients and those in your field to reinforce your message.

- Press reports will increase your credibility.

- ◆ Always include proof of nonprofit status, even with renewal grants.

- ◆ Keep staff and consultant bios brief.

- ◆ Don't include bulky items such as videotapes and books unless the funder has requested them.

18

Putting It All Together

In This Chapter

♦ Dotting the "I"s, Crossing the "T"s

♦ How to present your proposal

♦ Formatting the proposal to win friends

♦ Special presentations

♦ How to deliver your proposal to best effect

After you've completed what might be months of work on a proposal, you will want to make sure that it leaves your charity with the blessing of all involved. You also will want to ensure that it makes the best impression on the funder. The smallest details can make a difference, and no matter how trivial some details might seem, your proposal deserves to be received and seen in the best possible light.

When I prepare a proposal for submission, I look at the package as a little drama that will unfold as the funder opens and first looks at it. I not only carefully place the parts in the order I want them to be read, I take time deciding where page breaks occur (especially in the cover letter) and which paper it's printed on. Yes, I do get a little crazy about this, but it makes a difference. I'll give you some tips in this chapter on how to make a good impression—and how to avoid making a bad one.

Final Internal Review

Chances are, the proposal has changed a lot since the program officer (or clinic director, librarian, coach, and so on) last saw it. It's usually a good idea to give him or her one last chance to review the entire proposal, complete with attachments. (Remember to cover or exclude any confidential salary information when sharing the proposal with anyone who doesn't already have access to this information.)

Be sure to remind the program officer that you have to present the program in terms that will appeal to the funder. Just because his or her language has been largely left behind doesn't mean the program has changed. Offer to translate the proposal back into the original terms if necessary. If you think bringing program staff back into the process at this late stage will delay submission, you might skip this step with your executive director's consent.

Make sure you have notes for your own use that explain how each budget line was arrived at. You'll be asked to review this with the finance or program staff after the grant comes in, and believe me, in six months you will have forgotten how the printing line got to $6,000.

When I discussed customizing the proposal for each funder in Chapter 14, I asked you to create a checklist of the required parts of the proposal and attachments. Use that checklist now to make sure all the parts have been prepared. You might even ask a colleague to review the checklist with you. After the proposal has been completely assembled and all concerned have had a chance for a final review, it's time to prepare your package for the mail.

You Can Be Too Pretty

The cover letter should be printed on your charity's letterhead. If it takes more than a page, subsequent pages should be on blank pages of similar color and quality. Use regular photocopy paper for everything else. Using heavier paper looks wasteful. If you are fundraising for an environmental organization, always use recycled paper. Recycled paper will make a good impression on other socially conscious funders, too (and you'll be doing the environment a favor at the same time).

Twelve-point type is optimum for proposals and cover letters, but never use a font smaller than eleven points. Budgets and charts with numbers might use a font as small as 10 points if the spacing makes it easily legible. You might laugh at these guidelines, but the trustees who will read your proposal are mostly, like me, over 40 with eyesight that isn't what it once was. They'll appreciate receiving documents that can be read easily. In print,

> **CAUTION**
>
> **How to Say It**
>
> Whatever you say in your proposal, say it using a reader-friendly format. That means 12-point type, an extra space between paragraphs, margins of at least one inch on all sides, page numbers on everything except your cover letter, white paper printed one side, and no staples.

fonts with serifs (such as Times Roman) are easier to read than sans serif fonts (such as Arial). You'll also find you can get more words to a page using Times as opposed to using Arial.

Margins of at least one inch all around also make a document easier to read. Using a discrete header or footer that identifies your charity and gives page numbers can come in handy for the funder if pages get scrambled in the funder's photocopying process.

Words to the Wise

Don't put the funder's name in the header or footer. It's too easy to forget to change these when revising the proposal for a new funder and failing to do so will make you look incompetent.

Standard proposal formatting calls for paragraphs not to be indented. In addition, I like the paragraphs to be formatted flush left with a ragged right margin. Justified text might make pretty blocks on the page, but because justification compromises the spacing between letters and words, it ends up making the text harder to read.

Save your beautiful glossy folders for press packets and sponsorship proposals. Funders can be put off if you have obviously spent a lot on presentation materials.

To staple or to paperclip, that is the question—one with an easy answer. Paperclip always. Chances are, the funder will need to make additional copies of your proposal. Stapling will make this more difficult. I clip together each section separately (cover letter, executive summary/proposal, and each attachment) and then use a large clip for the entire package so that it comes out of the envelope in one piece. A thick annual report or other publication might not fit into the clip, but all the unbound sheets should.

You'll want to use an envelope that looks professional but not flashy. I think white envelopes are always best. The brown craft ones look too plain. Colored ones might make the proposal stand out in a stack of mail, but I don't think it does so in a positive way.

How to Say It

I like to make the cover letter stand out as the personal communication it's meant to be. Not only should it be on different paper (namely the charity's letterhead), you might also indent the paragraphs to distinguish it. Changing the font, however, might make it look too unlike the proposal.

Playing to Your Audience

Arts organizations, especially large ones, are expected to present themselves in a more dramatic manner. But even arts groups should consider the impression that very elaborate materials will make on the funder because of the expense involved in printing and mailing them.

Social service agencies, even large ones, usually have more simply produced materials. I once quit making contributions for several years to a social service agency that sent me an elaborate annual report, complete with vellum overlays and embossing. I suspected that the printing and design had been donated, but it was really off-putting, considering their mission, to receive such an expensive report.

There are, of course, exceptions to every rule. When going to the sponsorship office of a major company, you might want to gloss-up your presentation a notch or two. The people reviewing your proposal in this situation are more likely to believe that it takes money to make money and that a successful organization will not be shy about looking successful.

With the increasing sophistication of word-processing programs, it becomes tempting to format proposals using all the bells and whistles available. Don't. Rather than impressing the funder with your sophistication, you might give the impression that you spent too much time on the appearance of the proposal—time that could have better been spent creating and submitting additional proposals.

This is not to say that you should never include an illustration in a proposal. Charts and graphs created by a spreadsheet program can make a point better than dozens of words, and a photograph illustrating your program description can also be effective. But never add any kind of illustration just to break up the page or because it's a nice picture related to your organization. *Everything* in the proposal—words and images—exists to tell *one story only*. Don't confuse the funder with extraneous materials of any kind.

Words to the Wise

Ironically, some federal government agencies advise you to use any service other than the U.S. mail for your proposal because of irradiation requirements for mail going to government offices, which slows service and can destroy some types of enclosures. A quick phone call to the agency will help you to make the right delivery choice.

Words to the Wise

Even a short proposal should be mailed flat. If you fold it and the funder needs to make an additional copy, it will be that much harder for them.

Getting the Package Delivered

Unless the funder has specified some other method of delivery (such as electronically), send your proposal by U.S. mail whenever possible. Express delivery companies offer highly reliable service, but the funder will note the additional cost. This might send the wrong message about how your charity spends its money.

If you have planned ahead, you shouldn't need to send the proposal express, anyway. If you're running late, however, by all means use the express delivery rather than miss a deadline. If the funder has a firm deadline *and* you're running late, use a service (such as certified express mail) that will give you proof of mail date and delivery. If you've submitted your proposal well in advance, the proof of delivery will be unnecessary, because you can call and check on the receipt.

Many deadlines will be "postmark deadlines," which means your proposal must be postmarked by the post office by that date. The date on your metered postage machine doesn't count. Get a stamped receipt from the post office when you mail it, because frequently the "return receipt" you pay extra for will never be returned or returned unsigned.

So let's talk stamps. Yes, even the stamp is important, especially when sending a proposal to an individual. The larger the funder, the less important the stamps, since at a large foundation the person opening the mail will have no part in evaluating the proposal. Metered postage works fine in these cases.

Stamps have that hand-prepared look that sends a subtle message that a real person prepared this proposal just for them. When sending a proposal to an individual, use large commemorative stamps rather than the standard flag stamps or the small ones that look too much like third-class mail postage.

First impressions are always important. A perfectly written proposal can be sunk if it arrives out of order or hard to read. By making it easy for the funder to process your proposal, you're starting out with points in your favor. Formatting and presentation are simple things to do right, and they can make a real difference in how funders perceive your charity.

One last reminder: Follow the funder's instructions to the letter as to order and delivery, just as you did for content.

The Least You Need to Know

- Give those most involved with a program a final chance to review the grant proposal.

- Use a serif font in 12-point type on inexpensive plain white (or recycled) paper and similar paper for your envelope.

- Keep document formatting simple with flush left paragraphs, varying it only to make an important point.

- Paper clips win out over staples every time.

- Avoid expensive express delivery of proposals unless it's the only way to make a deadline.

- Follow the funder's directions for putting the parts of the proposal together and for mailing.

19

Other Types of Applications

In This Chapter

- ◆ Condensing your entire proposal into a letter
- ◆ Making foundation forms work for you
- ◆ Types of electronic proposal submission

Ninety percent or more of the proposals you submit will be prepared just as I've described in the preceding chapters, but there are some exceptions you need to be familiar with. With a full proposal, you have the most control over how the case for your program is presented to the funder, making some parts longer, others shorter, as best suits your program.

Other means of requesting grants—letters, forms, and electronic versions of these—reduce the flexibility while calling more on your ability to make your case creatively, in whatever form the funder wants to receive the proposal.

Letters

Many smaller foundations ask that you submit your proposal in the form of a letter, frequently specifying the maximum number of pages you can use. I gave you two examples of letter proposals in Chapter 6 in the discussion of proposals to individuals.

When foundation trustees have little or no professional staff to assist them, a letter proposal is a practical means to reduce the amount of

Words to the Wise

When a funder asks that you restrict your proposal to a set number of pages, don't employ formatting tricks such as smaller margins and fonts to squeeze in more words. You won't help your proposal and might, in fact, have your proposal rejected out of hand because it is too hard to read.

materials that they must evaluate in their grantmaking. Keeping that in mind, you should scrupulously respect any length restrictions. Don't depend on adding attachments that haven't been requested to get around the length restrictions. They won't be read.

This is not to say that letter proposals should not have any enclosures. Funders requiring a letter proposal will usually ask for a program budget and proof of nonprofit status to be attached at minimum. An organizational brochure enclosed along with the proposal will provide the funder with additional background without adding much in the way of bulk to the proposal. But remember that everything you need the funder to understand must appear within the letter itself.

A letter proposal must …

- Function as a cover letter by making a connection with the reader on a personal level and tying the proposal to the funder's interests.

- Act as an executive summary by presenting in condensed form the critical points of the proposal.

- Include all the parts of a full proposal such as the statement of need, process, goals and objectives, key personnel, and evaluation procedure.

- Provide a context for and references to the budget.

If you look back at the sample letters in Chapter 6, you'll see that those very short letter proposals do all these things.

- The personal connection is established by reference to the donor's friend, and their past support is included to show why the proposal has been sent to them. If this had been a foundation proposal there would have been a sentence or two tying the proposal to the foundation's interests.

- The need for the new animal shelter is established in a series of bullet points in executive summary fashion and the objectives for the new shelter appear in a parallel series of bullet points.

- Only the fundraising goal for the program is mentioned, but had the letters been longer, there could have been details on the costs of the building.

The letter proposal enables you to make a more personal appeal because the format encourages a "me and you" tone. I prefer this type of application to all others, even though it requires greater discipline to keep the length down while making all the important points.

Forms

The degree to which funders use forms varies widely. In many cases, the only form involved is a cover sheet that collects the basic contact information and gives broad strokes about the budget (such as a total for expenses and a total for income). These forms are just an adjunct to your full proposal. The forms to be discussed here will, in large part, substitute for a full proposal.

Forms give funders a means to ensure that they receive information in a uniform format from every applicant. This can make evaluating the proposals easier. Forms can also serve to decrease the distinctions between proposals submitted by large organizations with considerable fundraising resources and smaller ones with just one grant writer.

> **Philanthropy Facts**
>
> You are most likely to encounter form proposals when applying for government grants that will provide limited space for each section of the proposal. But even these forms usually also allow a few additional pages for the program narrative.

The quality of the writing, of course, comes to the forefront when formatting and presentation are made uniform. This means you have to do an even better job when preparing a grant application form. Having restricted space to make all your points requires everyone who edits your proposal to exercise restraint so that it does not exceed the allowable length.

A number of regional associations of grantmakers provide a standardized application that many of its members will accept. In most cases, these are little more than a cover sheet, an outline to follow when developing your proposal, and a budget form. Most of the associations offer the application only in PDF format, which requires the free Adobe Acrobat Reader software to download, but which you must then complete using a typewriter or by buying additional software.

There are a few sterling exceptions. The Donors Forum of Chicago (www.donorsforum.com) offers the usual PDF version, but also has a well laid out electronic form that can be downloaded and completed online or offline. The Minnesota Council on Foundations offers a form you can complete online and print out, a PDF version, and a MS Word version.

The regional associations intend their common applications to make it simpler for the grantseeker as well as the grantmaker. No matter how common the application requirements, you must still take all the care described in this book to customize your proposal for each funder. To their credit, the instructions for the regional associations remind you of this. In the end, I'm not sure how much time the forms save anyone, but the outlines each association offers are useful in organizing your proposal.

> **Philanthropy Facts**
>
> The Regional Associations of Grantmakers (www.rag.org), Foundation Center (fdncenter.org), GrantStation (www.grantstation.com), and other organizations offer access to many of the application forms accepted in different regions.

Chicago Area Grant Application Form

Working collaboratively, representatives from Chicago's foundations and corporate giving programs and a broad range of nonprofit organizations designed this form in order to streamline the grantseeking process.

Be strategic. Make sure that the goals, objectives, and amount requested in your proposal match the criteria of the funder you are approaching. A cover letter should be included with each proposal which introduces your organization and your request, and makes a strategic link between your proposal and the funder's mission and grantmaking interests. Information about many individual grant programs is available from each funder at the Library of the Donors Forum of Chicago.

Important notes

1. Please keep in mind that different funders have different guidelines, priorities, deadlines and timetables. In addition, funders who accept this form may require a preliminary concept paper or request additional information at any stage in the proposal process.

   Know each funder's grantmaking philosophy, program interests, and criteria.

   It is important to follow specific instructions from the funder.

   Be aware of each funder's application process, including timetable and preferred method of initial contact.

2. Include a cover letter that outlines the strategic link between your proposal and the funder's mission.

3. This form must be completed in its entirety.

4. Develop your proposal using the format on page 3.

Resources

Call or write each funder to obtain a copy of funding guidelines and/or annual report.

Use the Donors Forum of Chicago's Grantseekers Toolbox (at http://www.donorsforum.org/resource/gstool box1.html), Illinois Funding Source (at http://ifs.donorsforum.org), the *Directory of Illinois Foundations* and other local and national directories as a starting point to your research.

Visit the Donors Forum Library to conduct research on private grantmakers. The Library is open to the public and is located at 208 South LaSalle, Suite 735, Chicago, IL 60604. Regular hours are from 9:00 a.m. to 4:00 p.m. Monday through Friday and until 6:00 p.m. on the second and fourth Wednesday of each month. The Library's telephone number is (312) 578-0175; TDD 578-0159.

Foundations/Corporate Giving Programs that accept the Chicago Area Grant Application Form

Alphawood Foundation (fka WPWR-TV Channel 50 Foundation)	Circle of Service	GATX Corporation	C. Louis Meyer Family Foundation	Retirement Research Foundation
Aon Foundation	Community Memorial Foundation	Harris Bank Foundation	Michael Reese Health Trust	Hulda B. & Maurice L. Rothschild Foundation
The Baxter Allegiance Foundation	R.R. Donnelley & Sons Company	Hartmarx Charitable Foundation	The Elizabeth Morse Charitable Trust	SBC (fka Ameritech)
BP (fka Amoco Foundation)	EVEREN Foundation	IBM Corporation		Sears Roebuck & Co.
	Exelon Corporation/ Commonwealth Edison	ITW Foundation (fka Illinois Tool Works)	ONDEO-Nalco Foundation	Albert J. Speh, Jr. and Claire R. Speh Foundation
The Bufka Foundation	Company	Mayer and Morris Kaplan Family Foundation	New Prospect Foundation	Irvin Stern Foundation
Elizabeth F. Cheney Foundation	Jamee and Marshall Field Foundation	John D. and Catherine T. MacArthur Foundation	Northern Trust Co.	TCF National Bank
Chicago Bar Foundation	First United Church of Oak Park	The McCall Family Foundation	Peoples Energy Co.	VNA Foundation
Chicago Tribune Foundation	Lloyd A. Fry Foundation		Relations Foundation	Washington Square Health Foundation

Donors Forum of Chicago

This form from the Chicago Donors Forum (www.donorsforum.org) collects much of the information you'd include in a proposal, but note that your narrative is created apart from the form using their outline.

Chicago Area Grant Application Form

Grant Request   Amount requested: $ _____

This request is for: ☐ General operating support   ☐ Capital   ☐ Other: _____

☐ Program/project title: _____

Organizational Information

Organization name _____

Address, city, state, zip _____

Telephone _____ Fax _____ E-mail _____

Executive director _____ Telephone _____

Name/title of contact person _____ Telephone _____

Total organization budget for current year $ _____ United Way funded? ☐ Member ☐ Grant ☐ No

Date of incorporation _____ FEIN number (or equivalent) _____

Is your organization tax exempt under Section 501(c)(3)? ☐ Yes ☐ No   **Section 509(a)?** ☐ Yes ☐ No

If not, do you have a fiscal agent? *(please identify organization, contact person, and telephone number)* _____

_____

_____

Primary service category of organization *(check only one)*
☐ Arts & culture   ☐ Human services   ☐ Education   ☐ Environment
☐ Health   ☐ Civic / economic development   ☐ Other *(specify)* _____

Summarize the organizationís mission *(2-3 sentences)* _____

_____

_____

_____

_____

Geographic service area(s)
☐ City of Chicago   ☐ Northwest Indiana   ☐ Regional/national
☐ County *(specify)* _____   ☐ Suburbs *(specify)* _____
☐ Chicago neighborhood(s) *(specify)* _____
☐ Other *(specify)* _____

Provide percentages and/or descriptions of the populations your organization serves.

Race/ethnicity (if applicable)
____ African American   ____ Asian American/Pacific Islander
____ Caucasian   ____ Hispanic/Latino
____ Native American   ____ Other _____

Sex ____ Female ____ Male

Other (i.e. disabled, age, gay/lesbian, etc.)

_____

Staff composition in numbers

	Professional	Support
Paid full-time	_____	_____
Paid part-time	_____	_____
Volunteers	_____	_____
Interns	_____	_____
Other	_____	_____
Totals	_____	_____

Grant Request *(continued)*

Summarize the purpose of your request *(5 sentences or fewer)*

_____
_____
_____
_____
_____
_____
_____
_____
_____
_____
_____

Time frame in which the funds will be used: From _____   To _____

List other private and public funding sources for this particular request.
(If this is a request for general operating support, please see Attachment A6 on page 3.)

Funding sourcesóto date   *Amount*   *Date received*

_____
_____
_____
_____
_____
_____

Funding sourcesópending   *Amount*   *Anticipated receipt date*

_____
_____
_____
_____
_____
_____

Organizational Budget *(last fiscal year)* Expenses $ _____   Revenues $ _____

Program/project Budget *(if applicable)* $ _____

Signature of authorized official _____   Date _____

Name/Title _____

Proposal Narrative *Please provide the following information in this order. Do not use more than 5 single-spaced pages, exclusive of attachments. Please staple; do not bind your application.*

A. Background

1. Organization's mission, history, overall goals and/or objectives.
2. Description of current programs and activities. Please emphasize major achievements of the past two years.
3. Description of formal and informal relationships with other organizations.

B. Purpose of funding request

1. If applying for general operating support, briefly state how this grant will be used.
2. If your request is for a specific project or capital campaign, please provide the following information:

   The community and/or agency needs or problems that this effort will address, including population served.

   Describe how the project addresses these identified needs.

   Program or Capital Campaign description to include strategies employed to implement the proposed project: (1) goals and objectives, (2) timetable for accomplishing stated goals and objectives, (3) program methodology (program only), (4) staffing, and (5) collaboration with other agencies.

   If this is a collaboration, briefly describe the partners.

   If this request is for a specific program, explain how it will be supported after termination of the grant.

C. Evaluation

1. Explain how you will measure the effectiveness of your activities.
2. Describe your criteria for success.
3. Describe the results you expect to have achieved by the end of the funding period.

Required Attachments *Please provide in the following order.*

A. Finances

1. Audited financial statements for the last fiscal year, if available, or Form 990. If neither document is available, include unaudited financial statement.
2. Current year's operating budget to include both projected expenses and revenues. Categorize expenses under program, general and administrative, and fundraising.
3. Program budget (with narrative, if applicable).
4. If request is for a multi-year grant, include multi-year program budget.
5. Capital budget and a list of Campaign Committee members (if applicable).
6. A list of foundations, corporations, or governmental agencies which funded the organization in the last fiscal year, including amounts contributed ($1,000 and above).
7. Itemization of use of requested funds (if requested by funder).

B. Other Supporting Materials

1. Verification of the organization's or fiscal agent's tax-exempt status under Section 501(c) 3 and 509(a) of the IRS code. If using a fiscal agent, please include Letter of Authorization.
2. Grantee report (if previously funded).
3. Latest annual report or a summary of the organization's prior year's activities.
4. Current board list with related employment affiliation.
5. A description of ethnic and minority representation of Board of Directors in percentages (if requested by funder).
6. Qualifications of professional program staff (if applicable).
7. If the project for which funding is sought is a collaboration with other agencies, include letters of agreement from the collaborating agencies.
8. Letters of support and/or reviews (if applicable).

Donors Forum of Chicago

Online and E-Mail

Every year, more funders make it mandatory to submit grant proposals electronically. This includes proposals that are submitted by e-mail (and might be no different from a traditional proposal other than how you deliver it to the funder) and forms that are completed over the Internet.

On the face of it, online submission might sound like a great thing for the grant writer. No worrying about getting it in on time, just press the "submit" button. No decisions to make about paper, stamps, or other bothersome details.

Presentation, in fact, ceases to be a factor because every application will appear identically formatted. And that's the reason I don't like electronic submissions. They make it much more difficult to give your proposal personality that makes it stand out in the crowd. Because electronic proposal submission is still relatively new, many funders' online processes are still filled with bugs and do not take into consideration the electronic capability and Internet access of their potential grantees.

One prominent funder known for its online applications and sophistication issued an RFP for grants to help charities without online access. The only problem was that proposals could only be submitted online and were only advertised online. I never heard how many applications they ended up receiving.

With all the cosmetics of the proposal removed, the grant writer's talents become even more important. Everything you do must be done with words alone.

When faced with an online application, your first step should be to print out the entire application (so much for the paperless office). You'll need to look at the entire application before beginning completion of any part. If possible, save your work as you go to prevent an interrupted Internet connection or glitch when going to the next page from losing your hard work.

Words to the Wise

Don't unintentionally give the funder access to details about your budget process you might prefer they not know. Before submitting a budget by e-mail, I always copy the entire spreadsheet to a new one using the "Edit-Paste Special-Values Only" commands. That way, your formulas and cell comments don't get e-mailed along with the numbers.

If possible, download the application and all instructions so that various drafts can be worked through using the actual form. More likely, you'll have to work on each section separately in your word-processing program, pasting it into the form after all edits have been made. This gives you the advantage of spell-checking each section, but makes it hard for anyone else to review what you have written in the context in which it will finally appear. Remember that you'll probably lose formatting such as bold, underlining, and bullet points.

Online applications differ significantly depending on the sophistication of the programming. Some will consist of forms identical to ones you would submit through regular mail. These are the easiest to complete because they are the most like traditional printed forms. (For an example, see the Sample Government Proposal's application cover form on the accompanying CD-ROM.)

Some online applications are now structured so that you are asked a series of questions that determine the additional questions you will be asked and sections you'll be asked to complete. These can be frustrating in that they don't allow you to see the entire form at one time. At other times, this process can break down into manageable steps what might seem overwhelming when presented all at once. If you've applied to the funder before, consult the offline paper form you used in the past. The online form is probably very similar.

Words to the Wise

If you don't work in an office with Internet access, remember that most public libraries offer free access. Try to get there before school lets out, when competition for machines becomes more intense.

The New York State Council on the Arts' online application (introduced in 2003) uses the step-by-step procedure with the formerly fearsome budget form. Now, you are asked for each budget category one at a time, which feels less intimidating. The programming assembles all your figures into a completed form and does the math for you. Of course, you must be prepared to answer each of the budget questions as they are asked, which requires prior knowledge of what they want to know.

Before pressing the "submit" button with any online application, print out a copy of the completed application for proofing and for your files. If possible, save an electronic copy, too.

Don't wait until the last minute with online applications either. The flurry of people completing last-minute applications can overload the funder's server and prevent you from completing your application. At this writing, online applications are still relatively new and are likely to improve in the near future.

The Least You Need to Know

- A letter proposal must contain all the main elements of a full proposal but in condensed form.

- Common applications must be customized for each funder, just as if you were preparing a proposal from scratch.

- Access common applications and find out what funders accept them from your regional grantmakers association or the Foundation Center's website.

- Always print out online applications before beginning work to see how the sections fit together.

- Print out and proof carefully an application submitted by e-mail or online. After you press the "send" button, that's it.

Part 6

Post-Application

Waiting just might be the hardest part of the grant-writing process. It can take months. What should you do in the meanwhile? We'll discuss what can improve (and what can sink) your chances of receiving the grant.

And then the letter arrives! Whether the answer is yes or no, work remains to be done.

And for those of you who always looked at the answers in the back of the algebra book before working the problem, I've put together a whirlwind grant-writing course in one final chapter. There are references to previous chapters in case you want to dig deeper into a topic, but this chapter is truly the least you need to know.

Chapter

20

Waiting for and Receiving the Verdict

In This Chapter

- ◆ What to do after you've submitted a proposal
- ◆ Making the most of a rejection
- ◆ Making the most of an acceptance

You've spent months preparing your grant proposal—researching, cultivating, writing, editing, and formatting. Now comes the really hard part: waiting for the verdict. And there can be considerable waiting involved. Some funders might take eight to nine months to inform you of their decision. Fortunately, most will let you know in one to four months. I'll give you a few tips on what to do and *not do* while waiting.

No matter what the funder's verdict, you will need to respond in a way that makes the best of either situation. Receiving the money doesn't mean you can ignore the funder. And having your proposal declined doesn't mean giving up. I'll cover both possibilities in this chapter.

Don't Be a Nudge

If you submitted your proposal well in advance of the funder's deadline, you can wait a week before calling to make sure it was received. The funder's program officer might have a suggestion for additional information that will help your proposal or even suggest you rework a section. Most often, he or she will simply acknowledge that it has been received.

Always ask when you should expect to hear the result of their consideration of your proposal. Mark this date on your calendar, and follow up with them again somewhat after that date if you haven't heard from them. You might want to call earlier, but don't. The funder's staff has much more to do than keep you posted on the progress of your proposal.

These two calls are the only ones you should make while your proposal is under consideration, unless you have substantive information that could update your proposal. What's a substantive update?

It's not that your chorus will be performing the fifth Bach cantata rather than the fourth one, or the new soccer uniforms will be red instead of maroon. If, however, a famous conductor has been engaged to conduct one of the choral concerts, or the soccer team has made it to the state semi-finals, those would be worth informing the funder about.

CAUTION

How to Say It

Get good news about your program or other grants received for it to the funder as soon as you can. Not only can this strengthen your proposal, but it also reminds them of what you're doing. Don't report bad news unless it is so bad (such as all your funding falling through), that you need to withdraw the proposal or so public that you know the funders will discover the information on their own. In the latter case, contacting the funder allows you to try to put a positive spin on the issue.

Any changes that positively affect the funding of the program under consideration should be reported. This would include a grant that you had listed as "pending" coming through. (I wouldn't contact a funder to tell them a grant *didn't* come through. Bad news of this kind can always be dealt with later.) In-kind donations of space or materials might also be worth reporting, depending on the degree to which they affect your ability to carry out a program.

There might be times when you must withdraw a proposal. This has got to be one of the hardest things you'll ever have to do as a grant writer. If major funding from another source falls through, making it impossible for you to carry out the program, you have no choice but to withdraw the proposal. It's also feasible that your charity could decide to postpone or cancel a program between the time the proposal is submitted and a decision is expected from the funder.

Withdrawing your proposal in cases such as these will allow for a better long-term relationship with the funder. You never want to be in the position of sending back a check, which would be disrespectful of the time the funder spent in evaluating your proposal.

Of course, programs can also change after you receive a grant, but I'll discuss that situation in Chapter 21.

Handling Rejection

After carefully preparing a proposal that perfectly matches the funder's interests and was beautifully crafted, you receive a two-paragraph letter telling you that your proposal has been declined. Funders employ widely differing levels of tact and courtesy in their rejection letters.

The best letter (if there can be a "best" rejection letter) will tell you some specifics about why they did not fund your program. Other letters will make general excuses about previous commitments to other charities and limited funds.

> **CAUTION**
>
> **How to Say It**
>
> If a program officer has been helpful to you concerning why your grant application was not approved, a short note thanking him or her for speaking with you would be a nice touch. Even if you were told there was no point in reapplying, the note will help build your personal relationship with someone who a year later might be working at a different foundation and in a position to help you.

Then again, you might receive a letter like the one a colleague recently received that said they weren't being funded again (after 10 continuous years!) and shouldn't call to ask why because the funder wouldn't tell them. Their message got through loud and clear.

No matter what kind of rejection letter you receive, it will be a disappointment, but how you deal with rejection is a sign of maturity. Unless the funder expressly tells you not to contact them, it's wise and perfectly acceptable to call them to try to determine more than what you were told in the letter.

If one of your board members tried to help you get a grant, they should be told of the rejection. When informing them that the grant was not approved, be sure to thank them for helping. You don't want the board member to feel powerless because a grant didn't come through. The same board member might be able to help you get another one.

Where Did You Go Wrong?

In most cases, a phone call is the best way to follow up on a rejection. Asking the funder to write you an explanation creates more work for them, and if they were going to tell you in a letter, they already had a chance to do so. The rejection follow-up call can either improve your chances the next time you approach a funder or burn your bridges forever. Keep in mind the following points when making these calls:

- The call should be made to your contact at the funder. Don't try to go to the head of the foundation just because that's who signed the letter.

- Be polite, no matter what you might be feeling. If you're particularly disappointed by a rejection, wait a few days before calling.

Words to the Wise

The comments you receive as a result of a rejected proposal can be many times more valuable than information you get from a funder before applying. The rejection comments will focus directly on your program and can present a blueprint for your next proposal.

Words to the Wise

Try not to look at an unsuccessful proposal as a failure—there will be a lot of them. Instead, make it a growth experience by opening communications with a funder and getting feedback about the specifics of your proposal.

- Respect whatever your contact tells you. If he or she says that your proposal didn't meet the funder's criteria (even though you know they've made similar grants), ask how you might have modified your proposal to fit better with their interests. Never argue.

- Be open to using this conversation to mention other programs your charity conducts. Perhaps your program wasn't successful because they only fund after-school programs and your proposal was for activities that were part of the regular curriculum. Introduce the alternate program now to get feedback to use in preparing that proposal at a later time.

- Ask if there were parts of your program to which the trustees did respond positively.

- If it appears there is a possibility of receiving a grant from this funder in the future, ask how long you should wait before reapplying.

- Take careful notes of your call to use when preparing the next proposal.

- Review your notes with program and administrative staff so that everyone understands what might be done to receive funding in the future (or why you have removed the funder from the prospect list).

The Freedom of Information Act requires that federal government funders give you the reasons for a grant decision. Some agencies will require that you submit a request in writing and then make you wait some time before you receive them. Others will simply tell you over the phone what you need to know. Private funders are under no such obligation, but many, if not most, will share with you what they can within the funder's policies.

Persistence

"Three strikes and you're out" has many connotations these days, but I also use it as my general gauge as to how often to apply to a funder unsuccessfully before giving up on them. I figure that the first time I approach a funder, the "we're already committed to other charities" excuse is probably genuine. If I've subsequently done a decent job to cultivate them, that excuse begins to ring a little hollow the second time. By the third time, I know they are just being polite.

In the best cases, you'll receive comments from the funder that will either allow you to modify your proposal the second (or third) time to increase your chances of being funded, or allow you to eliminate them from your prospect list. In other cases, you will not know what went wrong. If your research tells you a funder should be open to your proposal, you should try more than once to give them the opportunity to fund your charity.

> **Words to the Wise**
>
> Never submit a proposal that was rejected by a funder to that same funder a second time. It's a waste of time, not to mention disrespectful of the funder's time and of your charity's investment in paying you to create proposals.

Acceptance

Congratulations! You received a grant. Now you're done, right? Wrong. Things just got more complicated.

Calling to say thank you to your contact at the funder is a courteous practice and a great first step in developing a relationship. The funder's program officer will remember you did this. Also, it's a good idea to ask for comments from the trustees or grant panel even when you are successful. Knowing what parts of your proposal appealed to this funder might help you focus proposals to others.

If you received the amount you requested (which is fairly rare), and other funding has been coming in, your program will be fully funded and can proceed as planned. It's still advisable to review proposals with program staff when the money is received so you can find out if they have already modified the program and take appropriate actions with the funders if needed.

> **Words to the Wise**
>
> The thank you letter is the first step in developing a long-term relationship with a funder. Take care that these letters are personal, specific to the grant, and free of boilerplate text (except for the required IRS language).

In some cases, reduced funding might make it impossible to carry out the program as described in your proposal. If this is so, the sooner you let all funders know about changes to the program the better.

In my experience, funders are understanding about changes to programs. If a program will still be able to accomplish its mission and goals (even if it's conducted in a different manner and serves fewer people), it's unlikely you will encounter a problem. Some funders will ask that you send them a letter noting the changes. It's important that you do this so that your reports will be based on the modified proposal rather than the original.

Remember: A grant is a contract between your charity and the funder. You have accepted the funder's money on the condition that your charity will carry out a certain program in a particular way in a specified amount of time. The funder has a right to know if any conditions of the contract will not be met.

A Prompt, Simple Thank You

Within a day of receiving a grant award letter, a letter acknowledging receipt of the grant and thanking the funder should go out signed by someone in authority at your charity. Ideally, the acknowledgement letter will be signed by the same person who signed the cover letter that accompanied the proposal. The acknowledgement letter can, however, be signed by the executive director, board president, or even the director of development. The important thing is that it be sent promptly.

An acknowledgement letter should contain …

- ◆ A thank you.

- ◆ A statement that the grant money will be used as stated in the proposal.

- ◆ A brief restatement of how the grant will assist your charity and/or its clients.

- ◆ A statement that the funder is receiving no benefit by making the grant (to satisfy IRS regulations).

Here's a general acknowledgement letter by way of example:

Dear Ms. Sterling:

The Community Clinic's staff faces an enormous challenge every day to meet clients' needs within the Clinic's own limited means. That challenge just got easier, thanks to your generous $6,000 grant. Your grant will be used to support the mobile unit that provides free blood pressure and blood tests in neighborhoods throughout the city. It will specifically be used to extend the number of hours the mobile unit operates, as described in our proposal to you.

Since we applied to the Sterling Family Foundation, Lifeline Pharmaceutical, Inc. made a grant of both cash and equipment that will allow us to update the mobile unit. The better equipment along with the extended hours made possible by your grant will make a significant difference in the number of people with heart disease that can be identified early and treated.

Your support of this program is greatly appreciated, and we look forward to reporting to you on the execution of the expanded program in due course.

Sincerely,

Herbert Washington, M.D.

Herbert Washington, M.D.

P.S. As no goods or services were received in connection with this grant, it is fully tax deductible under IRS regulations.

I like to put the legalistic IRS language in the postscript so as not to spoil the flow of the letter, but it just as easily could have been inserted before the last paragraph.

If one of your board members helped pave the way for a successful grant, you should write him or her a thank you, too. Depending on your relationship with the board member involved, an e-mail or phone call might do. If it is a particularly large grant, a letter or call from your board president to the helpful board member would also be in order.

No, I Really Mean Thank You

You can never say thank you too often. Especially with large grants or grants of any size from a new funder, it's a good idea to send a second thank you a few days later from someone else at your charity. This is especially important if, in order to get the acknowledgement letter out quickly, it did not have the same signer as the proposal cover letter.

The second thank you should not repeat any language in the first one. Only the acknowledgment letter should have the IRS language, so you have more freedom creating the second letter. And yes, it might be you writing all the thank you letters, too, no matter who signs them.

How to Say It

Keep a supply of plain note cards on hand for your executive director or board president to use when sending handwritten thank you notes to funders. If he or she has terrible handwriting, the note can be typed, but have someone with good handwriting address the envelope by hand, and use a stamp—not metered postage on important thank you letters.

Really, Really Thank You

A handwritten note from one of your charity's board members is a nice follow-up to the letters from staff. These letters should be reserved for the largest grants or when you used a board contact to help get the grant. These should be on the signer's personal stationary or even a note card. They can be very short, something like this:

Dear Mary,

I was thrilled to hear that the Sterling Family Foundation has made a grant to the Community Clinic. I know we have you to thank for this. It will mean a great deal to our clients to have the extended service, and it means a great deal to me personally to know that we have your support. Thanks so much.

Best wishes,

Cindi

The Least You Need to Know

- Limit your contact with a funder after submitting a proposal to one call to check on receipt and one to check on the result (only if they are late in responding to you).

- Accept rejections graciously, but call to see if your contact is free to share information about why you weren't successful.

- Gather as much information as possible in a rejection follow-up call to aid in crafting the next proposal.

- Don't give up on a funder with the first rejection unless you're told flat out not to try again.

- Acknowledge grants received immediately, including the required IRS language about tax deductibility.

- Follow the acknowledgment with one or more additional thank you letters from different people at your charity.

Chapter 21

Reporting on Success

In This Chapter

♦ How to extend the cultivation of a funder beyond the thank you letter

♦ Communicating with the funder about problems with a program

♦ Preparing financial reports

♦ Modifying a grant contract

♦ Reporting on successful and unsuccessful programs

In Chapter 10, I wrote about the importance of cultivating funders before asking for money. Cultivation doesn't end when you receive a check. In many ways, it's just begun.

Funders' requirements for reporting back to them on how their money was spent will vary, but all at least ask for a report a year from when the grant was awarded. You could wait twelve months before communicating with the funder, but in doing so you would be passing up golden opportunities to make the funder a long-term friend of your charity. This chapter will show you how to integrate the funder's reporting requirements with other communications to cement a relationship.

Developing a Relationship

The thank you letter represents the first step in cultivating the funder into a friend. If you send two or more thank you letters, you've established multiple lines of communication and possibilities for a relationship.

In working to develop a relationship with a funder, you're not just manipulating them to your own ends. In many cases, the funder will want to establish a relationship with your agency. Why? By furthering your work, they accomplish their goals as well. So don't be shy or hesitant about contacting funders after the grant has been made. True, some will want to remain distant and uninvolved, and they'll let you know that pretty soon, but you owe it to your charity to try to establish a lasting relationship.

When the funder believes they can work with you on any project related to your common mission, you'll find that they will contact you about new initiatives they plan to fund before the RFP ever goes out. They will also work closely with you to craft future proposals that get funded. This chapter is devoted to the various ways to cultivate and communicate with funders to give you the best possible chance at developing this kind of relationship.

Giving Credit Where Credit's Due

Publicly acknowledging the contribution you've received follows closely on the thank you letter in establishing good karma at the beginning of the funder/grantee relationship. To start with, you'll want to add the funder's name to the list of donors on your website or anywhere else you publish a list of donors. This could be your next concert program, a donor recognition wall, or any publication. On your website, you can also provide a link to the funder's website, if one exists.

Carefully note the spelling of the funder's name on its letterhead and use that form in all acknowledgements (unless the funder otherwise instructs you). Is it "The Smith Foundation" or just "Smith Foundation?" These little things can matter a great deal.

Occasionally, a funder will ask in the award letter that their grant remain anonymous. Always scrupulously honor this request. Mark their database record and let program and development staff know about this. If the letter says nothing about anonymity, you can assume the funder won't mind being listed, but if you intend to do anything else to publicize the gift, always ask for permission.

Your donor lists make your donors known largely to an internal audience (even if on your website), because only those seeking your services (or your colleagues at other charities looking for prospects) will be likely to read them. If you have received a major grant, you'll also want to let the world know about it by issuing a press release.

> **" "** **Words to the Wise**
>
> Out-of-date donor lists on websites occur far too often. Leaving out a current donor shows a disregard for the importance of their gift, and I believe leaving a donor on long after their gift can discourage subsequent gifts.

> **Philanthropy Facts**
>
> Although your charity's list of major donors is the only part of your 990 IRS form that is *not* open to the public, funders' 990-PF forms do have to list who they gave the money to, so eventually "anonymous" will be no more unless given by an individual or a corporate giving program.

Always get the funder's permission before issuing a press release. You'll want a quote from them for the release anyway, but also give them the option of seeing the draft press release before you issue it.

You can do a press release for an anonymous gift, but unless you've received a really large gift, the press won't be interested because one of the major facts (the donor's name) isn't available to them. And if you receive a really major gift (say, in the millions), some reporter will try to ferret out the identity of the donor and probably will succeed.

Timing

You'll want to keep your funders informed as your program progresses. It's critical to the development of a long-term relationship that you do this, but you don't want to overdo it and put them off. Good ways of keeping funders informed include ...

◆ Invitations to events related to the program they funded. These could range from formal events (such as a concert or dinner) to sessions for clients (when the privacy of clients is not an issue).

◆ Copies of positive news coverage of the program. If you receive negative coverage, you might need to inform the funder with an explanation of why the coverage was negative and possibly a copy of a letter to the editor you have written, whether published or not.

◆ Copies of your publications that report on the program, such as your newsletter or new information posted on your website.

◆ Copies of any special publications created for or by the program, such as application forms, catalogs, or books created by clients.

The funder will probably expect to receive these things from you. Sending them in advance of formal reports will help keep the relationship going.

> **Words to the Wise**
>
> Several charities have been rocked by scandals in the last few years. This has led to greater scrutiny and suspicion by the public. Should there ever be even a hint in the press about a problem in your charity, you will want to contact your funders right away. You might not be able to turn a story around, but you can assure funders that you share their concerns about how their grant money is spent.

You might be tempted to share right away with the funder thankful letters you receive from clients. I'd save these to include with a formal report.

Your charity might have other publications and events not related to the funded program. Be judicious in sending these to the funder. Just as with the proposal, you want to keep the funder's focus on the project they funded. You want to keep your charity in the forefront of the funder's mind, but you can go too far and be a pest. If the funder receives too much unrelated information, they might stop reading anything you send them.

Gathering Information

The grant writer acts as the pivot point between the funder and the program staff. You can't do a good job of keeping the funder informed unless you know how programs are progressing. Attend meetings where program staff discuss programs. Ask questions. Attend program activities whenever possible. (There's nothing quite like first-hand experience of a project to make your next report or grant proposal take on a whole new personal tone.)

You'll find it also helpful to let program staff know what kinds of information you will need to report to the funder. That way, they can solicit the information you need as the project progresses, rather than trying to make it up at the end. The information you'll need will relate directly to the goals and objectives stated in the grant proposal.

Progress Reports

Some funders will require that you submit a progress or interim report at a time they specify, typically six months. If a project started slowly, that doesn't mean you can delay or skip the interim report. Send it in on time, explaining any delays with the program.

Usually, the narrative portion of an interim report will be in letter form. Preparation of these reports should be done with great care. Anything stated in the progress report will form the basis for the final report. For example, don't get yourself in trouble by overstating the progress that has been made in the interim report.

Words to the Wise

Writing the funder to modify a grant proposal, although not something you want to make a habit of, is critical when a program does not go as planned. By modifying your proposal, your program's final results will be judged against it rather than the original one, allowing you to report successful completion of your program.

If the grant was to make possible 1,200 free meals and after six months you've only served 300, you should explain why now. Perhaps the program's start was delayed or the health department closed down your kitchen or bad weather kept clients away. It's better to take advantage of the interim report to explain why things aren't going as planned than to find yourself at the end of the grant period telling the funder the program failed. If adjustments in the goals need to be made, request them in an interim report.

An interim report will also include a financial report contrasting the proposal budget with actual expenses. Again, if there looks as if there might be a discrepancy at the end of the program, it's better to inform the funder in advance.

Funders realize that in an imperfect world, conditions affecting your charity change. Asking to modify the grant contract should not be a big deal. Going all the way to the end of a program and then telling the funder the project was unsuccessful is a big deal. Never let your charity get in that situation.

If one of your funders does not require an interim report, it would still be a good idea to send them something before the end of the grant period. In this case, it can be a feel-good letter of two to three pages reporting on progress that has been made. Of course, if problems are accumulating with the project, inform these funders as well as those requiring a report.

Here's an abbreviated interim report for the internship program for curators described in Chapter 14.

Dear Ms. Brown:

It is my pleasure to report to the Brown Trust on the Curatorial Internship Program since the awarding of your generous grant in September 2002. The program has thus far met or exceeded all our expectations and brought to us three very talented young curators.

City Art Museum conducted outreach for this program through letters sent to the career development offices at three local colleges with large minority populations and to six local galleries that are known for presenting the work of minority artists. We widely publicized the program through press releases, on our website, and on a number of Internet job-posting services. We also held a meeting for interested applicants at State College, which was attended by 60 potential applicants.

We received a record 30 applications as a direct result of these outreach efforts, which made it very difficult to select only three. The City Art Museum curators along with Sara Bright, curator of contemporary art at the Asian Art Museum, served as the panel to select the interns.

There were five applicants selected by the panel. Because of the intense working relationship between the curators and interns, it was not possible for us to accept all five, even if funding had permitted this expansion. One applicant when approached had already accepted another offer, so the next three in the panel's ranking were invited to join the program and all three accepted. The fifth candidate was encouraged to apply again next year.

The interns have since been working directly with the curators assigned to them on upcoming exhibitions. This has so far mostly included research using the Museum's library and other resources. The curators are very pleased with the interns' enthusiasm and resourcefulness.

We look forward to reporting to you again at the end of the program year, by which time the interns will have begun preparations for the exhibitions they will curate at the end of their second year. Should you have any questions about this report, I can be reached at (414) 555-1234 or schin@cartmuseum.org.

Sincerely,

Susan Chin

Susan Chin
Head Curator

Note that the report comes from the head curator, not the museum director, who most likely would have signed the grant proposal, nor from someone in the development office. Having a curator sign the report emphasizes the curators' direct involvement with the interns, from selection through their two-year term, and beyond. Needless to say, the grant writer actually wrote the letter.

Because the program just got started, the report of necessity concentrates on the selection of the interns rather than what they have done. Now let's look at the financial report that would accompany this letter.

Curatorial Internship Program

EXPENSES

Personnel	Year 1	Year 2	Total	6 Month Interim Report Actuals
Curators (3 @ 12%)	$27,000	$27,000	$54,000	$13,548
Registrar @ 5%	$3,500	$3,500	$7,000	$1,600
Librarian @ 5%	$3,000	$3,000	$6,000	$1,500
Fringe benefits	$6,365	$6,365	$12,730	$3,163
Subtotal salaried personnel	$39,865	$39,865	$79,730	$19,811
Intern Stipends (3)	$66,000	$66,000	$132,000	$33,000
Total Personnel	**$105,865**	**$105,865**	**$211,730**	**$52,811**
Program Expenses				
Marketing/outreach	$5,000	$500	$5,500	$4,921
Supplies	$600	$1,000	$1,600	$302
Travel	$1,000	$2,000	$3,000	$98
Photocopying	$800	$1,900	$2,700	$110

EXPENSES

	Year 1	Year 2	Total	6 Month Interim Report Actuals
Telephone	$100	$400	$500	$30
Postage/Delivery	$400	$400	$800	$338
Exhibition expenses	0	$40,000	$40,000	0
Contingency	$300	$1,200	$1,500	$15
Subtotal direct expenses	$8,200	$47,400	$55,600	$5,814
Indirect costs @ 15%	$17,160	$23,010	$40,170	$8,794
Total Expenses	**$131,225**	**$176,275**	**$307,500**	**$67,419**
Income				
Consolidated Arts Fund	$75,000	$75,000	$150,000	$75,000
Brown Trust	$50,000	$50,000	$100,000	$50,000
Bankers Bank	$10,000	$10,000	$20,000	$10,000
Community Trust	$8,000	$12,000	$20,000	$8,000
Jones Family Foundation	$7,500	0	$7,500	$7,500
Adams Family Trust (pending)	0	$10,000	$10,000	0
Total Income	**$150,500**	**$157,000**	**$307,500**	**$150,500**
Surplus/(Deficit)	**$19,275**	**–$19,275**	**0**	**$83,081**

Note that this budget covers two years, reflecting the program's two-year time frame. Because this report comes after six months, exactly half of all personnel costs for the first year have been included in the Actuals column at the far right. Other expense items are not evenly distributed. For example, virtually all of the outreach costs have already been incurred, but no exhibition costs are claimed, because that part of the program takes place in the second year.

Income for this program came from a variety of funders, most of which made two-year commitments. Because most are making the grant in equal installments, there will be a surplus in year one balanced by an equal deficit in year two.

CAUTION

How to Say It

A budget narrative might well be included with interim reports to explain the rationale behind the allocation of expenses. Even pointing out the obvious (such as the exhibition being part of the program's second year) might save the funder time in figuring it out for themselves.

For an interim report, it would have been acceptable to delete the columns for the second year and the total project costs. This would have made a simpler presentation, but I thought it would be more helpful for you to see the full presentation. This budget can also be found on the accompanying CD-ROM in spreadsheet format.

Spend the Money

It seems obvious that your charity will spend the money received from grants in the manner the funder agreed to. But I've seen many cases where this hasn't happened. Those running programs sometimes don't understand that the funder didn't just make a $5,000 grant—the funder made a grant of $3,000 to be spent on personnel, $100 to be spent on telephone service, $500 to be spent on travel, $600 to be spent on printing, and so on. If it turns out that no travel expenses were incurred, that doesn't mean that $500 can be spent on something else.

This might be an unrealistically strict interpretation of the use of grant money, but if you're not spending the money as planned, then the program probably hasn't been conducted as planned either, and that can present problems when reporting the program's results to the funder. A gentle inquiry of program staff as a program progresses about how the budgeted expenses compare to actual expenses might help avoid misunderstandings or at least nip them in the bud.

Grant Extensions and Exceptions

There will be times—other than when making an interim or final report—when you will need to communicate with a funder, especially if the program has experienced problems. It's not uncommon to ask that a grant's time period be extended. This could be because it began late, took longer to organize, unforeseen complications arose, or everything has simply taken longer than expected.

If it appears your program will need more time, ask for it. A time request should be submitted two months or more before the end of the grant period. It would be unusual for the need for more time to be discovered later than this, so submitting a request only a few weeks before the end looks sloppy at best.

When asking for an extension, be sure to ask for *all* the time you will need to complete the program. Not only will asking for a second extension make it appear that you are running the program carelessly, but funders will be much less likely to grant a second extension.

> **" " Words to the Wise**
>
> When submitting a request for a grant extension or modification, be scrupulous in the financial reporting. After you've reported an expenditure, you're stuck with it. Having to footnote your final financial report to point out discrepancies with the interim report does not present the picture of professionalism you want to cultivate with the funder.

Other requests to modify a grant proposal should be dealt with as soon as the need arises. This isn't something you want to do often, but it is much better than reporting to the funder at the end if the grant period that you have failed to achieve the program's goals, or you have spent the funder's money in ways not given in the proposal budget.

The Final Report

The final report should set the stage for your next grant request to a funder as well as reporting on the current project. But because reporting on the present grant is the primary purpose of the final report, I'll discuss that first.

Rarely will everything you outlined in your proposal have gone exactly as planned in the execution of a program. That's only to be expected, but the final report must give reasons for successes, failures, and near misses. Quotes from thankful clients sprinkled judiciously throughout the report will make it more real.

> ### Words to the Wise
>
> A published annual report makes a great marketing tool with funders, sponsors, individuals, and all kinds of other people you want to understand and appreciate your charity's work. You should send a copy to every funder, but this does not relieve you of creating a final report on your project or even your general operations. The details in an annual report usually fall short of what a funder wants to know about how their money was spent.

If you did a good job in your proposal of stating both goals (results) and objectives (measurable accomplishments toward the goals), the report will be a snap. Your final report narrative should include in relation to each goal and objective …

- A statement of the original goal or objective.

- A description of who was served in reaching this objective, providing metrics whenever possible.

- If the objective changed, an explanation of why and what the new objective was and how it was achieved.

And in relationship to the program as a whole, the narrative should include …

- Any challenges you encountered and how they were overcome.

- The method you used to evaluate the program.

- The major lessons learned from conducting this program.

◆ Future challenges for this program and the problem it sought to solve (other than funding).

◆ Any plans for continuation or adaptation of the program, including any funding received for a future period.

Funders have a vested interest in knowing of any problems or obstacles you encountered along the way and how you overcame them (or didn't). From your answers, they can gain knowledge that will assist them in evaluating similar proposals they might receive and in advising future applicants. Be frank about what it took to carry out the program. Who knows: If it was much harder than expected to carry out the program, the funder could see that as a reason to give you a larger grant the next time.

How to Say It

Reports should always be upbeat and find something positive, even in a disappointing program. The staff at the funder must present your report to the trustees, and they don't want to look as if they made a bad decision in recommending your charity for a grant.

The tone of your report should be upbeat, positive, and thankful. Receiving this grant was one of the greatest things to ever happen for your clients, and carrying out the program was a learning experience and a joy for everyone at your charity. Remember: *You are still selling your program.*

The interim report was done as a letter. Because of its relative brevity, this was an acceptable means of conveying the information. Because your final report will be more in-depth (and closer in length to the proposal), a cover letter is appropriate, followed by the formal report.

The cover letter in this case should thank the funder one more time, point out one or two of the major outcomes of the program, summarize how the program did financially, and close with a statement that leaves the door open for submitting another application. An anecdote about one client's experience of your program in your cover letter will put a human face on your program and engage the funder like nothing else.

You'll find a full final report with cover letter, narrative, and financial report in Appendix G and on the CD-ROM. Here is an excerpt from a different final report (based on an executive summary that appears in Chapter 16) to illustrate what I described earlier.

Final Report to the James and Mary Brush Family Foundation on a $10,000 grant to African American Literary Council

The James and Mary Brush Family Foundation's $10,000 grant to the African American Literary Council had a significant effect on the Council's ability to sustain the publication of *Black American Voices* and to serve a wider public. We are pleased to report on how this goal was achieved.

In August, we hired direct-mail consultant Mark Jacobs to revamp the subscription appeal we had been using for several years. Mr. Jacobs was able to suggest a number of simple changes in the cover letter and subscription form that resulted in dramatic increases in income.

One of his suggestions was to decrease the number of choices offered on the subscription form. Fewer choices result in a higher percentage return. He also suggested we add one new option: to become a "Friend of *Black American Voices*" for an additional $10. He also taught us how to re-mail to the best names, thus further increasing the return with very little additional expense. The 50,000-piece mailing went out in late October.

The combined effect of the changes in the subscription package was a higher percentage return and higher net income. In fact, the mailing nearly paid for itself. Our subscribers now number 7,200, nearly a ten percent increase in only one year. Just as important, 176 of the new subscribers paid the higher Friends fee. We will work to cultivate these Friends as donors with appeals to increase their contributions over the years.

In addition, we saw a slight increase in newsstand sales shortly after the direct mail campaign was launched. We attribute this to more people knowing about our magazine and buying a single copy rather than taking out a subscription. Time will tell if some of these readers later become subscribers.

As a result of this direct mail campaign …

- Subscriptions are up nearly 10 percent, providing a firmer financial basis for our magazine.

- We have 176 new names in our donor database.

- An additional 700 people per issue (including newsstand sales) read the work of our writers.

Your grant made all this possible. Yet much remains to be done. In the magazine business 30 to 50 percent of new subscribers typically do not renew, so to maintain the number of subscribers and to hopefully increase it, we must institutionalize an annual direct mail campaign. In addition, if advertising remains at its present level, we still need 10,000 subscribers for the magazine to be self-supporting.

Encouraged by the success of this new direct-mail campaign, we believe we can reach the magical 10,000-subscriber figure in three years. We have set ourselves a higher goal, however, of 12,000 subscribers so that the magazine can begin to subsidize the local literary activities.

We would welcome a meeting to review this report with you and discuss the details of our future plans.

This report was pretty easy, because the scope of the program was narrow. It is also shorter than the actual report would be, where more details would have been included on the changes in the mailing that resulted in so dramatic a change in return. A financial report and copies of the mailing would have been enclosed along with this narrative. The cover letter would have been brief and enthusiastic about the dramatic results of the mailing.

Combined Final Report and Renewal Request

In Chapter 14, I showed you how a proposal for general operating support using the outcomes method might consist of a list of notable accomplishments from the past year accompanied by plans for the coming year. With a little more attention to details about what you did in the past year, this same format works as a combined final report and request for renewed funding. You can do this in cases where you have a close relationship with a funder, but sending a separate report before asking for the renewal will serve you better in developing a relationship with a new funder. If you are seeking a large increase in support, you can set the stage for the increased request in a report, saving the ask for a new proposal that would follow it soon afterwards

> **Words to the Wise**
>
> When submitting your report and new request separately, use the intervening time to call the funder and ask for comments on your report. This will help you shape the new proposal.

You can take the same approach to submit a combined report and proposal for a program grant as well, assuming the program runs year after year with little change, the funder has a real commitment to the program, and you're not seeking a major increase.

With some larger (and more bureaucratic) foundations, combining the report with the new request won't work because of the particular ways they want to receive reports. In that case, you'll file your final report and submit a new request a few weeks later.

Educating and cultivating the funders, thanking them, keeping in touch, and giving them timely reports are all parts of good donor stewardship. If you take good care of your funders, they'll be more likely to continue to support your charity.

The Least You Need to Know

♦ Make all your communications with the funder, from thank you letter to final report, focus on the funded project and work toward developing an ongoing relationship.

♦ Interim reports (including a financial report) will be required by many funders, but are a good idea even if not requested.

♦ If a program does not go as planned, consider asking the funder to modify the terms of the grant.

◆ If you need more time to complete the program, request an extension at least eight weeks before the end of the grant period.

◆ Use the final report to set the stage for your next application by including information on areas not yet resolved or the need for continued similar activities.

◆ A final report should include information on each goal and objective listed in the proposal.

Chapter 22

Your First Grant

In This Chapter

- Research in brief
- Prospect development in brief
- Writing a proposal in brief
- Submitting a proposal in brief

Having read this book through, you're now well aware that grant writing is not a simple, one-dimensional process. Grant writing doesn't exist in a vacuum from other types of fundraising, involving as it does cultivation of funders, extensive research, financial acumen, and excellent writing skills. That said, there are technical aspects that you need to keep in mind when writing any grant proposal. In this chapter, I've streamlined the process, providing you with a quick grant-writing guide to remind you of the basics. You should find it particularly helpful when you're asked to produce a proposal in a few weeks rather than over several months.

This chapter covers all the basics with no frills so that you can quickly put together a grant proposal. You'll find references in parentheses throughout the chapter to other parts of the book where you can go for additional information. Words in italics can be found in the glossary.

Before getting to the grant-writing process, remember these three important facts about the grant-getting process:

Philanthropy Facts

Most foundations will not make grants to individuals, but individuals can gain access to foundation money by finding a nonprofit to act as their fiscal sponsor. A variety of service organizations and community foundations offer this service to individuals and organizations just getting started. Individuals seeking scholarship funds do not, however, need a fiscal sponsor.

1. Grants are usually made only to nonprofit, tax-exempt organizations, except for some grants made to individuals to carry out scholarly or artistic pursuits and some that are made to for-profit companies in special cases. If your group is not tax exempt, you might be able to receive grant through a *fiscal sponsor*. (For more details refer to Chapter 2.)

2. When an organization accepts a grant, it agrees to carry out the program it described in the grant proposal in the manner it was described. The grant proposal becomes in essence a contract between the nonprofit and the funder.

3. When preparing a grant proposal, always follow the funder's directions no matter what.

Gather Information Internally

The first step must always be gathering information from whomever runs the program for which you will be seeking grants. Try to get that person to write a first draft. Otherwise, use the questions relating to the parts of the proposal in Chapter 13 to coax the information from him or her.

Note the characteristics of the program that will be keys to finding funding:

♦ Can the description you have best be described as a discrete program, or does it involve major capital investments in equipment or other property? Is the grant to be for general operating support? (Refer to Chapter 2 for details.)

Words to the Wise

You'll find that "draft" is a magical word that will avoid all kinds of misunderstanding when working with a number of people to construct a proposal. By indicating at the top of your documents that it is a draft (and with the date), you let them know that you realize you don't know everything and are honestly asking for their opinions.

♦ How much money is needed to carry out the project? Are there funds already committed from other sources, including any fees from clients or participants? Has any existing money been received as a challenge grant?

♦ Is this for a new program or a continuing one? If it is new, does it break new ground or is it similar to programs elsewhere?

♦ What geographic area will be served?

You now have the basic information you need to begin researching potential funders: type of grant, amount needed (you might have to get several grants to cover all costs), new or continuing program, and geographic area served. These are categories that most funders will specify and with which most directories of funders are indexed.

Research Funders

Good research forms the foundation for successful grant proposals. A good grant writer does not mail dozens of identical proposals hoping to strike it rich with one of them. Instead, you will send out three to ten proposals for a program that has been written based on a thorough knowledge of what each of those funders would like to give money to.

There is no such thing as too much research. The more you know about each funder, its trustees, its giving patterns, and its stated interests, the greater your chances of success.

Start At Home

Start your prospect list by looking to see if your charity has received past support for the program, and if so, if those funders are prospects for renewed support. Also look at all your charity's current and past funders to see if any might be good prospects for this program. Don't leave out any major gifts ($1,000 to $10,000 or more, depending on what is major to your organization) from individuals. Note the names of all prospects with a short history of their support.

Words to the Wise

You will want to research not only the funders but also the people associated with the funders. Knowledge is power, and discovering a hidden relationship between a funder and someone in your charity will make a huge difference in your chances for success. Anything you can put into your proposal that acknowledges the personal interests of the person reading it will strike a chord with them that will place your proposal above all others.

Continue with Your Neighbors

There are probably other charities similar to yours in your geographic area. Do everything you can to obtain a list of the names of their donors. This might be as easy as checking their websites, or you might have to call and offer to exchange copies of annual reports. Make note of each of the major donors (again, relative to what that word means to your charity) with, if possible, an indication of how much they gave the other charity. Add these to your prospect list.

Finish with the Wide World

Armed with the information you've gathered, you're ready to begin to research prospects more broadly and gather important details about their funding. If you have Internet access, you'll save yourself hours of time. (See the extensive lists of online resources in Appendix B.) If not, plan to spend hours in a library. (For more details refer to Chapters 7 and 8.)

Start out with a general directory such as *The Foundation Directory*, published by the Foundation Center or *The Foundation Reporter*, published by the Taft Group, or either publisher's directory of corporate giving. (For details on resources see Chapters 3 and 4 and Appendix A.) Use the search criteria (or indices) to locate prospects. At this point you're not particularly interested in eliminating any potential funder, but look out for two instant eliminators:

- The funder does not accept unsolicited proposals.

- The funder does not make grants in your geographic area.

It will not be worth your time pursuing these funders. If you have a very well-connected board of directors, there is a chance one of them could contact a friend who is a foundation trustee and get them to solicit a proposal from you, but this is a long shot. (See Chapter 9 for more information.)

> **Philanthropy Facts**
>
> The many expensive directories on funders (both in print and online) are somewhat (or a lot) out-of-date. Don't rely solely on information you find in them. Always go to the funder's website or request copies of their brochures, guidelines, and annual reports to ensure you are working with the most current information.

Next look to see what government funding agencies (at the local, state, and federal levels) might support your program. If you are a very small or very new charity, most federal grants will be beyond your reach, so concentrate on grants closer to home. State and city websites are good places to begin your search for government grants, but also look at the sites of agencies related to your charity's work, such as Health and Human Services, Department of the Environment, or the Arts Council. (See Chapter 5 for tips on government funding.)

When you've completed a few days of research along these lines, you will have a list of 20 to 50 prospects. You won't be sending that many proposals, so now you'll work to narrow them down to the ones most suitable for your program.

Cross-Check and Refine Your Prospect List

In all likelihood, only three to five of your 20 plus prospects will be perfect matches for your program. To find them, you'll dig deeper into the specifics of what each has funded in recent years. Some foundations will list all their grants and their guidelines in their annual report or online. For others, you'll have to consult the informational returns they submit annually to the IRS. You can gain access to these returns (990-PF) from the Foundation Center or GuideStar websites. The 990-PF should also contain a brief description of the foundation's grant guidelines and a list of its trustees.

Compare each foundation's guidelines (including those of your current and past funders) with the grants they made. You'll probably find some grants that don't fit the guidelines at all. If one of these grants (for example, one made to a similar organization near you) was your only reason for adding this funder to the prospect list, you can eliminate them now. The grant was probably made through a personal connection at the foundation, which you probably don't have, so move on.

Words to the Wise

In the best of all possible worlds, you will be able to meet with the funder before or after submitting your proposal. There is no substitute for a face-to-face meeting for you to convey your passion for your program and to learn the specifics about what the funder wants to support. Unfortunately, few funders will meet with you before you submit a proposal, and only a few more will meet afterward.

If you are uncertain about whether or not to keep a funder on your prospect list, call them to discuss your program. Be sure you have at your fingertips a short description of the program and a general idea of what it will cost. Take careful notes of your conversation to use in preparing your proposal. (For more information see Chapter 11.)

When you have completed checking and cross-checking, you should have narrowed your list to five to ten prospects. Prepare a list of all of them, giving the funder's name and a complete list of its trustees. This document should be sent to everyone on your board of directors. You never know who might know the right person at a foundation. Should one of your board members know someone connected with one of your prospects, talk with that board member to decide how they can help pave the way for a positive reception of the proposal.

For government funders, get the application forms and guidelines and read them carefully to see if your charity meets all the eligibility requirements. If so, add these to your short list of grant proposals to prepare. (See Chapter 5 for details.)

If you had any individuals on your list, review them with the heads of your charity to see if they should be solicited to support this program. Some individuals might give through their family foundation (see Chapter 3). If they have given to you before, keep them on your list. If you found them on someone else's list of donors, you might send them something, but it will be a long shot without a personal connection with your charity. (For more information on individuals, refer to Chapter 6.)

Grant Talk _____

A number of funders will require that you submit an **inquiry letter** so they can judge whether your proposal will be of interest to them. This letter must be particularly strong, because it must provoke a positive response from the funder in a limited amount of space. If you clear this hurdle and they request a full proposal, you stand a very good chance of receiving the grant.

Note the deadlines of the remaining funders on your prospect list and compare them with your program's timeline. Timing might be unimportant (such as with general operating support) or the deciding factor (when you must have the money in hand by a certain date before making commitments to do the program).

At this point, you should have narrowed your prospects down to no more than five (excluding government applications). These are the funders for which you will be writing grant proposals.

Create a Grant Plan and Development Schedule

Before you begin writing, make a schedule based on the funders' deadlines. Remember that even funders with no specified deadline do have internal deadlines by which applications must be received to be considered at a particular meeting of its trustees. Try to find out when this is by calling them. (See Chapter 12 for help with scheduling.)

Plan to submit your proposal at least two weeks prior to the deadline, but a month or more ahead of time is even better. Early submission gives the funder time to request additional information or even ask you to revise part of your proposal.

Your schedule should also include any publications your charity will publish related to the program for which you are seeking funding between now and the consideration of your proposal. These should be sent to your prospects. Also, if your charity plans to hold an event related to the program, you might consider sending invitations to the prospects as well. Do not send them anything unrelated to the program you want them to fund. (For more details on funder cultivation, see Chapter 10.)

Outline the Entire Proposal

Outlining and organizing your proposal requires two steps. First you must accumulate all the information the funder will need to evaluate your proposal. In brief, the parts are …

- ◆ **Cover letter.** A one- to two-page letter introducing your charity and the program you want funded, including the amount requested, information on any past support from this funder (if any), and how the program fits within the funder's priorities (see Chapter 16).

◆ **Executive summary.** A one-page document that summarizes everything about the program, including purpose, needs, audience, evaluation, and budget (see Chapter 16).

◆ **Grant proposal narrative.** Your complete argument for funding. If the funder does not supply a list of what they want a proposal to contain, use the parts of the proposal that follow (and are described fully in Chapter 13) as your guide.

◆ **Statement of purpose.** A strong one-sentence description of the program followed by a brief elaboration on that theme.

◆ **Needs statement.** Why you are doing the program.

◆ **Process narrative.** A description of how the program will be carried out as well as its goals and objectives.

◆ **Key personnel.** Who will be responsible for carrying out the program.

◆ **Audience.** Who the program will benefit.

◆ **Evaluation.** Describe how you will know if the program has been successful, that is, if it has met its goals and objectives.

◆ **Summary.** A concluding paragraph restating the main reason your program should be funded along with the requested grant amount and a thank you to the funder for considering your proposal.

◆ **Budget.** A statement of the expenses directly related to the program (as well as a single number representing indirect expenses) and sources of income to support it. You might want to add a budget narrative if there are any exceptional expenses you want the funder to be aware of or to explain how other funds will be raised. (For a discussion of budgets, see Chapter 15.)

How to Say It

Whether you are raising money for a specific program, a capital project, or general operating support, you need to include all the parts of a proposal. Funders will want this level of detail no matter what kind of support you seek, and each funder will expect to find language that ties your request to their interests.

How to Say It

Will you or would you? "Will" conveys a can-do, assertive, positive approach. "Would" is conditional and weak. Always use "will" in writing a proposal. Be positive. Your program is the best thing since sliced bread, so of course it will be funded.

After this information has been gathered and is in reasonably literate form, you must look closely at how your program can address each funder's interests and goals. Don't just parrot back their *jargon*. Think about what the funder wants to accomplish through its grants, and customize your language throughout your proposal accordingly. Also remember that even if you seek support for general operations or to buy new computers for your charity, the proposal must reflect how these things will benefit the clients your serve. (For more details see Chapter 14.)

Some funders now suggest or require your proposal to be submitted on forms, either online or printed. The process of developing the proposal is no different in these cases, but you will probably have to edit down much of your text (as explained in Chapter 19).

Write It

To further organize your proposal and give it a point of view, structure it using the *process* or *outcomes* method. I prefer to use the outcomes method to stress the result the program has had in the past and will have again. For new programs or those that will develop a new methodology, describing the program in terms of the process might show it to greater advantage.

The outcomes method is the only practical method for *general operating support* proposals for charities with several programs. Describing the process by which you carry out each program would be endless, and a history is not a substitute for a general operating support proposal. (For more information on organizing your proposal, see Chapter 14.)

Internal Review

By now, some time has passed and much work has been done since the program person gave the first draft to you. It's a very good idea to take some time now to allow everyone involved with the program to review what you have written to make sure that nothing of substance has been changed or distorted in the writing and tailoring it for the funder. After any changes resulting from this review have been made, spell-check it and have someone else proof it as well.

> **Words to the Wise** _____
>
> Don't overstate or understate what your program will accomplish. You will have to write a report on the program based on the degree to which you accomplish all the goals and objectives in your proposal. Too many times, charities get themselves in trouble by making claims using big numbers and grand language they think the funder wants to hear without thought to what they'll say when the results are quite different.

When all reviews and revisions have taken place, print the cover letter on your charity's letterhead. Use regular photocopy paper for everything else. For best presentation, use 12-point Times Roman font and maintain at least a one-inch margin on all sides of the paper. Print only on one side of each page. (For more information see Chapter 18.)

Gather All the Parts

The funder will ask for specific bits of back-up materials to support your proposal. These will likely include proof of nonprofit status, a list of your board of directors, and a budget for your entire organization. Funders frequently will also ask for a list of all your other funders (as explained in Chapter 17).

You might be tempted to enclose any number of additional attachments. Restrain yourself. They probably won't be looked at, but here are some general guidelines about some of the things you might want to include:

- Publications (do so only if directly related to the program and then keep them at a minimum)

- Video tapes (don't include unless requested by the funder, this goes for CDs and DVDs, too)

- Testimonials and news clips (include no more than three examples combined)

- Miscellaneous brochures (don't include any unless related to the program, although a small brochure describing your organization would be okay)

Words to the Wise

No detail is too small to merit your close attention when putting together your proposal package. First impressions count, so keep everything in order and make the package as attractive as you can without glossing it up. If you can make it easy for the funder's staff to handle your proposal, you'll have earned important points.

Submit It

Assemble all the attachments using paper clips (never staples) and mail them in a plain white envelope (flat, not folded) by regular mail, unless you absolutely must use an express service or hand delivery to make a deadline. Use a return receipt with proof of delivery when a funder has a hard deadline and you submit your proposal at the last minute. Otherwise you can call a week after submitting to see if it was received.

After submission, keep the funder informed of anything that affects your proposal or any good news about your program (such as other funding coming through or a positive story in the press). Otherwise suffer in silence while awaiting the verdict. (For more information see Chapter 20.)

There. You've done it. Congratulations on completing your first grant proposals. Be sure you customized each proposal and followed each funder's instructions to the letter. Good luck!

Words to the Wise

Funders will actually accept proposals prior to the deadline. In fact, they prefer to do so. By waiting until the last minute, you cause yourself extra stress, waste money on express delivery, and make it impossible to alter or resubmit the application should the funder want you to do so.

Elements of a Grant Proposal

Cover letter (1 to 2 pages)

- Introduces the charity and the activity to be funded.
- Provides a reason for funding based on the funder's interests.
- Connects with the funder on a personal letter.
- Asks for the money.

Executive Summary (1 page only)

- Briefly introduces the charity and the activity to be funded.
- Summarizes all the key points in the proposal narrative.
- Provides a context for the budget.
- Asks for the money.

Proposal Narrative (3 to 15 pages)

- Covers all the areas requested by the funder.
- Presents an orderly, logical argument for funding.

Program Budget (1 to 2 pages)

- Lists all main expense categories directly related to the program, including personnel and any expense that would not be incurred if the program did not take place.
- Shows an allocation of indirect expenses that support the program (such as rent and administrative personnel) but are not directly related to it.
- Lists sources of income for the program, including other grants received and those pending, and any income that will be earned from fees or other activities related to the program.
- Includes footnotes or a narrative highlighting the main expenses and explaining how additional funds will be raised.

Attachments (vary according to funder requirements)

- Proof of tax-exempt status
- Audited financial statement
- List of your board of directors with their professional affiliations
- List of other funders
- Organizational budget
- Organizational history
- Press clippings, client testimonials, programs, brochures, flyers, and so on that directly relate to the proposal

Hallmarks of Good Research

- Does not rely on one source for information.
- Compares a funder's stated interests with the grants it makes.
- Includes research on the individuals associated with a funder.

Hallmarks of Good Grantwriting

- Follows all of the funder's instructions.
- Strives for succinctness and to be jargon free.
- Remains focused on the activity needing funding.

Hallmarks of Good Funder Stewardship

- Educates and cultivates a funder before soliciting a grant.
- Keeps the funder informed of the progress of a funded activity.
- Submits a thorough and timely report on every grant.

The Least You Need to Know

- ◆ Follow each funder's instructions to the letter.

- ◆ Research carefully to determine each funder's interests, and confirm everything directly with the funder.

- ◆ Tie your proposal to the funder's interests by restating their purposes in your own language in relation to your program.

- ◆ Always use "will" rather than "would" to describe how your program will proceed and be positive.

- ◆ Submit all proposals weeks before the deadlines whenever possible, having checked and rechecked spelling and grammar.

- ◆ Keep every communication with the funder—before, as part of, and after the proposal submission—focused only on the program you want funded.

Offline Resources

A few publishers have made a specialty of books dealing with fundraising and nonprofit management. In addition to the books listed here, you might also check the catalogs of the Allworth Press, Aspen Publishers, Foundation Center, Oryx Press, The Taft Group, and John Wiley & Sons.

Funder and People Directories

Baker, Deborah J., ed. *Corporate Giving Directory, 26th Edition*. Farmington Hills, MI: Taft Group, 2004.

———. *Foundation Reporter*. Farmington Hills, MI: Taft Group, 2003.

———. *Prospector's Choice*. Farmington Hills, MI: Taft Group, 2004. (The same information as in the *Foundation Reporter*, but on CD-ROM.)

Clark, David L., ed. *National Directory of Corporate Giving*. New York, NY: The Foundation Center, 2002.

Directory of Directors Company, Inc. *Directory of Directors in the City of New York and Tri-State Area*. Southport, CT: Directory of Directors Company, Inc., 2003.

Foundation Center. *FC Search. The Foundation Center's Database on CD-ROM*. New York, NY: The Foundation Center, 2002. (Also available by subscription on the Internet.)

———. *Grant Guides*. New York, NY: The Foundation Center, 2002. (Twelve volumes based on sector.)

Goddard, Mollie Mudd, ed. *Grants for At-Risk Youth, 2003 edition*. New York, NY: Aspen Publishers, 2003.

Jacobs, David, ed. *The Foundation Directory*. New York, NY: The Foundation Center, 2003.

Jacobs, David, and Melissa Lunn, eds. *Guide to U.S. Foundations, Their Trustees, Officers, and Donors*. New York, NY: The Foundation Center, 2003.

Marquis Who's Who. *Who's Who in America*. New Providence, NJ: Marquis Who's Who, 1999.

Martindale-Hubbell. *Martindale-Hubbell Law Directory*. New Providence, NJ: Martindale-Hubbell, 2001.

Miner, Jeremy T., and Lynn E. Miner. *Funding Sources for Community and Economic Development 2002*. Westport, CT: Oryx Press, 2002.

New York City Social Register Association. *Social Register*. New York, NY: New York City Social Register Association, 2002.

Orxy Press. *Funding Sources for K-12 Education*. Westport, CT: Oryx Press, 2001.

Romaniuk, Bohdan, ed. *Fund Raiser's Guide to Religious Philanthropy 2000*. Farmington Hills, MI: Taft Group, 1999.

Writing Guides

Procio, Tony. *In Other Words*. New York, NY: Edna McConnell Clark Foundation, 2000. (Available free at www.emcf.org.)

Strunk Jr., William, and E.B. White. *The Elements of Style, 4th edition*, Needham Heights, MA: Allyn & Bacon, 2000.

The University of Chicago Press. *The Chicago Manual of Style, 14th edition*. The University of Chicago Press: Chicago, IL: 1993.

Research and Grant Writing Guides

Blum, Laurie. *Complete Guide to Getting a Grant*. New York, NY: John Wiley & Sons, 1996.

Colvin, Gregory L. *Fiscal Sponsorship: 6 Ways To Do It Right*. San Francisco, CA: Study Center Press, 1993.

Dropkin, Murray and Bill LaTouche. *The Budget-Building Book for Nonprofits*. San Francisco, CA: Jossey-Bass, 1998.

Geever, Jane C. *Guide to Proposal Writing, Third Edition*. New York, NY: Foundation Center, 2001.

Quick, James Aaron and Cheryl Carter New. *Grant Seeker's Budget Toolkit*. New York: NY: John Wiley & Son's, Inc., 2001

Schladweiler, Kief, ed. *The Foundation Center's Guide to Grantseeking on the Web*. New York, NY: Foundation Center, 2001. (Available in print and on CD-ROM.)

Seymour, Harold J. *Designs for Fund-Raising*. New York, NY: McGraw-Hill, 1966.

Resources for Individual Grant Seekers

Brogan, Kathryn Struckel, ed. *2003 Writer's Market*. Cincinnati, OH: Writer's Digest Books, 2003.

Edelson, Phyllis, ed. *Foundation Grants to Individuals, 13th edition*. New York: NY, Foundation Center, 2003.

Ferguson, Jacqueline. *Grants and Awards for Teachers*. Alexandria, VA: Capitol Publishers, Inc., 1998.

PEN American Center. *Grants and Awards Available to American Writers*, PEN American Center, 2002-03 edition.

Palgram MacMillan. *The Grants Register, 21st Edition*. New York, NY: Palgram MacMillan, 2002.

Miner, Lynne and Jeremy T. Miner. *Directory of Biomedical Health Care Grants, 2003*. Westport, CT: Oryx Press, 2002.

———. *Directory of Research Grants, 2003*. Westport, CT: Oryx Press, 2002.

Sova, Kathy *et al.*, eds. *Dramatists Sourcebook 2002–03 Edition: Complete Opportunities for Playwrights, Translators, Composers, Lyricists, and Librettists*. New York, NY: Theatre Communications Group, 2002.

Useful Organizations in the United States

Council on Foundations
1828 L Street, N.W.
Washington, DC 20036
202-466-6512
www.cof.org

The Foundation Center
75 Fifth Avenue, 2nd Floor
New York, NY 10003
212-620-4230
fdncenter.org

The Foundation Center
312 Sutter Street, Suite 696
San Francisco, CA 94108
415-397-0902

The Foundation Center
1627 J Street, N.W., 3rd floor
Washington, DC 20006
202-331-1400

The Foundation Center
Kent Smith Library
1422 Euclid Avenue, Suite 1600
Cleveland, OH 44115
216-861-1933

The Foundation Center
Suite 150, Grand Lobby
Hurt Building, 50 Hurt Plaza
Atlanta, GA 30303
404-880-0094

Useful Organizations in Canada

Canadian Center for Philanthropy
425 University Avenue, Suite 700
Toronto, ON M5G 1T6
416-597-2293
www.ccp.ca

Philanthropic Foundations Canada
1 Place Ville Marie, Suite 1511
Montreal, QC H3B 2B5
514-877-6626
www.pfc.ca

Appendix B

Internet Resources

Websites change every day. In the course of my research, I found that some sites I had used recently no longer existed. Others were still there, but the URL had changed.

If you are unable to find a page where I have given an address for an inner page (such as www.cfda.gov/public/granttopics.asp), try searching again by taking off the letters after one or more backslashes (for example, try www.cfda.gov/public or www.cfda.gov) until you get the correct website, then use the site search or site map to locate the topic you need. Of course, you can also use any general web search site like Google or AllTheWeb to find the organization if all else fails.

General Information on Grant Writing and Research

Association of College and Research Libraries
www.ala.org/acrl/resjuly99.html
The ACRL provides grant resources links in a number of disciplines.

Chronicle of Philanthropy
www.philanthropy.com
This is the nonprofit world's newspaper of record. Issued biweekly, it includes articles on trends in philanthropy. It also reports on recent grants by foundations and companies. Skimming this listing is a great way to pick up some prospects for further research, but you'll have to be a subscriber to the paper edition to access all of them.

Corporation for Public Broadcasting
www.cpb.org/grants/grantwriting.html
This site provides a grant writing guide from beginning to end in seven pages.

The Foundation Center

fdncenter.org

This site is usually your first stop when researching foundations (private or corporate). It provides extensive online databases and reference materials.

GuideStar

www.guidestar.org

This database of every nonprofit organization in the United States includes foundations (private and corporate) and provides links and several years of tax returns for each.

Internet Prospector

www.internet-prospector.org

The Internet Prospector provides dozens of links to sites to research most everything you'll need information on.

Management Assistance for Nonprofits

www.mapfornonprofits.org

MAP provides much free information on their website, but the section about evaluations entitled "Basic Guide to Outcomes-Based Evaluation for Nonprofit Organizations with Very Limited Resources" is particularly useful.

Medical University of South Carolina Grant Guides

research.musc.edu/ord/granttips.htm

The Medical University of South Carolina has compiled these links to grant writing guides, focusing on medical research proposals.

The NonProfit Times

www.nptimes.com

The NonProfit Times provides articles about nonprofits beyond fundraising to include management issues.

Society of Research Administrators International

www.srainternational.org

This site offers information on RFPs and issues in research.

TechFoundation

www.techfoundation.org

The TechFoundation makes technology grants as its name implies, but also offers information on other funders and a newsletter about grants for technology.

Government Resources

StateLocalGov.Net

www.statelocalgov.net

Use this site to find websites of state and local government agencies nationwide.

GovSpot

www.govspot.com

GovSpot is an exhaustive set of links to state agencies plus subject listings for federal agencies.

Catalog of Federal and Domestic Assistance

www.cfda.gov

You can research federal grants here. Also use the federal government's most user-friendly interface for searching for grants by topic at www.cfda.gov/public/granttopics.asp.

Federal Register

www.gpoaccess.gov/fr/index.html

Use this site for new grant opportunities and every minute thing your federal government does every day.

FirstGov

www.firstgov.gov/Business/Nonprofit.shtml

FirstGov provides links to grants, nonprofit registration and tax information, and a number of other topics.

Federal Emergency Management Association

www.fema.gov

FEMA is the agency that assists in the recovery from natural disasters like floods and hurricanes, and these days, unnatural disasters like terrorist attacks. FEMA has an office in every state, the address of which you can find on the website.

National Endowment for the Arts

www.arts.gov

Most grants are for organizations, not individual artists.

National Endowment for the Humanities

www.neh.gov

The NEH funds research of all kinds in the arts and humanities, including documentary films.

National Science Foundation

www.nsf.gov

This is a portal for locating government grants in science and engineering.

Small Business Administration

www.sbaonline.sba.gov

Most programs are for for-profits.

U.S. Department of Education

www.ed.gov

The Department of Education makes thousands of grants, but many are to state agencies only. Read the eligibility requirements first when reviewing these RFPs.

U.S. Department of Health and Human Services

www.dhhs.gov

The U.S. Department of Health and Human Services is one of the government's largest grantmakers.

U.S. Department of Housing and Urban Development

www.hud.gov

HUD makes many grants to community organizations to improve neighborhoods, as well as larger grants to state agencies.

U.S. Environmental Protection Agency

www.epa.gov

Check out their free tutorial on how to write a grant for the EPA. It takes you through each part of the application, offering tips on what to include and how to say it along the way at www.epa.gov/seahome/grants.html.

Federal Grants and Contracts Weekly

www.aspenpublishers.com

Newsletter from Aspen Publishers.

For state websites, try the state name and ".gov," for example, www.oregon.gov or www.illinois.gov.

Foundation Resources

The Council on Foundations

www.cof.org

This site has links to many foundations and other associations. Convention information is worth a quick scan for buzzwords of the moment.

The Foundation Center

fdncenter.org

This site is usually your first stop when researching foundations (private or corporate). Extensive online databases and reference materials.

Grantmakers Concerned with Immigrants and Refugees

gcir.org

This site provides links to foundations and tips on grant writing.

Grantmakers in Health

www.gih.org

There are no links to foundations, but there are lots of links to studies that might provide backup for your proposal's assertions.

Grantmakers in the Arts

www.giarts.org

Grantmakers in the Arts provides all types of funders from foundations to corporate giving programs and grantmaking public charities in a listing with links.

GrantStation

www.grantstation.com

Many fewer foundations are included here than in the Foundation Center's databases, but more complete information is given here for most of the foundations that might help you. This is a strictly pay service, except for a free weekly newsletter.

GuideStar

www.guidestar.org

This database of every nonprofit organization in the United States includes foundations (private and corporate) and provides links and several years of tax returns for each.

Regional Associations of Grantmakers

www.rag.org

This site provides you with links to the numerous regional associations and their standardized application forms.

SchoolGrants

www.schoolgrants.org

Maintained entirely by volunteers, the site offers links by state as well as national funders, along with other information particular to education funding. Not comprehensive, but a good place to start.

Major Foundation Sites

The Dana Foundation (New York, NY)

www.dana.org

Principal interests are in improved teaching of the performing arts in public schools and in health, particularly neuroscience and immunology.

The William Randolph Hearst Foundations (New York, NY and San Francisco, CA)

www.hearstfdn.org

They fund nationally, but with an emphasis on the two cities where they have the strongest corporate presence. The website gives details on each grant and links to grantees.

The James Irvine Foundation (San Francisco, CA)

www.irvine.org

They give in California, primarily for higher education, workforce development, civic culture, sustainable communities, and children, youth, and families.

The Joyce Foundation (Chicago, IL)

www.joycefdn.org

They make grants for urban issues in Chicago; improvement of schools in Chicago, Cleveland, Detroit, and Milwaukee; poverty in the Midwest; the natural environment of the Great Lakes; election finance reform; and gun control. They also make grants to individuals whose work falls within these areas.

W.K. Kellogg Foundation (Battle Creek, MI)

www.wkkf.org

Their primary interests lie in health; food systems and rural development; youth and education; and philanthropy and voluntarism. They also make special grants in their local community.

The Rockefeller Foundation (New York, NY)

www.rockfound.org

Their wide-ranging interests include the arts; civil society; feeding and employing the poor; medical research, training, and distribution of services; revitalization of the African continent; and more. They also run a conference center in Italy for scholars, scientists, artists, writers, policymakers, and others to conduct creative and scholarly work.

Robert W. Woodruff Foundation, Inc. (Atlanta, GA)

www.woodruff.org

Interests of this foundation include K-college education; health care and education; human services, particularly for children; economic development; art and cultural activities; and the environment. They prefer one-time capital projects of established private charitable organizations.

Family Foundation Sites

The Arthur M. Blank Family Foundation (Atlanta, GA)

www.blankfoundation.org

The founder of Home Depot gives to arts and culture, athletics and fitness, education enhancement, environment (including outdoor activities), fostering understanding, and organizational effectiveness in Georgia, Maricopa County, Arizona, Coastal South Carolina, Park and Gallatin Counties, Montana, and New York City.

The Brown Foundation, Inc. (Houston, TX)

www.brownfoundation.org

They support public primary and secondary education in Texas; services for children, especially in the Houston area; and the visual and performing arts.

The Milken Family Foundation (Santa Monica, CA)

www.mff.org

Although there are a number of family members among the trustees, several non-family members are also on the board. Grants are made mostly in education and medical research (especially cancer research) and mostly in California. They make a large part of their grants through awards and fellowships.

Community Foundation Sites

Community Foundation Silicon Valley (Santa Clara, CA)

www.cfsv.org

This is one of the fastest growing community foundations in the United States with assets of $583 million in 600 funds. The founders of eBay are among their donors. They serve Santa Clara and southern San Mateo Counties in California.

The Greater Kansas City Community Foundation (Kansas City, KS)

www.gkccf.org

This is a model of clarity in laying out their different funds and how to apply, including detailed lists of current RFPs.

Operating Foundation Sites

Russell Sage Foundation (New York, NY)

www.russellsage.org

This foundation is devoted to research in the social sciences, supporting scholars who study at their facility or at other institutions. They also publish books and hold seminars.

Carnegie Endowment for International Peace (Washington, DC)

www.ceip.org

International affairs and U.S. foreign policy are pursued through research, discussion, education, and publications by this beneficiary of Andrew Carnegie.

KnowledgeWorks Foundation (Cincinnati, OH)

www.kwfdn.org

Educational initiatives in Ohio are the sole concerns of this foundation, which does, however, make grants.

Venture Philanthropy Foundation

Robin Hood Foundation (New York, NY)

www.robinhood.org

This foundation focuses mainly on children.

Corporate Resources

The Council for the Advancement and Support of Education (CASE)

www.case.org

This site maintains the most complete and up-to-date information on corporate matching gift programs.

EDGAR database

www.sec.gov/edgar.shmtl

Although the information in the Securities and Exchange Commission's EDGAR database is probably more esoteric than you will need, you should be aware that you can gain access to all SEC filings.

EDGAR Online

www.edgar-online.com

This site is more user friendly than the related EDGAR section on the SEC site. A lot of this site is only available to subscribers, but the people profiles might provide just the information you need.

The Foundation Center

fdncenter.org

This site is usually your first stop when researching foundations (private or corporate). It has extensive online databases and reference materials.

GuideStar

www.guidestar.org

This database of every nonprofit organization in the United States includes foundations (private and corporate) and provides links and several years of tax returns for each.

Gifts in Kind

www.giftsinkind.org

This site provides a catalog of donated products of all kinds.

The International Events Group

www.sponsorship.com

IEG provides the most complete information on corporate sponsorship. They publish a newsletter, have a helpful website, and hold seminars across the United States.

LexisNexis

www.lexis-nexis.com

This is a very expensive tool that provides access to a database with information on some 200 million households and 700 million phone numbers, among other information. You might be able to gain free access at some business and academic libraries.

Tech Soup

www.techsoup.org

This site handles the software donations for a number of software companies, in addition to many other services.

Company Sites

AT&T Foundation

www.att.com/foundation

Grant proposals are accepted by invitation only. They make grants for uses of technology in education, public policy, and the arts and culture. They make no in-kind contributions of products or services. There is no official corporate contributions office. Local AT&T affiliates make some grants to local charities.

Delta Air Lines Foundation

www.delta.com/inside/community/foundation_guide/index.jsp

They handle employee matching gifts as well as making direct grants for child welfare, civil rights, community development, and international affairs. There is no staff dedicated to the foundation. Their grants are limited by the income produced by the foundation's endowment.

Delta Air Lines Inc. Corporate Giving Program

This office covers much of the same territory as the company's foundation, but also makes grants in the arts. In-kind gifts for free air travel are made through this office. Donations come from allocations of current company revenues.

The Gap Foundation

www.gapinc.com

Most of the foundation's grantmaking is aimed at programs that assist young people, although they also make some grants in health, human services, the arts, and the environment. Grants are made "worldwide," according to their website.

Sears, Roebuck and Co. Contributions Program

www.sears.com/sr/misc/sears/about/communities/community_main.jsp

"Cause-related marketing" and sponsorships come from this office, as well as the huge donations in products. Local organizations can apply directly to local stores for contributions. Note that the Sears Foundation does not have a website.

People Research

AllTheWeb

www.alltheweb.com

This is a great all-purpose search engine.

American Medical Association

www.ama-assn.org

The American Medical Association will give you doctors by name or specialty with office addresses and educational background.

AnyWho

www.anywho.com

Based on AT&T information, AnyWho offers free national online telephone directories. Search results will usually return a complete address as well as the phone number.

Directory of Directors

www.directoryofdirectors.com

The Directory of Directors (a pay site) enables you to search by person or organization for information on both nonprofit *and* corporate affiliations.

EDGAR database

www.sec.gov/edgar.shmtl

Although the information in the Securities and Exchange Commission's EDGAR database is probably more esoteric than you will need, you should be aware that you can gain access to all SEC filings.

EDGAR Online

www.edgar-online.com

This site is more user friendly than the related EDGAR section on the SEC site. A lot of this site is only available to subscribers, but the people profiles might provide just the information you need.

FindArticles

www.findarticles.com

This site enables you to search on all periodicals (which will usually give you too many hits) or by sector (arts, business, science, and so on). Newspapers and magazines are included.

Google

www.google.com

Google is one of the best general search engines on the Internet.

LexisNexis

www.lexis-nexis.com

This is a very expensive tool that provides access to a database with information on some 200 million households and 700 million phone numbers, among other information. You might be able to gain free access at some business and academic libraries.

Martindale Directory of Lawyers

www.martindale.com

This site includes business address, area of practice, and the law school each lawyer graduated from.

Princeton Research Links

www.princeton.edu/Giving/devres/researchlinks.html

Researchers at Princeton have developed an excellent resource page for researching individuals.

Who's Who

www.marquiswhoswho.com

Who's Who (a pay site) has a long history of compiling biographical data on (according to their website) millions of people worldwide. Marquis is the publisher of the most comprehensive Who's Who.

Individual Grantseeker Resources

Community of Science
www.cos.com
The Community of Science offers information for the "global research and development community." You can sign up for a free weekly e-mail alert of new opportunities.

Grants for Individuals Online
gtionline.fdncenter.org
This is the Foundation Center's online directory of grants for individuals in all areas. This is an inexpensive pay service.

Michigan State University Research Links
www.lib.msu.edu/harris23/grants/3subject.htm
Researchers at Michigan State University have compiled this extensive list of links for grants for individuals. Because it is a university, it's not surprising that they have concentrated on scholarships.

NYFA Source
www.nyfa.org/source
This free database of more than 7,000 opportunities for artists in all disciplines includes dance, film, music, theatre, literature, and visual arts.

Poets & Writers
www.pw.org
This site lists recent grants and awards as well as classified ads and limited free access to Poets & Writers Magazine.

Society of Research Administrators International
www.srainternational.org
The Society of Research Administrators International offers information on RFPs and issues in research.

Writer's Digest
www.writersdigest.com
This site is full of information on the publishing business, although it's better for commercial (as opposed to literary) publishing.

Fiscal Sponsors

Dade Community Foundation (Miami, FL)
www.dadecommunityfoundation.org/Site/creating/types3.jsp
Sponsorship of projects of all kinds in the Miami, Dade County area are listed on this site. Many community foundations provide this service to area groups.

Dance Theatre Workshop (New York, NY)
www.dtw.org
Information about sponsorship for dance and music projects is provided.

Film Arts Foundation (San Francisco, CA)
www.filmarts.org/sponsoredpr/whatis.html
This organization offers sponsorship for film projects.

New York Foundation for the Arts (New York, NY)
www.nyfa.org/fs
Information on NYFA's sponsorship of emerging arts organizations and artist projects
in all artistic disciplines is described here. NYFA also offers an extensive list of other
arts fiscal sponsors at www.nyfa.org/files_uploaded/OtherFSPrograms.pdf.

The Rose Foundation (Oakland, CA)
www.rosefdn.org/grants/fiscal.html
The Rose Foundation sponsors environmental protection and community regeneration
projects.

Third Sector New England (Boston, MA)
www.tsne.org/section/36.html
Sponsorship for community coalitions and regional or national projects that share their
mission of creating healthy, sustainable communities and active democracy can be
found at this site.

Canadian Resources

Canadian Center for Philanthropy
www.ccp.ca
The CCP offers similar services to the U.S. Foundation Center, including publications
on philanthropy and funder directories. Its online directory includes 1,200 Canadian
foundations. In addition to the types of searches offered by the Foundation Center, the
CCP service enables you to narrow your search by the type of foundation and total
grants made—a very useful enhancement.

Canadian Environmental Grantmakers Network
www.cegn.org
This site provides a database of funders to environmental causes in Canada, all with
links to their websites. Membership in the Network gives you access to additional
information.

Philanthropic Foundations Canada
www.pfc.ca
This site provides a series of links to member foundation sites and to sites covering various aspects of philanthropy from a national membership organization for Canada's
independent, grantmaking foundations.

Sample Foundation Grant Proposal

The proposal that follows was sent to a large corporate foundation that had not previously funded us. Before the proposal was sent, a board member called her contact at the foundation to ask for a meeting, and the executive director subsequently met with the company foundation's president.

Because this was a new funder, a capsule history of New York Foundation for the Arts (NYFA) and some recent accomplishments are given in the cover letter. Note that the cover letter and the proposal both seek to provide a context for the grant that extends beyond NYFA's own needs. It expresses how the grant will increase service to our constituencies. It also speaks to how the technology upgrade will provide greater efficiency in operations. There is no "knowing of your interest" phrase in this cover letter, but this foundation's interest was in increasing institutional capacity, so the entire proposal indirectly addresses their interests.

The section headings in the proposal are from this funder's guidelines, but they are similar to what most funders will want.

This foundation awarded us a $25,000 grant.

Ms. Ann Smythe
President
Company Foundation
89 Center Street
Anytown, CT 06400

Dear Ms. Smythe:

On behalf of the New York Foundation for the Arts, I am writing to request support from Company Foundation in the amount of $40,000 for a major, organization-wide technology upgrade at the New York Foundation for the Arts (NYFA). This upgrade will increase our organizational capacity and strengthen the long-term effectiveness of our service to artists and arts organizations in New York and beyond.

Established in 1971 as an arts service organization to facilitate the development of arts activities throughout the State, NYFA serves individual artists, promotes their freedom to develop and create, and provides the broader public with opportunities to experience and understand their work. Throughout its history NYFA has explored multiple ways of developing and providing grants, technology planning, and informational services to respond to the needs of a diverse and ever-changing arts community.

Entering its thirty-first year of operation, NYFA has firmly established itself as the leading arts service organization in New York, and is now poised to enter a critical juncture in its institutional development. Many members of the corporate and foundation community have a long-standing relationship with NYFA, and have leveraged their investments on NYFA's success in providing artists with the support and practical assistance they need to move from the initial inspiration to creating art. In recognition of significant support for NYFA's technology upgrade, the Fidelity Foundation would receive logo exposure on our Web site and recognition in NYFA's donor newsletter, our quarterly arts journal, *FYI*, which is available nationally and has a readership of 70,000, and in our biennial report.

Repeatedly, both artists and funders turn to NYFA to help meet the most pressing needs of the arts community. During the past twelve months, there have been three prominent examples of this involving all parts of the arts community:

- *Culture Counts: Strategies for a More Vibrant Cultural Life for New York City*, the culmination of a year-long study of the impact of arts funding by the NYC Department of Cultural Affairs

- New York Arts Recovery Fund, a comprehensive effort to address immediate, short-term, and long-term challenges facing New York's artists and arts organizations most affected by the 9/11/01 national tragedy

- Development of a national information service for artists in collaboration with the Urban Institute

The first two initiatives required a high degree of cooperation and participation from New York's diverse cultural community. NYFA was able to obtain this and as a result has made significant contributions to the cultural life of New York City. The third project called on NYFA's expertise in providing information to artists in all disciplines to a degree unequalled by any organization in the United States.

Over the past ten years, NYFA's programs and services to the field have expanded and undergone many changes, our organizational budget has grown from $5.5 to $16.7 million and NYFA's staff has grown by 35 percent. As the next step of NYFA's long-term technology plan, we will be upgrading workstations and software, networking hardware, server, and server software to increase efficency and aid in communication—all with the aim of more effectively fulfilling our mission to invest in individual artists and the broader arts community.

Although NYFA has been a pioneer in exploring new possibilities enabled by the recent information technology revolution, convening landmark conferences on the intersection of arts and technology, and in providing financial support and services to artists and arts organizations seeking to use the Internet or build organizational capacity, it has never received a significant donation for the sole purpose of upgrading internal technology systems. We have received small donations of second-generation equipment from individual donors and corporations, but the vast majority of our computer workstations, printers, and various file servers have been leased and/or purchased on an ad-hoc basis with funds from general operating support.

A grant of this magnitude from the Company Foundation would be an investment in the contemporary artists and artist-centered organizations we serve at a key moment in NYFA's institutional history, bringing our infrastructure up to a level more appropriate to our preeminence among arts service organizations.

I am grateful for your kind consideration of this request, and welcome any questions or suggestions you might have regarding NYFA, its programs, or its goals. Please contact me at 212-555-1212 extension 201 or by e-mail at exec@nyfa.org should you have any questions about this proposal.

Sincerely,

Executive Director

Proposal to the Company Foundation for a grant of $40,000 to implement NYFA's Technology Plan

Introduction

The New York Foundation for the Arts (NYFA) was established in 1971 as an arts service organization to facilitate the development of arts activities throughout the State. NYFA serves individual artists, promotes their freedom to develop and create, and provides the broader public with opportunities to experience and understand their work. NYFA also collaborates on the development of regional, national, and international initiatives.

As one of the country's preeminent arts-service organizations, much of our work is conducted using computers and information technology. Over the past ten years, NYFA's programs and services to the field have expanded and undergone many changes, our organizational budget has grown from $5.5 to $16.7 million and NYFA's staff has grown by 35 percent. We have gone from conducting only a portion of our work on computers to conducting almost all of our programs and internal tasks using various forms of new technology.

NYFA is in a leadership position regarding issues arising from the intersections of arts, arts organizations, and technology. In 1997 NYFA became the first organization in the country to offer Artist Fellowships ($7,000 unrestricted cash grant) in the Computer Arts. The 1988 Orcas Conference, "Creative Support for the Creative Artist" gave rise to NYFA's Arts Wire program, the first national online network to provide the arts community with a communications network that incorporated the Web sites of individual artists, and community-based cultural groups, and offered technical assistance and information regarding online and computer arts. In 1998, in partnership with the New York State Council on the Arts (NYSCA), NYFA planned and coordinated the Governor's Conference on Arts & Technology "Circuits @ NYS—the arts in the Digital Age." Our Knowledge In Technology (KIT) program has provided technology planning workshops to groups of arts organizations located in various regions of New York and the greater Northeast (including Arts Boston), and Washington, D.C., and The Arts & Technology Technical Assistance Program (TechTAP) provides subsidies for computer systems consultants, staff training, and/or professional development.

As with so many nonprofits that are primarily program-focused, we had never stepped back to make or implement our own comprehensive, organization-wide Technology Plan. This we did between February and September 2001, working first with a cross-department committee before involving the seasoned expertise of outside consultants and the entire staff in the process. The result was a clear direction and mission for NYFA's technology needs.

The external section of the plan calls for a reassessment of our Web site and the development of a strategy of employing e-mail effectively, both of which are in progress. The main needs identified in the internal section of NYFA's Technology Plan were to ...

◆ **Unify databases:** Each department maintained separate databases, making for overlaps and inaccuracies.

◆ **Configure a group calendar:** Keeping all of NYFA's 50 employees current on NYFA activities is difficult at best. An electronic group calendar was a crying need, as was an Intranet to post everything from the graphic style manual to the news of the day.

◆ **Upgrade workstations:** Computers had been added as staff was added, with the newest employees usually receiving the newest machines and (at that time) current basic software. Older machines were seldom upgraded to match, resulting in employees working side by side on similar tasks with greatly varying tools to accomplish them.

Since completion of the plan, three of the five major databases at NYFA have been combined, making a marked change in how those three departments operate and immediately increasing cooperation among them. In addition, an Intranet site was begun in December 2001 and continues as a work in progress. The group calendar feature requires new software and hardware that is part of this proposal, as well as the workstation upgrade.

Project Description

With assistance from our network consultants, NYFA has developed a plan for an organization-wide computer equipment and network upgrade. The workstation and file server upgrade is the next—and critical—step in the implementation of the larger technology plan, addressing concerns such as optimizing time management, increasing overall systems efficiency, and standardizing programs and processes.

Currently, 22 out of 48 workstations use the all-but-obsolete Windows 95 operating system, 20 use the later model Windows 98, and the others use the newer Windows 2000. This mix of platforms means that various staff members do not have access to the same tools; for example, those with Windows 95 cannot upgrade other software such as Internet Explorer to the current versions. Also, the older machines simply work slower, making it impossible for employees to work at their maximum capabilities. In addition many older machines lack CD drives, which means that they cannot access files sent to them on CD from outside the organization. Perhaps more importantly, this means that adding any new software is more laborious, because the CD has become the preferred means for new software to be distributed.

Under the IT upgrade, old workstations will be replaced with new, Pentium IV machines operating with Windows XP platforms, along with new Microsoft Office XP software. This organization-wide workstation consistency will make training new employees easier (because everyone will be working with the same system) and allow future upgrades to be done in a consistent and efficient manner.

It is also necessary to upgrade the file server at the same time as the individual workstations. NYFA is now using an IBM NT Server leased since 1997. Though it was state of the art in 1997 computer technology, it falls significantly short of the capacity and speed needed to run a 48-station network today. As part of this systems upgrade, NYFA will purchase a new IBM Series 240, Pentium III Server, with the complementary software. The new server has the capacity to create a parallel copy of all data on a separate drive. With this facility, should the main hard drive fail, a new one can be installed while the network continues to operate off of the "ghost" drive. In addition, the greater capacity of the server necessitates a new backup drive and tapes. Data security is critical to any system, and particularly at NYFA, which is a national clearinghouse for information and resources artists rely on for their career needs.

Rationale

Strategy: NYFA recently completed a strategic plan for institutional advancement, the primary goals of which are to 1) conduct research and analysis about artists, art making, and arts funders, 2) sustain and create programs of the highest standards, and 3) primarily serve individual artists but always recognize the critical dynamics among art making, arts organizations, donors, and the public perception of artists' value to society. NYFA's Technology Planning Committee took these goals into consideration in prioritizing the implementation process and underscored the primary need for standardized operating systems and increased server capacity.

Tangible results: As mentioned in the previous description, the systems upgrade will:

♦ Make training new and present employees much quicker and easier, increasing workflow and freeing up time for senior staff.

◆ Make CD drives standard technology in each workstation, increasing the ease of adding new software or viewing of CDs sent from outside the organization.

◆ Optimize the speed and reinforce the security of the file server, which not only saves time, but often means the difference between having an accessible and reliable archive and being unprepared.

Long-term organizational potential: With more and more artists and others wishing to take advantage of NYFA's services, but with funding relatively static at best, we must work more efficiently to continue to serve our constituencies. The technology upgrade's major long-term benefits will be in optimizing staff time and workflow, increasing service to the field, and enabling efficient time management.

Agenda

Implementation and evaluation of the NYFA computer systems upgrade will take one year to complete:

June to August 2002	inventory/consolidation of organizational file server
August to September	begin purchase and installation of new equipment, staff training
October to December	purchase remaining equipment and assess progress, launch some new program components
March to July 2003	organization-wide, program-wide evaluation of systems upgrade
August 2003	generate final report

Evaluation

To ensure that NYFA's technology equipment upgrade is properly implemented and brought to optimal effectiveness, NYFA will follow a rigorous evaluation procedure throughout the year. We will survey staff on special software needs and inventory all existing hardware to determine if any parts are upgradeable. We will then refine the purchase documents. We will seek evaluations of all staff following the initial training on the new machines and provide additional training based on those findings. We will again ask staff to evaluate the functionality of their new equipment after two months of use and make adjustments based on that evaluation.

Past Technology Support

Although NYFA has been a pioneer in exploring new possibilities enabled by the recent information technology revolution, convening landmark conferences on the intersection of arts and technology, and in providing financial support and services to artists and arts organizations seeking to use the Internet or build organizational capacity, it has never received a significant donation for the sole purpose of upgrading internal technology systems. We have received small donations of second-generation equipment from individual donors and corporations, but the vast majority of our computer workstations, printers, and various file servers have been leased and/or purchased on an ad-hoc basis with funds from general operating support.

Attachments [only the Project Budget is included here]:

◆ Project Budget

◆ NYFA Organizational Profile

◆ FY01 Audited Financial Statement

◆ FY02 Organizational Budget

◆ Funders List

◆ IRS 501(c)(3) determination letter

◆ Biennial Report for FY00 and FY01

New York Foundation for the Arts
Information Technology Systems Upgrade Project Budget

EXPENSES		July 02–June 03	
	Hours	Rate	Total
PERSONNEL			
Staff allocation			$22,000
Fringe Benefits			$3,960
Server installation and setup (consultants)	32	$135	$4,320
Workstation installation and setup (consultants)	52	$135	$7,020
Subtotal			**$37,300**
PROJECT COSTS	Unit	Qty.	Total
Workstations			
Pentium 4 processors w/Windows 2000 Professional	$1,104	33	$36,432
E74 17-inch Black CRT Monitor	$194	20	$3,880
Microsoft Office Professional Upgrade	$284	44	$12,496
GHOST Corporate Edition Licensing	$31	33	$1,023
Media kits (CDs) for MS Office and GHOST	$41	1	$41
Subtotal			**$53,872**
Server and Networking Hardware			
24-prog HP ProCurve Switch (hardware connect to workstations)	$899	3	$2,697
IBM X Series 240 Pentium 3 1 GHZ Server w/4 36.4 GB hard drives, RAM upgrade	$7,006	1	$7,006
250W HS Redundant Power Supply	$224	1	$224
APC Smart Uninterruptible Power Source	$670	1	$670

continues

continued

New York Foundation for the Arts
Information Technology Systems Upgrade Project Budget

PROJECT COSTS	Unit	Qty.	Total
Backup Tape Drive (100/200GB LTO Int. SCSI)	$3,035	1	$3,035
Backup LTO Tapes	$107	12	$1,284
Subtotal			**$14,916**
Server Software and Accessories			
Lotus Notes calendar software and customization for server	$5,200	1	$5,200
Windows 2000 Server License	$704	1	$704
Windows 2000 Server Client Access License and Media	$32	44	$1,408
Backup Exec. NT Windows 2K 8.6 Server, Open File opt.	$935	1	$935
Accessories	$74	1	$222
Subtotal			**$8,469**
SUB-TOTAL: PROJECT COSTS			**$77,257**
TOTAL EXPENSES			**$114,557**
INCOME			
Requested from Company Foundation			$40,000
Other pending foundation proposals			$40,000
Allocation from FY02 GOS			$34,557
TOTAL INCOME			**$114,557**
SURPLUS/(DEFICIT)			**$--**

Sample Corporate Grant Proposal

In this case, a meeting with the funder helped guide what we would apply for to this corporate giving program, which you'll note from the address was in the Public Affairs department. The letter reads much like a sponsorship proposal it is backed up with a proposal similar to a foundation proposal; however, note the prominent section on "public visibility." Note also that the amount requested is a range ($10,000 to $25,000) such as would appear in a sponsorship proposal. This hybrid approach is common when seeking corporate support, particularly if applying to an office other than a corporate foundation.

Cover Letter

Ms. Janet Kinard
Manager
Strategic Giving, Public Affairs
Big Corporation, Inc.
987 Main Street
New York, NY 10000

Dear Janet,

Thank you for taking the time to meet with me yesterday to discuss how the New York Foundation for the Arts and Big Corporation, Inc. might work together on a project. Artists in the Branches presents an excellent opportunity for Big Corporation, Inc. to make a significant impact on access to the arts on a grassroots, community level. Furthermore, any grant you make will release an equal amount from the challenge grant we have recently received from the New York City Department of Cultural Affairs.

A full description of the project is enclosed. This project will:

♦ provide increased access to the arts through branch libraries in neighborhoods with limited arts programming,

♦ introduce local artists to their surrounding community,

♦ help support artists by providing an honorarium and helping them to develop an audience for their work, and

♦ develop a publicity and marketing kit that will be used for the regular Artists & Audiences Exchange program for years to come.

The pilot program involves ten events (two in each borough) over a period of six months, reaching an audience of around 1,000. The publicity and marketing kit developed through this pilot will be used annually by as many as 100 community organizations statewide for years to come. Event sponsors include community centers, senior centers, public schools, local arts groups, and groups working with young people. Please see the enclosed list of sponsor organizations from the last two years. Although events take place statewide, 70 percent were held in New York City.

As a major funder to this project, Big Corporation, Inc. will be prominently credited in:

♦ the programs prepared for each event,

♦ flyers announcing each event distributed to and posted at community arts, education, and social service groups,

- bookmarks distributed throughout the New York, Brooklyn, and Queens library systems,

- advertisements taken in neighborhood newspapers (such as the *Amsterdam News*, *The Brooklyn Skyline*, *New York Press*, *Village Voice*, *Bronx Times Reporter*, *Asian-American Times*, and *Queens Times*),

- all press releases,

- announcements and reports on the project in NYFA's quarterly newsletter, *FYI*, with a subscription base of more than 24,000 statewide and a readership of nearly 80,000,

- NYFA's annual report, and

- NYFA's website.

A publicist will be working with us to get the word out for each event and to help develop the publicity and marketing kit. *Big Corporation, Inc.'s support for this pilot program would also be prominently acknowledged on this kit*, which we expect will be used by more than two hundred community groups within the following three years.

We must raise $24,500 by June 1 to meet the challenge grant requirements, and we hope that Big Corporation, Inc. will join us in this project with a contribution of $10,000 to $25,000.

Should you have any questions or need any additional details about the pilot project, I can be reached at (212) 366-6900, ext 211, or via e-mail at wt@nyfa.org. Your kind consideration of this proposal is greatly appreciated.

Sincerely,

Waddy Thompson
Director of External Affairs

Enclosed:

- Full program description

- Program budget

- Background

- List of sponsor organizations [not included as part of this example]

- Copy of 501(c)(3) letter [not included here]

- Audited financial statement [not included here]

Proposal

Proposal to Big Corporation, Inc. to Support Artists in the Branches

The New York Foundation for the Arts respectfully requests a grant from Big Corporation, Inc. in the amount of **$10,000–25,000** to support NYFA's **Artists in the Branches** program. This grant would be applied toward a $24,500 matching grant from the New York City Department of Cultural Affairs to provide free arts events throughout New York City.

One of the conclusions of the recent study completed by NYFA, *Culture Counts*, indicated that a majority of New Yorkers wanted to attend more cultural events than they currently are able to attend. The greatest impediments to attending cultural events were transportation and price. NYFA's Artists & Audiences Exchange program surmounts both these obstacles by providing free arts events in local communities.

The Exchange is part of NYFA's signature program, Artists' Fellowships, which invests in the creative potential of individual artists. Since 1985, this program has provided direct financial assistance—$7,000 merit-based cash awards—to emerging artists living and working throughout New York, in sixteen artistic disciplines—providing resources critical to an artist's ability to focus time, energy, and money on his or her work. From 140 to 160 artists each year receive these fellowships. Artists' Fellowships has a track record of identifying and supporting major artists early in their careers. Past recipients include 5 winners of the Pulitzer Prize and 15 of the MacArthur Foundation's "genius awards."

The Exchange encourages Fellows to present their work through free public events (readings, workshops, lectures, performances, demonstrations, or other activities) in collaboration with a non-arts, nonprofit host organization to reach audiences that might not seek out arts events.

For Artists in the Branches, NYFA will coordinate and promote 10 Exchange events around New York City involving 10 to 28 artists of various disciplines based on the Artists & Audiences Exchange program. We expect the events to average 100 attendees, giving the program an audience of 1,000. To tie these events to local communities, the events will be presented in collaboration with branch libraries. Each event will be free and open to the public. Like the Exchange, Artists in the Branches is a crucial means to promote greater awareness and understanding of the artist's craft and creative process, as well as a means to reach out to New York communities with limited exposure and access to the arts. These events differ from other free arts offerings through the inclusion of living creative artists (composers, writers, choreographers, painters, and so on), many of whom live and work in the same communities as those who attend the events.

Audiences will be able to identify contemporary art as something that is alive and part of their own community. Through this grassroots approach, the minds of the audience will be awakened to the possibilities of art in their lives and the image of the creative artist will be enhanced.

Artists will be chosen through a Request for Proposals that will be sent to 3,000 past Fellows by NYFA's Grants Department. In this way, NYFA will be able to choose artists who demonstrate a desire to work with the community and whose artistic abilities have already been evaluated through the Fellowship program's peer panels. After initial review by program staff at NYFA, final selection of artists will be coordinated with the events department at each of the three library systems. A program coordinator will oversee the RFP process, selection of artists, and execution of events.

Public Visibility: Publicity and marketing for the events will be handled by NYFA through means such as press releases to community publications, bookmarks with event information distributed through the libraries and local schools, and guerrilla marketing techniques such as posting flyers on community bulletin boards and in local gathering spots such as bookstores and restaurants.

NYFA normally plays a passive role in Exchange events, limited to paying the artist upon confirmation that the event took place. With Artists in the Branches, NYFA will take an active role by connecting artists with communities now lacking free events such as these and will take the lead in publicizing the events—something usually falling to the sponsoring organization. The benefits of this approach are many.

- ◆ Underserved areas will have new art events.

- ◆ Libraries will be able to market to new audiences.

- ◆ Fellows will receive additional exposure through greater attendance at these events.

- ◆ NYFA will gain new visibility in these communities.

As the conclusion of this project, NYFA will create a model public relations kit for sponsors to use in future years. The goal of the kit is to improve the publicity of all Exchange events and help local sponsors articulate the value of individual artists to their communities. By developing improved communications mechanisms, this project will indirectly benefit the 150 to 165 Fellows who participate in Exchange events in subsequent years.

Evaluation: Each Artists in the Branches event will be attended by a senior NYFA staff member. NYFA staff will also be available to assist libraries in securing any special equipment needed for the presentations. A meeting will be held with the library event coordinators at the conclusion of the project to receive feedback from the libraries. It is hoped that the bonds formed during the execution of this program will lead to branch libraries sponsoring more of the regular Artists and Audiences Exchange events.

Conclusion: Artists in the Branches is just one of the programs that helps fulfill NYFA's mission to serve individual artists, promote their freedom to develop and create, and provide the broader public with opportunities to experience and understand their work. This project allows NYFA to concentrate on the neighborhoods of New York City in which free arts events are not a regular occurrence. It also allows Fellowship recipients make their work known to a wider public.

Funding from Big Corporation, Inc. will help NYFA meet the Department of Cultural Affairs' Challenge to match their $24,500 award, and in turn, provide communities throughout the city with free access to the arts that they might not normally have.

Budget

Artists in the Branches

Expenses

Personnel

Project coordinator @ 30%	$11,800
Communications officer @ 5%	$2,000
Fringe @ 18%	$2,484
Subtotal salaried personnel	$16,284
Artist fees	$24,000
Total personnel	$40,284

Direct expenses

Space rentals/utilities (in-kind by libraries)	$15,000
Equipment rental/supplies	$2,250
Postage	$1,000
Travel/transportation	$750
Advertising/promotion/marketing	$5,200
Printing of model PR kit	$2,000
Total direct expenses	$26,200

Indirect expenses @ 12%	$8,016

Total Expenses	**$74,500**

Income

Requested from Big Corporation, Inc.	$20,000
Department of Cultural Affairs (committed pending a 1:1 match)	$24,500
Library systems in-kind	$15,000
A. Family foundation (pending)	$10,000
H. Family foundation (pending)	$5,000

Total Income	**$74,500**

Surplus/(Deficit)	**$0**

Background

Background

The New York Foundation for the Arts was established in 1971 as an independent arts service organization to facilitate the development of arts activities throughout New York. NYFA supports the creative evolution and development of individual artists and arts organizations in all artistic disciplines. From its inception, the Foundation has functioned as a creative development corporation, catalyst, and incubator for innovations in the arts.

The New York Foundation for the Arts serves individual artists, promotes their freedom to develop and create, and provides the broader public with opportunities to experience and understand their work. NYFA accomplishes this by offering financial and informational assistance to artists and organizations that directly serve artists, by supporting arts programming in the larger community, and by building collaborative relationships with others who advocate for the arts in New York and throughout the country.

NYFA's current programs include: *grants* that empower artists to create and share their work and promote public understanding of the arts; *services* that help artists and arts organizations find the tools they need to survive, including fiscal sponsorship, technical assistance, administrative support, and financial aid; *technology* initiatives that create communication networks, provide access to resources and information, and offer training and support in addressing new technology trends; *education* opportunities that enable schools and communities to implement or improve their arts in education programs and allow artists to apply their expertise in the public forum, expanding the cultural and educational opportunities available to artists, children, educators, administrators, and the general public.

NYFA was recently awarded a Challenge Grant from the New York City Department of Cultural Affairs to enhance Artists & Audiences Exchange, the public service component of NYFA's Artists' Fellowships program. Artists in the Branches will consist of collaboration between current and previous NYFA Fellows and public libraries to provide additional free events throughout the five boroughs of New York City. Two events will take place in each borough from July through December 2001, allowing communities to have direct, intimate access to award-winning emerging artists and their work, while providing Fellows with additional exposure and responses from new audiences. A major element of this project is a concentrated publicity and marketing campaign that will be developed to serve as a model for all Exchange events.

Sample Sponsorship Proposal

Although sponsorship proposals not really grant proposals, many grant writers are asked to create these proposals as well. The differences between the two are described in Chapter 4.

The following proposal is for a fictional bicycle ride-a-thon to support the local AIDS service organization. Other than this short letter and one page giving the specifics the marketing director will want to know, the only enclosures would be no more than three press reports and one sample of a printed item from a previous year's event showing prominent sponsor credit.

It is particularly important not to bulk up sponsorship proposals with extraneous information. They won't be looked at. There is very little here about this agency's good works. The good works are not the point here. The agency's reputation and the audience it can deliver are the selling points.

Note that at the end of the fact sheet the overhead rate for the event has been given. This is not something you would ordinarily do. Big fund-raising events such as this, however, have been criticized in the press in recent years for the very low percentage returned to the charity (sometimes as low as 20 percent). By letting them know that 75 percent of the money raised goes to the charity, a potential concern has been averted before it is raised. A budget is not enclosed with this initial request, but would be supplied on request from the company.

Cover Letter

February 1, 2003

Mr. Martin Doyle
Marketing Director
Anytown Daily News
1 News Square
Anytown, SC 29000

Dear Mr. Doyle:

Thank you for speaking with me this afternoon about Anytown Daily News' sponsoring the AIDS Ride 2003. Anytown Daily News has covered this event in the past, attesting to the interest it holds for the entire community. The presence of Morgan Whitney (fresh from her recent box-office busting film) is sure to attract attention from a wide range of electronic and print media.

The money raised from this event is as important today as it was when we held the first AIDS Ride in 1990, but maintaining the public's interest in conquering this disease has become increasingly difficult. This is why a partnership with Anytown Daily News is so important to the success of the event. The pro bono advertising we discussed will be critical in recruiting riders and will also play a role in increasing public awareness of the dangers that risky sexual behavior continue to present.

Community AIDS Services has a constituency that we believe Anytown Daily News will find very attractive, especially the young demographics that advertisers relish. Through signage at the event and press reports (including television and radio), Anytown Daily News will be presented as an important supporter of this worthwhile cause.

I've outlined the benefits we can offer you, as well as given specific demographics on the audience based on past events on the enclosed sheet. As we discussed, for status as a category exclusive sponsor, we would be looking for a cash donation of $5,000 to $10,000 in addition to pro bono advertisements of a quarter page or larger in each of the four weeks leading up to the event.

Please consider everything in this letter a point of departure for additional conversations. I look forward to working with you to refine this partnership to our mutual advantage.

Sincerely,

Betty Sanders
Director of External Affairs

Demographics and Details Sheet

Benefits to Anytown Daily News as Exclusive Media Sponsor of AIDS Ride 2003

1. Exposure to the 11,000 people either participating in or attending the start and finish of the AIDS Ride 2003

2. Exposure to the 4,000 supporters of Community AIDS Services through monthly newsletter

3. Prominent acknowledgement in all press releases, advertisements, and mailings associated with the AIDS Ride 2003

4. Celebrity participation (actress Morgan Whitney) is likely to draw significant press attention

5. Status as sole media sponsor excludes any competitors from participating

6. Opportunity to be associated in the minds of all who hear of the event with the local agency that has done more than any other in Anytown to provide services to people living with HIV/AIDS

Audience Demographics

Riders: average age 31, 60 percent male, household income between $40,000 and $55,000, college degree or higher

Starting and finish line audience: average age 29, 70 percent female, household income between $40,000 and $55,000, some college

Supporters of Community AIDS Services: average age 42, 65 percent female, household income $55,000 to $75,000, some college

Event Details

Date:	June 16, 2003
What:	Bicycle ride to raise money to fight AIDS
Where:	A 13-mile route starting and ending in front of City Hall with a route through the main business district and City Park
Who:	800 riders and an estimated 10,000 spectators

All funds raised will support Community AIDS Services programs for people with AIDS. Donated labor and products allows this event to operate with a low overhead of 25 percent.

Sample Government Grant Proposal

This is an application for the Federal Technology Opportunities program, which the Department of Commerce refers to as the TOP program. Typical of many government grant applications, this one combines a form with a formal written proposal.

This grant is for a fairly complicated project involving services to several constituencies, requiring us to build a case for the needs and benefits of each audience. This contributed to the application's length. The section headings are those requested by the funder. The form follows the narrative portion of the application. This proposal was still under consideration when this book was written.

OMB Approval No. 0348-0043

Application for Federal Assistance

2. DATE SUBMITTED 04/22/2003	Application Identifier

1. TYPE OF SUBMISSION:		3. DATE RECEIVED BY STATTE	State Application Identifier

1. TYPE OF SUBMISSION:

Application
- ☐ Construction
- ■ Non-Construction

Preapplication
- ☐ Construction
- ☐ Non-Construction

4. DATE RECEIVED BY FEDERAL AGENCY	Federal Identifier
	1783 (Rev 6)

5. APPLICANT INFORMATION

Legal Name New York Foundation for the Arts	Organizational Unit Information & Research

Address *(give city, county, state, and zip code)* 155 Avenue of the Americas 14th Floor New York, NY 10013 - 1507 New York	Name and telephone number of the person to be contacted on matters involving this application *(give area code)* Mr. Theodore S. Berger 212 - 366 - 6900 Ext. 201 tberger@nyfa.org

6. EMPLOYER IDENTIFICATION NUMBER (EIN):

2 3 — 7 1 2 9 5 6 4

7. TYPE OF APPLICANT: *(Enter appropriate letter in box)* ☒ N

A. State
B. County
C. Municipal
D. Township
E. Interstate
F. Intermunicipal
G. Special District

H. Independent School District
I. State Controled Institution of Higher Education
J. Private University
K. Indian Tribe
L. Individual
M. Profit Organization
N. Other *(specify)* non-profit organization

8. TYPE OF APPLICATION:

■ New   ☐ Continuation   ☐ Revision

If revision, enter appropriate letter(s) in box(es): ☐ ☐

A. Increase Award   B. Decrease Award   C. Increase Duration

D. Decrease Duration   E. Other *(specify)*:

9. NAME OF FEDERAL AGENCY:

National Telecommunications and Information Administration

10. CATALOG OF FEDERAL DOMESTIC ASSISTANCE NUMBER: 11.552 TITLE: Technology Opportunities Program	11. DESCRIPTIVE TITLE OF APPLICANT'S PROJECT: Empowering Communities through Interactivity

12. AREAS AFFECTED BY PROJECT *(cities, counties, states, etc.)*
1) New York's 8th Congressional District
2) All Congressional Districts throughout the United States as well as U.S. Territories

13. PROPOSED PROJECT:

Start Date	Ending Date
10/01/2003	06/30/2005

14. CONGRESSIONAL DISTRICTS OF:

a. Applicant	b. Project
8	All congressional districts

15. ESTIMATED FUNDING:

a. Federal	$	248,700	.00
b. Applicant	$	25,000	.00
c. State	$	0	.00
d. Local	$	0	.00
e. Other	$	233,000	.00
f. Program Income	$	0	.00
g. TOTAL	$	506,700	.00

16. IS APPLICATION SUBJECT TO REVIEW BY STATE EXECUTIVE ORDER 12372 PROCESS?

a. YES THIS APPLICATION WAS MADE AVAILABLE TO THE STATE EXECUTIVE ORDER 12372 PROCESS FOR REVIEW ON:

DATE _____

b. NO ☐ PROGRAM IS NOT COVERED BY E.O. 12372

■ OR PROGRAM HAS NOT BEEN SELECTED BY STATE FOR REVIEW

17. IS THE APPLICANT DELINQUENT ON ANY FEDERAL DEBT?

☐ Yes If "Yes," attach an explanation   No ■

18. TO THE BEST OF MY KNOWLEDGE AND BELIEF, ALL DATA IN THIS APPLICATION/PREAPPLICATION ARE TRUE AND CORRECT. THE DOCUMENT HAS BEEN DULY AUTHORIZED BY THE BOVERNING BODY OF THE APPLICANT AND THE APPLICANT WILL COMPLY WITH THE ATTACHED ASSURANCES IF THE ASSISTANCE IS AWARDED.

a. Typed name of Authorized Representative Mr. Theodore S. Berger	b. Title Executive Director	c. Telephone Number 212 - 366 - 6900
d. Signature of Authorized Representative		e. Date Signed

Previous Edition Usable

Standard Form 424 (REV 4-92)
Prescribed by OMB Circular A-102

Authorized for Local Reproduction

BUDGET INFORMATION - Non-Construction Programs

OMB Approval No. 0348-0044

SECTION A - BUDGET SUMMARY

Grant Program Function or Activity (a)	Catalog of Federal Domestic Assistance Number (b)	Estimated Unobligated Funds		New or Revised Budget		
		Federal (c)	Non-Federal (d)	Federal (e)	Non-Federal (f)	Total (g)
1. NTIA/TOP	11.552	$	$	$ 248,700	$ 258,000	$ 506,700
2.						
3.						
4.						
5. Totals		$	$	$ 248,700	$ 258,000	$ 506,700

SECTION B - BUDGET CATEGORIES

6. Object Class Categories	GRANT PROGRAM, FUNCTION OR ACTIVITY				Total (5)
	(1) FEDERAL	(2) NON-FEDERAL	(3)	(4)	
a. Personnel	$ 90,000	$ 94,000	$ 0	$	$ 184,000
b. Fringe Benefits	16,700	17,400	0		34,100
c. Travel	0	200	0		200
d. Equipment	0	3,000	0		3,000
e. Supplies	0	400	0		400
f. Contractual	70,000	70,000	0		140,000
g. Construction	0	0	0		0
h. Other	50,000	50,000	0		100,000
i. Total Direct Charges (sum of 6a-6h)	226,700	235,000	0		461,700
j. Indirect Charges	22,000	23,000	0		45,000
k. TOTALS (sum of 6i and 6j)	$ 248,700	$ 258,000	$ 0	$	$ 506,700
7. Program Income	$	$	$	$	$

Authorized for Local Reproduction

Standard Form 424A (Rev. 7-97)
Prescribed by OMB Circular A-102

Previous Edition Usable

Executive Summary

New York Foundation for the Arts

The New York Foundation for the Arts (NYFA) requests a $248,700 grant through the Technology Opportunities Program for Empowering Communities through Interactivity, by way of NYFA's Web site.

Primary Goal of Empowering Communities through Interactivity: to continue the evolution of the most comprehensive, innovative, user-friendly, all-encompassing set of information resources for those who work in, create, and enjoy the arts.

We will develop and implement new tools to increase interactivity with our professional constituencies (artists; arts organizations), online learning opportunities to create artist entrepreneurs, and enhanced informational resources for the public. These will include:

- An online interface for foundations, publications, and arts organizations nationwide to submit updates to their listings in the opportunities database (NYFA Source). This will allow us to use staff time more efficiently and encourage organizations to keep information current.

- An online interface for more than 3,300 artists in the NYFA Artists gallery to submit work samples and update biographical and contact information online. This, too, will increase staff efficiency and keep the information current.

- Online business tutorials to foster artist entrepreneurs that can take charge of their careers and move away from a patronage system

- New offerings for the art-curious public; we will develop original content for the site, link to resources offered by others and develop innovative ways to integrate the two.

Anticipated Outcomes:
-greater ease of use and greater information resources for artists in all disciplines

-updated information on opportunities in the arts, assisting both the artists who use the information and the organizations whose information is posted

-more NYFA artists being better represented on our Web site, increasing their public recognition

-more artists being empowered to create and take advantage of business opportunities

-the public gaining a better understanding of what contemporary artists (in all disciplines) are about, and be willing seek to experience contemporary art as consumers, thus rewarding the artist entrepreneurs.

Continued engagement with the Urban Institute and Carnegie Mellon University's Center for Arts Management and Technology will provide research and programming services, continuing a relationship of over 3 years.

Federal Identifier: 1783 (Rev 6)

Proposal

NYFA Interactive—Empowering Communities through Interactivity

I. Organizational Mission: Project History

NYFA

The New York Foundation for the Arts (NYFA) serves individual artists, promotes their freedom to develop and create, and provides the broader public with opportunities to experience and understand their work.

Through its leadership in groundbreaking programs and large collaborative projects, NYFA has shown itself to be one of the most important cross-disciplinary institutions working on behalf of individual artists and arts organizations in New York State and nationwide. Established in 1971 as an arts service organization to facilitate the development of arts activities, NYFA offers financial and informational assistance to artists and organizations, supports arts programming in the larger community, and builds collaborative relationships with others who advocate for the arts in New York State and throughout the country.

As it reaches more and more artists and arts organizations nationally, and as the home of a multi-disciplinary artist information center with a national impact, NYFA is widely recognized as the "go to" organization by funders and arts practitioners when it comes to information for artists.

NYFA Interactive
Information & Research Department: History and Evolution

1992	With the introduction of **Artswire.org**, NYFA became the first arts organization to have a national online network for artists in all disciplines, and followed this development with the first email newsletter in the arts, *Arts Wire Current*.
1996	NYFA became the permanent home of the innovative and forward-looking **Visual Artist Information Hotline**, which provided visual artists with a person-to-person information service to empower them in the business aspects of their careers free of charge.
1999	NYFA's second Web site and first online home (www.nyfa.org) was launched as a comprehensive online brochure and catalogue of NYFA's mission, history, and programs.
2001	As part of a major national study of the support structures available to individual artists, NYFA entered into collaboration with the Urban Institute and Carnegie Mellon University's Center for Arts Management and Technology on the *Investing In Creativity* project. As a part of this project,

NYFA embarked on the creation of the **NYFA Source,** a free, national, comprehensive online information database for artists at all stages in their careers working in any of the disciplines.

2002 NYFA launched **NYFA Interactive,** the first step in consolidating what is the most comprehensive and diverse artist information resource in the world. NYFA Interactive is now the online center for all of NYFA's information programs: **NYFA Quarterly**, **NYFA Current**, and **NYFA Source**. Based on Web Trends reports, we estimate that the site will serve more than 800,000 unique users in its first full year.

II. Project Purposes

The primary purpose of **Empowering Communities through Interactivity** is to continue the evolution of the most comprehensive, innovative, user-friendly, all-encompassing set of information resources for those who work in, create, and enjoy the arts.

Needs and Solutions

By fall 2000, NYFA's Visual Artist Information Hotline was the most comprehensive resource of its kind in the country. This fact brought it to the attention of the Washington, DC-based **Urban Institute** (UI) as they began their two-year study of support mechanisms for U.S. Artists, culminating in the *Investing in Creativity* report (to be published this year). The need in the community was certainly there: NYFA Hotline's annual usage grew from approximately 4,000 artists per year in 1996 to over 38,000 in 2002. During 2001–2002, UI worked with NYFA, as well as **Carnegie Mellon University's Center for Arts Management and Technology**, to create the new NYFA Source database. Built upon the foundation of the former Hotline's resources, the new database was developed and implemented with a range of new technological features.

A. Individual artists

According to the National Endowment for the Arts, 80 percent of American artists (including actors, musicians and sculptors, among others), hold a second job. The moonlighting rate among artists is 40 percent higher than other professional workers. A recent report from a long-term study called ArtistFacts by the Research Center for Arts and Culture at Columbia University points out that over the past decade:

- the time artists spend working on their second jobs continues to increase,

- the time artists spend on their artwork continues to decrease,

- a decreasing number of artists own their workspaces, and

- a decreasing number of artists have health insurance.

It is for this reason that artists need free, efficient, and effective information resources. These resources can work toward both increasing artists' independence from traditional funders and resources, and increasing the national impact of art service organizations' programming. Toward these ends, NYFA has continued to adapt and expand its programs to help artists become better advocates and administrators of their own careers. NYFA Interactive is, in many ways, the heart of a network of free information services for artists, and visits have increased from 400,000 to 800,000 annual unique users as a result of the improvements of Phase I. In light of reduced funding in all sectors, it is important for users to have this resource at their fingertips.

Solutions

♦ During Phase II of NYFA Interactive, NYFA will create a new online feature that allows users to store the results of searches, building resource lists of foundations, publications, and other resources for future reference. This will be similar to many portal sites such as Yahoo. Users may then check the Web site as needed to view updated information on their programs.

♦ NYFA will design and launch an interactive online Business of Art tutorial for individual artists that provides artists with lessons and resources on how to become "artist entrepreneurs." This tutorial will include information such as setting goals, the arts universe, career and employment options, artist portfolio/ press package development, traditional and emergent venues for exhibition, making public presentations, marketing and public relations, grants management and proposal writing, income and taxation, and legal issues.

In the past, NYFA has offered this information to artists in all-day workshop format. NYFA has also recently developed this same kind of business of art information into a one-semester course to be taught at six Masters in Fine Art programs across the country starting this fall. However, information concerning the business of art needs to be made available on a much broader basis. With about 75,000 users monthly, NYFA's Web site would be the most suitable location to develop this information.

♦ NYFA will create a new online interface in the NYFA Artists ("gallery") pathway on NYFA's Web site that enables the more than 3,300 contemporary artists currently listed to self-submit updated information, including biographical changes, new work samples, and contact information. The NYFA Web site currently provides individual web pages for each artist, which, according to many artists, have been a tremendously visible tool for marketing their work. Artists have been including their new Web site information on applications for grants, residencies, and press materials. Currently, however, all edits and updates must be e-mailed to NYFA staff which then get uploaded to the Web site—usually on a weekly basis. A new online interface would allow artists to self-update their information and encourage them to keep their web pages up-to-date.

For artists nationwide, a new classified and event-listing service will be constructed and made available online. This service will provide artists, arts organizations, event organizers and others with low-cost, high-profile listings on NYFA's Web site designed to increase the visibility of contemporary arts events, literary and film releases, and performances nationwide. These listings will be circulated and referred to through the other areas on the site—such as the art curious section—in an effort to bring the constituencies we serve together through art and interactivity.

Phase II of NYFA Interactive will result in a savvy new cadre of independent artists who understand the intricacies and protocols for working and sustaining careers in competitive contemporary arts markets—both in the United States and abroad.

B. Foundations, art service organizations, and cultural institutions

As artists become more adept in administering their own careers, it is also evident that the practices of institutions and organizations working in the cultural sector are becoming more ambitious, transparent, proactive, and sensitive to the needs of artists and the larger arts sector in America.

Funders have become more aware of the needs of the field, as well as more hands-on in their approaches to support. **Arts service organizations** have diversified their programs and support structure for individual artists, and, in developing their programs with a knowledge of the field provided by NYFA Interactive, will be more able to leverage more support and advocacy to the needs of artists and creative communities they feel are the least adequately addressed. Many **Cultural institutions** have adapted their programming to be more responsive to the needs of artists and emerging arts groups, and in many places have entered into more interactive relationships with artists, arts service organizations, and their surrounding communities in an effort to more effectively serve their constituencies and missions. All of these developments require more detailed information and data regarding the support structures for artists and how these are used, so that the programs being developed for the field respond to the way that artists operate.

Solution

We will design and launch a new online interface for NYFA Source that enables arts organizations nationwide to submit and update their program listings directly on the Web site. With more than 3,400 organizations and over 7,000 programs listed, an online submission/correction form will allow NYFA to use staff time more efficiently and encourage organizations to keep their information current. Currently, organizations must mail, fax, or e-mail their program updates to NYFA staff in order to be updated. Turnaround time is generally a few business days to a week. The online interface would greatly speed up the updating process, allowing NYFA staff more time to seek out new programs and provide technical assistance to NYFA Source users by telephone and e-mail.

C. Art-curious public

It is important to provide the general public with greater access to the richness and diversity of the contemporary arts as well as encouraging them in supporting the arts. With a long history of outreach to marginalized communities, artists and audiences exchanges, and public programs, NYFA continues to expand its interaction with the broader public, and has engaged in efforts to cultivate understanding and appreciation of the arts.

Solution

We will increase content, including articles, interviews, links, and so on, available through the For Art Curious pathway on NYFA Interactive. As a direct result of its highly visible and respected national profile, NYFA is often looked to as a meeting point between artists, arts organizations, the philanthropic community, and the public. However, unlike an arts presenting organization with a fixed physical space such as a theater or gallery, NYFA can only assume the role of arts educator, mediator, and advocate through its Web site. In November 2002, NYFA launched its redesigned Web site featuring a new pathway called For Art Curious. Using hyperlinking to the fullest extent, we will develop programs that will enable the public to explore any area of contemporary arts on the Internet. For example, beginning with an article on contemporary music, the visitor will be able to click through to hear sound samples of composers' work, visit an opera company's Web site to read about the production of a work, go to a record store and purchase a CD, find a list of composers working in a similar style to explore in the same way, or find a calendar listing in their area of where they might hear contemporary music live. Through development of original content and exploiting the connectedness of the Internet, we will provide a unique experience for all those users who are art curious.

III. Innovation

Already, the NYFA Web site is becoming one of the most innovative tools for capacity building in the arts sector. Based squarely on the belief that knowledge is power, NYFA Interactive collects, collates, and disseminates a highly specialized form of information free-of-charge. Of course, NYFA Interactive would not be what it is without a diverse network of information services and peripherals, including:

- two artist information telephone hotlines
- a weekly arts digest, NYFA Current
- the most popular job-posting site for arts in the country
- a quarterly print publication, NYFA Quarterly
- business of art workshops
- one-on-one consultations
- public presentations

The primary goal of Empowering Communities through Interactivity is to continue making the site more interactive, and thereby more useful to the entire arts field. In essence this will include multiple types of interaction:

◆ Arts organizations will be able to update and modify content in the NYFA Source database.

◆ Artists who are either NYFA-supported artists or have artist projects being fiscally sponsored by NYFA will also be able to more readily update, improve, and change their content on the NYFA Artists pages.

◆ Artists nationwide will be able to advertise their upcoming performances, exhibitions, and other events.

◆ Online tutorials will guide individual artists through a professional development process that will assist them in becoming better entrepreneurs in their own careers.

◆ Offerings for the art-curious will provide a wide range of accessible interactive essays linking out to online galleries and other sources to assist those less familiar with arts in understanding what contemporary artists do and why they do it.

NYFA Interactive Phase II will introduce an entirely new component for administrative and business practices of artists and emerging arts organizations. Artists producing projects will be able to handle a large portion of their administrative duties online, effectively solving what is often cited as the biggest obstacle to independent arts production. And with the event listing capability, artists will be able to market their projects and events at one-third the market cost of these services.

The design of NYFA Interactive is based almost solely on two things: *accessibility* and *clarity*. In constructing NYFA Interactive, we specifically chose not to employ any technology that would slow the process of information retrieval, or prevent users with low-tech machinery to view it. In Phase II, NYFA will keep with this commitment.

NYFA Interactive already has begun to affect the way that other organizations in the arts sector conduct their business and relate to each other, particularly through NYFA Source, and NYFA Current. In Phase II, organizations and institutions offering services to artists will be able to post their own programs and materials as they evolve and change, and measure the visitors and users of the database to their programs. More than anything else, this will have a radical impact on the way that organizations market their programs and services. But this centralized resource will also enable a much more comprehensive picture of the entire field, making it easier for organizations to share resources, information, and statistics, and even modify their programs according to what exists in the field.

IV. Community Involvement

The New York Foundation for the Arts has worked with artists and the broader arts community for over 31 years. It is widely recognized as the best national resource for information for individual artists. NYFA Interactive is an information network providing a wide range of services to *all* those who work in the arts, across all disciplines, throughout the United States. Throughout NYFA's history, we have worked to develop tools with which artists can more readily access vital information.

We have developed the Visual Artist Information Hotline, NYFA Current, and NYFA Interactive—which now serves as a centralized home for all of these services, and makes them accessible *free-of-charge*. NYFA Interactive is also the best place on the Internet to find out about contemporary art, and provides a wealth of information to foundations and researchers about the opportunities available to artists in the United States. The evolution and development of NYFA Interactive and all of its services have at every step been formed in response to the needs of the populations that NYFA serves.

To make the site's tools more readily usable, NYFA will design an entire range of tutorials modeled on the one that is already available for users of the NYFA Source. These tutorials will empower new users and those unaccustomed to the Internet in utilizing the resources and programs available on NYFA Interactive.

Evaluation

To ensure that its programs are of the highest quality and effectiveness, the New York Foundation for the Arts treats the evaluation process as a learning tool to review and improve each individual program area. The main elements of the evaluation process will include the following:

◆ Beta testing of the new elements, first through a small focus group and then through a wide and diverse set of users to determine functionality.

◆ Modifications to the program will be made prior to public release (based on the results of the previously mentioned tests).

◆ NYFA will solicit feedback from all NYFA Interactive users through short evaluation and comment forms placed on the Web site.

◆ Responses post-launch will be carefully tracked to aid in implementing additional improvements to ease of use and clarity of instructions.

◆ Programmers' contracts would extend through the evaluation phase to make changes immediately.

◆ Senior Program staff and the Program Committee of NYFA's Board of Directors provide further evaluation of all programs.

◆ An external evaluation will be conducted by The Conservation Company, which uses a team approach in the evaluation process, and which has conducted very effective evaluations of NYFA and various programs in the past.

NYFA Interactive Dissemination and Marketing Plan

The marketing campaign of NYFA Interactive will be targeted to inform all of the four major constituencies that NYFA serves: artists, small- to mid-sized arts organizations, foundations, and the art-curious public. For each of these target populations NYFA Interactive, and the network of services it houses, will make certain elements of their operations much easier:

◆ Artists can virtually work independently to find solutions to almost any of their needs, be they funding, materials, insurance and legal, marketing, financial, and so on.

◆ Artists and emerging arts organizations in NYFA's Fiscal Sponsorship program—again, the largest of its kind in the country—will be able to rely on NYFA Interactive for the interface to a number of their administrative operations as well as their temporary presentation on the internet.

◆ Arts service organizations, foundations, and arts councils will benefit from both having a centralized resource with current information for research related to program development, and they will benefit from a user-friendly marketing device for their grant programs and services.

◆ The general public will benefit from a wealth of digestible information on and exposure to the work of contemporary artists.

The Director of External Affairs and the Development Officer Communications will head up these efforts. The marketing plan below is designed using our current resources, along with the outside PR consultant and pro-bono work done by Marketing Committee members and others.

Advertising

By strategically placing advertisements, we intend to attract artists, foundations, and the art-curious public to the site. And by concentrating our ads around the first of the month of the launch rather than spreading them over a longer period, we will obtain one of the key elements in successful advertising—repetition—to a degree necessary to filter into the minds of our target audiences. One outlet for reaching all our audiences is public radio, which accepts "sponsorships" from profit and nonprofit organizations. Public radio sponsorships consist of a short (usually 10 seconds) announcement such as "The Listening Room is sponsored by the New York Foundation for the Arts' NYFA Source, providing all the information on grants and other resources that artists of all kinds need to succeed at www.nyfa.org."

All of NYFA's constituencies are contained within the demographics of public radio: both the high net worth individuals, arts workers, and artists. By targeting particular markets through specific radio programs, we can reach the artists, foundations, and the art-curious who are already interested in contemporary art and therefore will most likely be interested in our services. These announcements will appear nationally.

E-Marketing

We will also send an e-mail notice to the 6,000 names on various NYFA lists announcing the launch. We can also reach the network of family and friends of these people by asking each person on the NYFA list to forward the message on to those they know who might be interested in this news. This will expand out message well beyond our current audience to potentially 36,000 or more. (This method was highly successful during our launch of NYFA Interactive's Phase I.)

Public Relations

Working with our outside publicist, we will generate press releases for publications, both discipline-specific (Art in America, Dance Magazine, Film Comment, Back Stage) and general interest (e.g., daily newspapers). In addition, through the Artist & Audience Exchange requirement of the fellowships, NYFA is associated with as many as twelve events each month. The postcards announcing the launch will be distributed at all of these events taking place in the fall.

V. Use of Technology

Technical approach

Using the best practices and methodology employed during Phase I of NYFA Interactive, NYFA's Information & Research staff will work closely with Carnegie Mellon University's Center for Arts Management and Technology (CAMT) to identify, acquire, and install the technological necessities for evolution to Phase II. Although NYFA is committed to utilizing technology that is widely available even on older processors, some of these new technologies may include more advanced products.

Organizational capacity

One need only look at the difference between NYFA's old Web site and the new NYFA Interactive to see the value and depth of NYFA's relationship with the people at CAMT, which stretches back to 1992.

Privacy and security

NYFA Interactive is designed to protect the privacy of all its users. At present the site does not employ cookies. Some of the new features in this next development might require them but they will be employed only to the degree necessary to maintain functionality. Since the beginning of our online endeavors, NYFA has protected the privacy of end users, and there is an organization-wide policy not to share our list-servs with anyone.

Longevity

Designed to operate without a permanent Webmaster, NYFA Interactive is supported as part of NYFA's general operations, with continued support from a number of foundations. NYFA Source, the most labor- and cost-intensive program on NYFA Interactive, is supported through annual contributions from a Consortium of public and private funders.

Timetable

Steps	Objectives	Dates
1.	**Planning**—Identification of all goals and methodology; shopping for software; agreement upon timetable, administrational workflow.	11/03–2/04
2.	**Lay-out**—Work to create a comprehensive site-map; creation of wire-frames.	2/04–4/04
3.	**Design**—Redesign and enhancement of templates, graphic textures of site, peripheral program materials.	4/04–6/04
4.	**Building**—Construction of actual site, pages, links; database administration interface, ASP pages.	6/04–10/04
5.	**Testing**—Beta-testing, controlled public testing.	10/04–1/05
6.	**Public launch**—Artists and Organizations Interfaces Outreach activities, press releases, marketing campaign, ongoing email blasts, public demonstrations.	1/05, ongoing
7.	**Public launch**—Art curious general public outreach activities, press releases, marketing campaign.	4/05, ongoing
8.	**Evaluation**—Ongoing user evaluation, Senior Staff and Board evaluation, external evaluation by Conservation Company.	3/05–6/05

Budget Narrative

Category	Description	Total
A. Personnel	The personnel involved in this project include: Director of Programs, Senior Program Officer in Information & Research, and one Manager of Information Systems.	$184,000
B. Fringe Benefits	Fringe benefits are set at 18.5 percent of total staff expenses.	$34,100
C. Travel	The travel costs involved in this project are negligible, and have been included as a miscellaneous expense.	$200
D. Equipment	The equipment expense here is solely based on use of pre-existing equipment for the development, testing, and operation of the program by the Program Officers.	$3,000
E. Supplies	Self-explanatory; no special requirements.	$400
F. Contractual	This will include programming, interface development, and design.	$140,000
G. Construction	None.	$0
H. Other	National marketing and visibility campaigns.	$100,000
J. Indirect Costs	Indirect expenses for this project are calculated at 10 percent of the total project budget.	$45,000

Statement of Matching Funds

The Applicant will contribute the following:

- ◆ $22,600 in salary and fringe benefits for Director of Programs, Senior Program Officer, Manager of Information Systems, and other administrative personnel

- ◆ $2,000 for Equipment being used on-site for the purposes of the project

- ◆ $400 for supplies

Total Applicant Contributions: $25,000

Contributions from Funders to Program Income:

Foundation 1	$15,000
Foundation 2	$5,000
Foundation 3	$45,000
Foundation 4	$2,000
Foundation 5	$2,000
Foundation 6	$25,000
Foundation 7	$10,000
Foundation 8	$2,000
Foundation 9	$10,000
Foundation 10	$15,000
Foundation 11	$15,000
Foundation 12	$15,000
Foundation 13	$1,500
Foundation 14	$2,000
Foundation 15	$5,000
Foundation 16	$2,500
Company	$25,000
Other foundations	$33,500
Total Contributions from Others:	**$233,000**
Grand Total Match:	**$258,000**

Appendix G

Sample Final Report

This report is for the literacy program described in Chapter 14 for The Ralph Goodson Literacy Project (a fictional organization) that addresses literacy issues in three ways. This funder earmarked its funds for one part of the program. Please review the condensed proposal in Chapter 14 before reading the following report.

Cover Letter

Mr. Martin Szebo
President and CEO
Community Trust Company
456 Main Street
Anytown, IL 60000

Dear Mr. Szebo:

We are pleased to enclose a report on the Ralph Goodson Literacy Project's family program. The Community Trust Company's $50,000 grant was instrumental in making it possible for us to continue a program that requires a high degree of personal attention to each client. Although costly, the personal attention is key to the program's success.

Over the past year, we have continued to help families help themselves by gaining essential skills in reading and writing. 85 families that included 140 children and 118 parents participated in the program for at least 6 months. A full 90 percent of these continued with us for an entire year.

The benefits to the families and the community are striking. Grades in all subjects went up by one to two levels for 90 percent of the children participating. Of the 62 parents who were seeking work at the beginning of the period, 49 had found work. Few other programs of any kind can point to such dramatic results, which attests not only to the Literacy Project's ability to run this program but also how essential basic literacy skills are to other kinds of success.

A new corporate sponsor (Firetown Tire Company) and a new source of service fees from training teachers working for other agencies will provide some security for the program in future years. As you read this report, we hope you will consider the long-term value of this program and consider becoming an ongoing partner with us in this important effort.

Should you have any questions about the report or the program in general, I can be reached at (312)555-4567 or fgsmith@goodson.org. Thank you again for your generous support.

Sincerely,

Florence Goodson Smith
Executive Director

Enclosed:

- Final Report
- Budget
- Program brochure [not included here]

Final Report

Report to the Community Trust Company from the Ralph Goodson Literacy Project

We are pleased to present this report to the Community Trust Company on the $50,000 grant awarded in August 2002. The past year has been a challenging one as we struggled to maintain and expand programs during a period of recession. It was also a time when our services were most needed. There were many successes and several remaining challenges that we would like to report to you.

Family Literacy

The family literacy program seeks to improve reading and writing skills in families with multi-generational illiteracy. Your grant helped make possible our family literacy program, which served 85 families in this, its tenth year. Ralph Goodson, our founder, was himself a child of illiterate parents, which is why he began this organization with the family literacy program. It is because of the success of this program that it has remained our signature program.

Illiteracy too frequently becomes a tradition handed down from parents to their children. Many adults have learned to function well enough that few people, even those close to them, realize that they are illiterate. But illiteracy holds them back and is the major contributor to the poverty in which these families inevitably live.

The Social Thinkers Forum's 1999 report on children in our state with inadequate reading and writing skills found that "in the majority of cases studied, children's literacy problems stem from having illiterate or barely literate parents." The Ralph Goodson Literacy Project's family literacy program seeks to end this cycle of poverty and illiteracy.

Getting to the families that can most benefit from this service requires a number of strategies. Illiteracy is not something adults readily admit to. The Goodson Project seeks to identify and address these families by:

- ◆ Working through schools. We hold an orientation meeting for elementary school reading teachers and counselors twice each year to acquaint them with our programs. In addition, we help them understand the signs present when a child might have illiterate parents. By asking parents in for counseling sessions with a staff member from the school and from the Goodson Project, we are able to broach the topic of the parent's literacy through a discussion of the problems their child is experiencing.

- ◆ Working through job training centers. We meet regularly with counselors at the major job training sites throughout the county. These counselors are trained to work with illiterate adults, but we ask that they call us in when they discover the adults are parents. Many adults are more comfortable approaching literacy training as another job skill rather than as some shortcoming.

◆ Working through employers. Twelve of the county's largest employers of un-skilled and low-skilled laborers work with us to offer literacy training as a job benefit. When adults see the clear relationship between job advancement and literacy, they are typically more willing to address this problem. We work with other literacy organizations so that we can concentrate our efforts on those employees with children.

Through these outreach efforts, 142 families with multi-generational literacy problems were identified last year. Teachers from the Goodson Project began work with each of these families, but the drop out rate continues to be around 40 percent, which left us with 85 families participating in the program for at least 6 months, a minimum period of time in which to make a significant and permanent difference in their literacy skills.

Goodson Project teachers worked with families in several ways:

◆ Sessions with the children alone to reinforce what they are being taught in the classroom

◆ Sessions with the parents to overcome any embarrassment they might feel in front of their children because of their lack of reading and writing skills

◆ Sessions with parents and children in which they are able to share their skills by reading aloud together and working on family writing projects

The sessions with parents and children are the key to the program's success. By making the activities of reading and writing family activities, the shared skills become an integral part of how the family relates to one another, thus strengthening these skills and the family bonds.

Most family sessions are held at the Goodson Literacy Project facilities, although teachers frequently make "house calls" to families for which transportation to downtown is a hardship.

One parent participating in the program last year told us that "being able to read with my kid has brought us closer than ever before." Another parent commented that "My Sara is so bright that I have to stay up late studying to keep up with her, but it's worth it to see her doing so much better in school." The program equally affects the children. Billy, one of three children in a family, let us know that "we all look forward to our weekly session with Ms. Thomas. The new books she brings us are great, and she even finds ones my dad wants to read."

Evaluation

In the past year, of the 140 children participating, the 123 for whom we were able to access school records all recorded significant advancement in their schoolwork. For 90 percent, grades in all subjects went up by one to two levels. Of the 62 parents who were seeking work at the beginning of the period, 49 had found work.

One of the truest measures of the program's success is the length of time families remain in it. As mentioned before, there is a considerable attrition in the first few months. Of the families that participate for four months, 90 percent complete a year in the program.

The Context

This program is complemented by our work with preschool children who come from families representing all economic and educational levels. The preschool program's goal is to make reading a joy and a lifelong occupation. We also work with the after-school programs with the county's elementary schools, providing tutoring in reading and writing. There were 29 children involved in these programs who were also clients of the family literacy program.

Present and Future Challenges

Overcoming the natural reluctance many adults feel in admitting to a lack of skill usually possessed by five-year-olds will always be a challenge. Frequently, even in two-parent households, one of the parents refuses to participate in the program. Addressing literacy as a job skill like mechanics or other manual skills has made the greatest inroads to this hard-to-reach group.

The extremely high teacher to client ratio of this program (1:4 per session, and 1:18 overall) provides the dramatic results for which the program is known. It also makes it a very expensive program to run. We believe that, given the higher levels of employment it creates for the present and the next generation and the contribution it makes toward more stable families, the program is actually quite cheap.

Funding will always be a problem, but we are pleased to report that the local factory of Firetown Tire Company has become our first corporate sponsor, making a five-year funding commitment and providing space at the factory for us to meet with clients.

A literacy center in Monroe County has approached us to provide training to its teachers in the family program beginning next month. This will provide us with modest service fees to complement the contributed income.

We hope you share in the pride we feel at the success of the family literacy program and all the programs of the Ralph Goodson Literacy Project. By acquiring literacy skills, the cycle of poverty can be broken, lives are made richer, and children will be allowed to reach their full potential. On behalf of all our clients, we thank you again for your generous support.

Budget Report

Ralph Goodson Literacy Project: Family Literacy Program

Final Report for the Year July 2002 through July 2003

Expenses		Budget	Actual	Variance
Personnel				
Teachers (15)	100%	$570,000	$570,000	$0
Teaching supervisors (3)	75%	$135,000	$135,000	$0
Executive director	5%	$4,000	$4,000	$0
Teaching assistants (4)	72%	$77,760	$77,760	$0
Subtotal salaried personnel		$786,760	$786,760	$0
Fringe benefits	16%	$125,882	$125,882	$0
Total Personnel		**$912,642**	**$912,642**	**$0**
Direct Expenses				
Telephone		$600	$589	–$11
Travel		$950	$1,095	$145
Supplies		$3,000	$3,498	$498
Printing		$1,200	$818	–$382
Postage and delivery		$700	$650	–$50
Mailing costs		$400	$350	–$50
Advertising and marketing		$500	$380	–$120
Web site		$500	$500	$0
Membership and subscriptions		$250	$250	$0
Equipment		$600	$800	$200
Contingency		$400	$0	–$400
Total Direct Expenses		**$9,100**	**$8,930**	**–$170**
Indirect Expenses	11%	$98,758	$98,740	–$18
Total Expenses		**$1,020,500**	**$1,020,311**	**–$189**

Expenses	Budget	Actual	Variance
Income			
Community Trust Company	$75,000	$50,000	–$25,000
State Department of Education	$800,000	$800,000	$0
Firetown Tire Company*	$0	$40,000	$40,000
United Charity Drive	$28,000	$22,000	–$6,000
Anytown Community Foundation	$100,000	$100,000	$0
Anytown Legal Association	$2,500	$0	–$2,500
Stars Fund	$15,000	$0	-$15,000
Smith Family Foundation	$0	$3,500	$3,500
Consolidated Electric	$0	$5,000	$5,000
Total Income	**$1,020,500**	**$1,020,500**	**$0**
Program Surplus (Deficit)	$0	$189	**$189**

Firetown Tire Company grant represents the first installment of a five-year grant.

Glossary

ask   As in "the ask," the actual request for a specific amount of money in a grant cover letter or proposal.

board of directors   Governing body of a nonprofit organization or foundation. Board members may also be known as *trustees*.

budget   A statement of a program's or organization's expenses and sources of revenue (income).

budget narrative   An explanation of key expenses or income items in a budget that is used to highlight particular expenses critical to the program, explain any exceptionally high or low expenses a funder might question, and describe how additional income for a program will be raised.

buzzword   A term used to obfuscate rather than elucidate.

capital support   Grant for a major project that will have a long-term effect on a charity, usually for a building or endowment.

challenge grant   Grant made by a funder to encourage additional contributions toward a program. The challenger's grant is made conditioned on a specific amount being raised to match it.

community foundation   Public foundation receiving contributions from a wide segment of the population to support charitable purposes in a specific geographic area.

competitive grants   Grants that are awarded on merit rather than financial need. All grants referred to in this book are competitive grants.

corporate foundation   Legally no different from other private foundations and governed by the same IRS regulations.

corporate giving office Office in a company responsible for making grants without the legal restrictions borne by the corporate foundation. Frequently the source for gifts of products.

corporate sponsorship *See* sponsorship.

cover letter Letter accompanying a grant proposal to introduce the proposal and the organization to the funder.

cross-tabs Tabulations used in evaluation data whereby one set of data is counted in relationship to another set of data, such as counting the number of people from large charities rating the workshop excellent and comparing it to the number from small charities giving it an excellent rating to see which group was better served by the workshop.

cultivation Means of educating a funder or donor about a charity in preparation for a solicitation. Can be done through events, meetings, newsletters, and other methods of contact.

development *See* fundraising.

discretionary grants Trustee-designed grants that might lie outside the funders' guidelines.

earned income Revenue not dependent on grants. Popular with funders, because more earned income means lesser dependence on grants. Earned income can come from service fees, products sold, or even interest income.

executive summary Section of a grant proposal that puts forth the major reasons for the grant request with references to the budget and all major aspects of the proposal.

family foundation A foundation controlled by family members of its primary donor.

fair market value That part of a contribution that is not tax deductible because the donor has received something of value in return (such as the meal at a benefit dinner).

final report A report required by most all funders at the end of the grant period describing the results and how the program was conducted along with a budget showing how the funder's grant was spent.

fiscal sponsorship A formal relationship between a nonprofit organization and an individual or an organization that is unincorporated or in the process of seeking nonprofit status. The relationship is formed so that the organization or person without nonprofit status has access to contributions from foundations, corporations, individuals, and government agencies.

501(c)(3) status Reference to the paragraph in the tax code that defines which types of organizations are recognized to be free from federal income taxes, defined as "organized and operated exclusively for religious, charitable, scientific, testing for public safety, literary, or educational purposes …." *See also* tax-exempt status.

formula grants   A type of government grant to reimburse your charity for services you have already performed based on a mathematical formula that, for example, might multiply the number of your clients by the average cost of providing a service in your city by some percentage the government has decided on.

foundation   A private organization formed to make grants or carry out specific programs. *See also* operating foundation.

funder   A generic term used to refer to foundation, corporation, and government grantmakers as a group.

fundraising   The practice of soliciting money from a wide variety of sources for use by a nonprofit organization in pursuit of its mission. One aspect of fundraising is grant writing, but it also includes membership, direct mail, special events, and planned giving.

general operating support (GOS)   A grant to pay for the everyday expenses all organizations have, such as rent, utilities, and insurance and also for personnel who are not involved in programs (like the grant writer). GOS support can also help pay for programs, which is sometimes necessary when a program is just getting started.

goals   What will have been achieved at the end of a program. *See also* objectives.

grant writing   The skill or practice of asking for money in the form of a grant from a foundation, corporation, government agency, or individual by crafting a well-considered document (the proposal) that outlines how the money will be used, what receiving the money will accomplish, and who will undertake the tasks described in the proposal. Grant writing is one aspect of *fundraising*.

indirect expenses   A portion of a charity's general operating expenses that although not a direct result of a program is necessary to maintaining the organization so that it can run the program. Indirect expenses include rent, utilities, insurance, payroll charges, and administrative and fundraising personnel.

indirect rate   A percentage that expresses the relationship between the total costs of running a charity and the portion of those expenses that are allocated to a particular program.

informational meetings   Meetings with funders to pave the way for a grant proposal while pretending simply to be gathering information.

in-kind gifts   Free goods or services donated by a funder in lieu of or in addition to a cash grant.

inquiry letter   A letter written to a funder to see if a program would be of interest. Usually precedes a grant proposal and is required by some funders.

interim report   A report required by some funders before the end of the grant period giving a report on progress made. Usually required when asking that a grant period be extended.

jargon A term used to obfuscate rather than elucidate.

matching grant A grant made to help meet a challenge grant. *See also* challenge grant.

metrics A term common in the corporate world meaning the *measurable* outcomes of a project.

need What a nonprofit's program seeks to satisfy, which is the justification for seeking a grant.

need-based grants *See* formula grants.

990 form An informational return required by the Internal Revenue Service for all nonprofits with incomes of $25,000 or more and for all foundations. Foundations file a special version of the form, the 990-PF.

nonprofit Used to describe an organization "organized and operated exclusively for religious, charitable, scientific, testing for public safety, literary, or educational purposes" by the IRS. A nonprofit can make a profit (called a budget surplus); it's just that profit is not the motivating factor. (Note that "non-profit" is also acceptable.)

objectives The measurable steps that will be taken to reach a program's goals or achieve the intended results. *See also* goals.

operating foundation A foundation that exists to carry out its own programs, usually making few if any grants.

organizational budgets A charity's total operations, including all personnel and expenses and all sources of income.

outcomes method A means of organizing a grant proposal that focuses on the results that are anticipated at the end of the program. *See also* process method.

process method A means of organizing a grant proposal that focuses on the way a program will be carried out. *See also* outcomes method.

program Activities carried out to achieve a limited set of goals and objectives within a set period of time.

program budget All expenses directly related to a program and all income raised specifically for it.

program or **project grant** A competitive grant to support a particular program.

program officer/foundation An employee of a foundation whose job is to answer questions from potential and current grantees, conduct initial proposal review, and prepare acceptable proposals for consideration by the foundation's trustees. The responsibilities of the job vary by foundation.

program officer (or staff)/nonprofit   Employee of a charity whose purpose is to carry out programs. These might be service providers from librarians to doctors to research assistants, but the term can also refer to a choral director or soccer coach.

Program Related Investment (PRI)   A means of funding used by foundations that allows them to "invest" in a nonprofit endeavor in hopes of the funds being returned to the foundation at some point with interest.

proposal   A document prepared to solicit a grant from any source. See Chapter 13 for the parts of a proposal.

regrants   Grants made by a charity with funds it has raised for that purpose. When seeking a grant to support regrants, be sure the funder allows this—many don't, including many federal grants.

request for proposal (RFP)   A pro-active means funders employ to encourage proposals for a program established by the funder.

renewal grant   A grant from the same funder to continue the same program. It can be a loaded phrase. On the one hand, it signifies a continuing relationship with your charity, which is a good thing to remind them about. On the other, it might imply to a funder that you expect the funder to continue supporting your charity and maybe even take their continued support for granted.

social responsibility   A corporate euphemism for a corporate contributions program.

sponsorship   A grant made usually by a corporation to a nonprofit or a for-profit in return for tangible benefits to the corporation, usually through marketing.

stewardship   Usually used to mean the practice of looking after a group of people or managing affairs, but in our parlance it refers to looking after donors to ensure their continued interest (and donations).

tax-exempt status   A designation by some level of government that an organization is a charity and is not subject to taxes imposed by that government body. *See also* 501(c)(3) status.

trustee   An official at a foundation or at a nonprofit organization who holds the assets of the organization in trust for the public good. Also sometimes known as a member of the board of directors. At a foundation, the trustees hold the authority to make grants and determine policy.

venture philanthropy   A trendy form of grantmaking that usually involves greater reporting requirements and greater involvement by the funder in the charity's program.

Appendix

What's on the CD-ROM?

The CD-ROM that you'll find in the back of this book has been put together to provide you with quick resources to make your research and grant writing easier. In addition to some of the examples found in the chapters or appendixes, you'll also find worksheets to keep your work organized and a budget worksheet to save you time and prevent errors.

Exploring the Contents

The CD-ROM contents are organized into two folders: Proposals and Budgets. The Proposals folder contains the following:

- ◆ Corporate Grant Proposal (from Appendix D)
- ◆ Corporate Sponsorship Proposal (from Appendix E)
- ◆ Foundation Grant Proposal (from Appendix C)
- ◆ Government Grant Proposal (from Appendix F)
- ◆ Final Report Goodson Literacy Project (from Appendix G)
- ◆ Thank you letters (from Chapters 20 and 21)

The Budgets folder contains these sample budgets and worksheets:

- ◆ Program Budget Workbook
- ◆ Budget Showing Grant Request as Separate Column
- ◆ Goodson Literacy Project Report Budget
- ◆ Multi-Year Budget with Interim Report Numbers (from Chapter 21)
- ◆ Funding Plan Worksheet (from Chapter 12)

◆ Prospect Worksheet

◆ Grant Schedule Worksheet (from Chapter 12)

The Program Budget Workbook is unique to the CD-ROM. It has been designed to enable you to calculate your charity's indirect rate and allocate personnel costs, all of which will be automatically fed into a program budget form. The other budget samples and worksheets are provided for you to use as guides when forming your own budgets and to help you organize your prospects and your work.

The CD-ROM also contains the same list of Internet resources that you find in Appendix B; however, on the CD-ROM, these sites are only a click away. You can access this list by clicking the Internet Resources link after launching the CD-ROM.

Launching the CD-ROM

Turn on your computer, place the disc in the CD-ROM tray, and then close the tray. On a Windows system, the main menu of the CD-ROM should appear momentarily. If it doesn't, choose Start → Run from the Windows desktop and type **x:\index. html** in the Open text box (where **x** is the drive letter of your CD-ROM drive). Click OK or press Enter to launch the CD.

On a Macintosh system, the CD-ROM doesn't launch automatically. Instead, you can access the contents by double-clicking the icon representing the CD-ROM drive.

Requirements

Your will need the following in order to have full access to the materials on the CD-ROM:

◆ Microsoft Word 95 or later

◆ Microsoft Excel 95 or later

◆ Microsoft Internet Explorer 4.0 or later or a compatible web browser

◆ Adobe Acrobat Reader

◆ An Internet connection (to access the online resources)

Your system must meet the following minimum requirements:

◆ Processor: 486DX or higher

◆ Operating system: Microsoft Windows 95/98/NT/XP or Mac OS/OS X

◆ Monitor: VGA, 640x480 or higher with 256 colors or higher

◆ Input device: Mouse or compatible pointing device

Index

G

J-K

L

M

N

Q-R

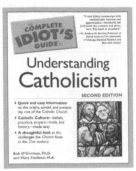

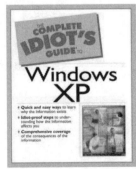